Cognition, Education, and Deafness

Cognition, Education, and Deafness

Directions for Research and Instruction

David S. Martin, Editor

Gallaudet College Press
Washington, D.C.

Gallaudet College Press, Washington, DC 20002
©1985 by Gallaudet College. All rights reserved
Published 1985
Printed in the United States of America

Library of Congress Cataloging in Publication Data

Main entry under title:
Cognition, education, and deafness.

   Includes bibliographies and index.
   1. Children, Deaf—Education—Addresses, essays,
lectures. 2. Cognition in children—Addresses, essays,
lectures. I. Martin, David S.
HV2430.C58   1985   371.91′2′019   85-12992
ISBN 0-930323-12-2

Gallaudet College is an equal opportunity employer/educational institution.
Programs and services offered by Gallaudet College receive substantial financial support from the U.S. Department of Education.

Contents

5 Cognitive Strategies and Processes

8 Measurement of Cognitive Potential in Hearing-Impaired Learners

9 The Effects of Cognitive Intervention Programs

Foreword

Our country has a well-deserved reputation for a broad range of achievements, including the resolution of many economic and social ills. In recent decades programs for the handicapped have been the fortunate target of some of this Yankee ingenuity. Compared with other health, social, and educational problems, however, hearing impairment has not received an equitable level of attention. Over the years, no problem affecting such a large portion of the population has received such a small share of our nation's research dollars or of its remediation efforts.

Fortunately, researchers and practitioners in a number of fields have "discovered" deafness as an interesting and fruitful area of investigation. Our knowledge about cognition and deafness has burgeoned (comparatively speaking, at least) in recent years. The International Symposium on Cognition, Education, and Deafness, which provided the stage from which prominent researchers and practitioners could present their work and viewpoints, and this volume, which represents the results of that symposium, are especially timely. Thanks are due primarily to Professor Clarence Williams who, more than 2 years ago, planted and nourished the seed from which this work grew. His untimely death halfway through the planning process, though tragic, served to harden the resolve of others on the task force to make the symposium and this report an extraordinary success.

This book represents the range of diversity in the field. Although no claims are made with regard to its completeness, it does provide the best summary to date of state-of-the-art information on topics related to cognition and deafness. The volume comes highly recommended as a veritable treasure to the serious student and to the practicing professional concerned about helping deaf persons help themselves by developing a greater portion of their cognitive potential.

Gallaudet College   Doin Hicks
Washington, D.C.

Acknowledgments

An enterprise such as this analysis and synthesis of papers from the 1984 International Symposium on Cognition, Education, and Deafness can never become a reality without the significant involvement of many dedicated people. Inevitably, some of these people work almost invisibly; regrettably, they may not receive the proper acknowledgment.

A great debt of gratitude is owed to Doreen Dixon for deliberate and precise work in word processing; Elaine Costello of Gallaudet College Press for essential guidance and support; Ivey Pittle of Gallaudet College Press for painstaking, thorough, and intelligent editing of the entire manuscript; Doin Hicks (Vice-President for Research at Gallaudet College) for encouragement and financial backing; and all of the obviously well-qualified contributors and analysts in this volume, without whose work there would be only blank pages after this page.

Careful and comprehensive notes of each symposium session were kept by a corps of hard-working graduate assistants. Their work proved to be essential to the contributors who analyzed each theme grouping of papers in this volume. Consequently, appreciation is expressed to the following recorders: Linda Savard for parts 4, 5, and 7; Carielyn Kelly for parts 6, 7, and 9; Karla Cowell for parts 3, 8, and 9; and Theresa Sternat and Renee Herbert for part 9.

A special expression of indebtedness and appreciation is owed to the late Clarence Williams, Director of Faculty and Student Research at Gallaudet College. His professional inspiration and energy were essential to the original conceptualization and initial planning for the symposium from which this book grew. He is much missed by all who knew him.

David S. Martin, Editor

Contributors

Felicie Affolter
Center for Perceptual Disturbances
St. Gallen, Switzerland

David F. Armstrong
Gallaudet College
Washington, D.C.

Irene Athey
Rutgers University
New Brunswick, New Jersey

Eileen Biser
National Technical Institute
  for the Deaf
Rochester, New York

Jeffery P. Braden
California School for the Deaf
Fremont, California

Richard P. Brinker
University of Illinois
Chicago, Illinois

Paula M. Brown
National Technical Institute
  for the Deaf
Rochester, New York

Roger Bruning
University of Nebraska
Lincoln, Nebraska

George Buranyi
University of Alberta
Edmonton, Alberta, Canada

Harold W. Campbell
Johns Hopkins University
Baltimore, Maryland

Edward E. Corbett, Jr.
Gallaudet College
Washington, D.C.

Ceinwen Cumming
University of Alberta
Edmonton, Alberta, Canada

Beth Davey
University of Maryland
College Park, Maryland

Pat Spencer Day
Kendall Demonstration Elementary
  School
Washington, D.C.

Gary S. Dell
University of Rochester
Rochester, New York

Thomas J. Diebold
Ohio State University
Columbus, Ohio

Charles H. Dietz
Model Secondary School for the Deaf
Washington, D.C.

Kenneth I. Epstein
Gallaudet College
Washington, D.C.

Jenny Friedman
Northwestern University
Evanston, Illinois

Joan M. Gibson
State University of New York
Buffalo, New York

Harley Hamilton
Atlanta Area School for the Deaf
Atlanta, Georgia

Vicki L. Hanson
Haskins Laboratories
New Haven, Connecticut

Richard Harding
University of Nebraska
Lincoln, Nebraska

Mary Hockersmith
Model Secondary School for the Deaf
Washington, D.C.

Bruce S. Jonas
Gallaudet College
Washington, D.C.

Irmina Kaiser-Grodecka
Jagiellonian University
Krakow, Poland

Kevin J. Keane
Trenton State College
Trenton, New Jersey

Anna Knobloch-Gala
Jagiellonian University
Krakow, Poland

Jane M. Krahe
California School for the Deaf
Riverside, California

Carol A. Kusché
University of Washington
Seattle, Washington

Carol LaSasso
Gallaudet College
Washington, D.C.

Lynn S. Liben
Pennsylvania State University
University Park, Pennsylvania

Edward Lichtenstein
National Technical Institute for
  the Deaf
Rochester, New York

Barbara Luetke-Stahlman
Northern Illinois University
DeKalb, Illinois

Pamela Luft
Kendall Demonstration Elementary
  School
Washington, D.C.

John P. Madison
Gallaudet College
Washington, D.C.

Lynne F. Mann
University of Virginia
Charlottesville, Virginia

David S. Martin
Gallaudet College
Washington, D.C.

Kathryn P. Meadow-Orlans
Gallaudet College
Washington, D.C.

Donna M. Mertens
Gallaudet College
Washington, D.C.

Margery Silberman Miller
Montgomery County Public Schools
Rockville, Maryland

Donald F. Moores
Gallaudet College
Washington, D.C.

Janis Morariu
University of Maryland
College Park, Maryland

Beverly Muendel-Atherstone
University of Alberta
Edmonton, Alberta, Canada

Virginia Murphy-Berman
University of Nebraska
Lincoln, Nebraska

Keith E. Nelson
Pennsylvania State University
University Park, Pennsylvania

Diana Pien
David T. Siegel Institute for
  Communicative Disorders
Chicago, Illinois

Philip M. Prinz
Pennsylvania State University
University Park, Pennsylvania

Ron B. Rembert
Texas Wesleyan College
Fort Worth, Texas

Michael Rodda
University of Alberta
Edmonton, Alberta, Canada

Cindy Rohr-Redding
Model Secondary School for the Deaf
Washington, D.C.

Philip S. Saif
Gallaudet College
Washington, D.C.

Irving E. Sigel
Educational Testing Service
Princeton, New Jersey

Manjula B. Waldron
Ohio State University
Columbus, Ohio

Robert Lee Williams
Gallaudet College
Washington, D.C.

Lee Witters
University of Nebraska
Lincoln, Nebraska

Anthony B. Wolff
Gallaudet College
Washington, D.C.

Steve Wolk
Gallaudet College
Washington, D.C.

Abraham Zwiebel
Gallaudet College
Washington, D.C.

1 Introduction

Introduction

David S. Martin

One definition of a symposium in *Webster's New World Dictionary* (1970, p. 1443) is a "free interchange of ideas." The essential nature of the International Symposium on Cognition, Education, and Deafness (Gallaudet College, June 1984) was indeed an opportunity for the exchange of important ideas on this subject.

For many years scholars, educators, and researchers in education and psychology have wrestled with the problem of the cognitive performance of the hearing-impaired learner. Indeed, much recent research in that area has provided some answers where there was previously only speculation. But, as with any field of investigation, each small answer creates exciting new questions to be explored.

The idea for holding an international symposium on cognition, education, and deafness came from several members of the Gallaudet community who realized that simultaneous investigations were under way in many different locations. They also realized that no systematic project coordination or plans for interchange existed. Thus, they proposed that a symposium be held to allow for discussion and analysis of the research, theories, and educational practices currently being investigated.

Review of Related Literature

Rationality has now begun to be the central focus of psychology. While some early psychologists (e.g., Thorndike, Hull, and Ebbinghaus) were interested in understanding reasoning, they used behaviorism as their strategy for inquiry; this strategy proved to be reductionist. When one begins the study of reasoning at the lowest stages, it becomes very difficult to move the study up to higher levels; hence, these psychologists' initial stage of inquiry became the field itself. This approach had the additional problem of being independent of context (Shulman, 1984).

The Gestaltists, on the other hand, emphasized frames of reference and schemata. With the possible exception of Dewey, however, they never seemed to have a significant impact on education.

A major change in the study of reasoning came during the 1950s with the rediscovery of cognition through the information-processing model. Piaget's work on stages of development, Bruner's on cognitive processes, Chomsky's on language, and Miller's on limitations all led the way to the era in which we are now working. As a result of that movement, reasoning resumed the center of study; today, the focus is on the study of how humans transform the world so as to deal with its problems (Shulman, 1984).

It is now apparent that other social sciences, such as sociology and anthropology, have also rediscovered this latter emphasis, with the result that in the past 10 years, psychology has received an increasing influence from these other disciplines. Psychologists must now look not only at individuals but also at groups (Shulman, 1984).

Let us now set the context for the papers, summaries, and analyses that follow in this volume by reviewing some of the high points of prior research on cognition and the hearing-impaired learner.

The authors of one particular thinking and language skills program for hearing-impaired students have pointed out that thinking skills are not only essential to the development of reasoning and critical thinking, but also are fundamental to the child's total learning ability. These skills include the ability to recognize relationships, store and recall information, recognize logical order, evaluate information, do original thinking, adapt the known to new situations, do trial-and-error thinking, and acquire an understanding of different types of concepts (Pfau, 1975, p. 4).

Furth has defined logical and conceptual thinking as the tendency toward an intellectual grasp of reality undistorted by symbols (1964, p. 187). Bruner (1969) has described thinking as a process originating with problem-solving strategies that are originally developed in acquiring specific skills. While Furth's latter point about symbols in the thinking process is debatable, these definitions provide a working tool for examining the need for curricular interventions for hearing-impaired populations, as will be discussed later.

An interest in cognitive training began to emerge in the late 1960s and early 1970s when researchers from several different orientations within special education began to focus on self-control processes. A longer tradition exists in teaching general and task-related strategies to exceptional children (Meichenbaum, 1980, p. 84). Among the relatively recent trends is a technique called *cognitive behavior modification* (CBM), which is defined as the student acting in some way as his or her own trainer or teacher through self-control, self-verbalization, self-instruction, and self-reinforcement. Verbalization by the student of what the student is doing is another trait of this technique. CBM also often involves identifying a series of steps or strategies for problem solving (Lloyd, 1980, p. 53). Unlike CBM, in which a single general strategy is taught, another approach called *strategy training* teaches specific strategies for specific types of problems through a rote set of subskills and rules for combining them as applied to a class of problems (Lloyd, 1980, p. 59).

A characteristic of some CBM programs is *metacognition*, which is defined as one's cognitions about cognitions, or the thinking about one's own thinking. The processes involved here include analyzing the problem, reflecting on what one knows that may be appropriate to a solution, devising a plan, and checking one's progress (Brown, 1978). Exceptional children have been considered to be deficient in metacognition as well as in certain academic areas.

Impulsivity is another characteristic of some learners who are achieving below their potential. One deficiency in the impulsive learner has been in the area of well-developed habits of self-observation (Gutentag & Long-fellow, 1977), which is related to the skill of metacognition. Jerome Kagan's work (1971) has been significant in identifying impulsivity (versus reflectivity) as a learning style and the attendant problems that impulsivity brings. A number of teaching strategies have been evolved for teaching the impulsive learner; among them, strategy-training has been experimentally demonstrated to be effective in making the learner operate in a more reflective manner (McKinney & Haskins, 1980, p. 48). The research on field-dependence and field-independence is also related to cognitive style, and it has important implications for hearing-impaired learners, as will be seen in several parts in this volume.

Systematic intervention programs, then, for working with the cognitive deficits of exceptional children are not new phenomena. Such intervention techniques as those just mentioned have had varying success. That success has been related to certain identified variables. For example, it has been shown that a child's concept of causal relationships influences his or her reaction to an intervention program (Henker, Whalen, & Hinshaw, 1980, p. 23). In addition, individual differences in language and cognitive maturity are also considered to be influences on the appropriateness and effectiveness of cognitive training interventions (Keogh & Glover, 1980, p. 79). One unresolved question is whether an intervention that is ineffective may be trying to use nonexistent prerequisite skills in the child when it should be developing those prerequisites (Keogh & Glover, 1980, p. 81).

Intervention programs used until now have had limited success in the critical area of generalizability (i.e., the transfer by the learner of learned skills to other areas where those skills can be appropriately applied). It has been suggested that generalizability may be limited by the strategies themselves; that is, transfer to a novel task with similar stimulus and response properties presents no difficulty, but transfer to a task involving different materials and responses is often not obtained (McKinney & Haskins, 1980, p. 49). On the other hand, generalizability across training programs appears more likely as a child matures because older children are more aware of the strategies available to them (Loper, 1980, p. 6). It has been recommended that generalizability can be enhanced if the training procedure ensures explicit feedback and includes direct instruction in generalizing (Meichenbaum, 1980, p. 86).

While few of the previously mentioned researchers have focused on the hearing-impaired learner, their work with exceptional learners in the cognitive realm suggests particular points of rationale for this volume.

Studies of cognition in relation to the hearing-impaired population have also been numerous in recent years. After an initial focus on IQ, the center of attention now is on the processes involved in cognition and perception. It appears to be a well-accepted fact that hearing-impaired subjects have the normal range of intelligence when tested on the performance, rather than the verbal, subtests of various IQ instruments (Drever & Collins, 1928). An exception is found in students who have neurological impairments in addition to their hearing loss (Vernon, 1968, p. 8). In a more detailed examination of hearing-impaired subjects by specific etiology of loss, Vernon found some differentiation in performance; for example, the mean IQ for genetically deaf students was reported to be 114, while that for postmaternal rubella deaf students was 95 (1968, p. 7). We also know that when the influence of age is controlled, statistical data on hearing-impaired children indicate strong relationships between achievement test scores and variables such as age of onset of hearing loss, cause of loss, degree of loss, additional handicapping conditions, ethnic background, and type of special educational program (Jensema, 1975).

It is useful to review what researchers have reported in regard to specific cognitive skill performance in hearing-impaired subjects, skill by skill.

1. *Memory:* Research conducted over the last 80 years indicates that profoundly deaf subjects perform less well than do normally hearing subjects on short-term memory tasks as well as on certain other cognitive tasks (Karchmer & Belmont, 1976, p. 1). In a report on the results of a cognitive laboratory study, deaf subjects benefited greatly by adopting particular strategies that explicitly tailored the primary and secondary memory systems to the demands of information processing. These strategies brought their performance up to the levels that the hearing subjects had achieved using self-selected strategies (Karchmer & Belmont, 1976, p. 4). Karchmer and Belmont concluded that what is often seen as a performance deficiency is instead a strategy deficiency, as opposed to some type of structural deficiency related to the physiological fact of deafness (1976, p. 8).

    Meadow reported that hearing-impaired children could better remember words that had a sign equivalent than words that did not. Further, she found that hearing-impaired children found it easier to remember geometric shapes than to remember digits (1980, p. 73). Thus, classroom intervention programs (as discussed later in this volume) that stress the direct teaching of particular strategies for cognitive tasks should hold promise of improvement of hearing-impaired subjects performance in cognitive problem-solving situations.

2. *Concept Application:* Furth asserted that "the deaf" can comprehend and logically apply concepts as well as the hearing can (1964, p. 168). More recently, Meadow reported that hearing-impaired subjects learn concepts in the same sequence as hearing subjects, but at a later time (1980, p. 72). Furth remarked that the difficulties experienced by hearing-impaired subjects in several skill areas indicated that they have difficulty with the discovery of a concept rather than with its comprehension or use (1964, p. 146).

3. *Parts-Wholes:* Furth found no difference in the performance of deaf as compared to hearing children (1964, p. 146).

4. *Opposition:* Furth found inferior performance among deaf subjects on this dimension (1964, p. 146), and the same finding was reported later by Meadow (1980, p. 72).

5. *Sameness:* Furth found the deaf subjects to be "equal" to the hearing subjects on understanding of sameness (1964, p. 146), and Meadow reported "little retardation" for hearing-impaired subjects in this domain (1980, p. 72).

6. *Analogy:* Meadow reported that hearing-impaired children had difficulty in this area (1980, p. 72).

7. *Superordinate Reasoning:* Meadow found this area posed difficulty for the hearing-impaired subjects (1980, p. 72). Johnson (1981) has reported that both the vocabulary and concept of cause-effect relationships are also more difficult for hearing-impaired youth.

8. *Symmetry:* Both Furth (1964, p. 146) and Meadow (1980, p. 72) found little, if any, difficulty for hearing-impaired children in this skill.

9. *Classification:* Prior research has reported that hearing-impaired children perform less well than hearing children on classification tasks that depend on verbal interaction with the environment (Best & Roberts, 1975). However, more recently, Meadow has found little retardation among hearing-impaired learners in this skill area. (1980, p. 72).

10. *Spatial Reasoning:* Research thus far on this area suggests that because hearing-impaired children depend primarily on visual and tactile senses to a greater degree than hearing children, they may develop a different concept of space (Hauptman, 1980, p. 43). In a separate study, Parasnis and Long (1979) found that deaf students are more field-dependent when compared to hearing students and that spatial skills are significantly related to performance on a field-dependence test. They have suggested that the effect of auditory deprivation and/or knowledge of sign language for congenitally deaf individuals may be weak cerebral lateralization and thus greater field-dependence.

    Thus, we can anticipate that a hearing-impaired child, whose cognitive style preference is for spatial reasoning, will have difficulty with nonspatial cognitive tasks. Some researchers assert that a hearing-impaired child who uses visual communication systems may be using the right hemisphere of the brain; therefore, cognitive tasks of a logical/sequential nature requiring left-hemisphere activity may be understandably difficult. This area remains controversial.

11. *Working with More Than One Type of Data:* Recent research (Ottem, 1980) indicated that hearing-impaired learners experience more difficulty on tasks requiring reference to two items of data than do

hearing individuals. This research placed the fault with the hearing world, which has imposed on the deaf population a requirement about simple and unambiguous communication that is obtained by referring to single events.

12. *Linguistic Abstraction:* Hearing-impaired adults are reported to be able to abstract and integrate the semantic content of sentences into holistic semantic ideas (Brewer, Caccamise, & Siple, 1979, p. 22). Brewer et al. suggested that the abstraction process itself is a basic cognitive process whose functioning is "quite ubiquitous" and that the way in which the process operates in an individual is related to world knowledge and experience as well as to linguistic skills. But, they note that further research on children is needed in this area. Moores (1978) also challenged the traditional notion that hearing-impaired children are concrete thinkers, and he found no evidence to support that hypothesis (p. 137).

13. *Use of Symbols:* Furth (1964) remarked that deaf people grow up without a symbol system for communication, but a careful reflection on the nature of manual systems would seriously challenge his point. Manual systems of communication are also clearly based on symbols. More recently, however, Furth has implied that deaf people do use symbols. He noted that among deaf adolescents, symbolic life is simpler, more reality-oriented, and more firmly anchored in the self (1973, p. 49). He also made a useful differentiation between *symbol discovery* as a process and the use of symbols, and he reported a study in which 16-year-old deaf students were found to be significantly behind their hearing peers in discovery of symbols (1973, p. 59).

The crux of Furth's approach was the assumption derived from Piaget's work that intelligent thinking is not based on language, but is an internal process independent of language (Furth, 1964, p. 228). Moores challenged Furth's position as failing to demonstrate that deaf people lack language or are inferior at the formal operational level (Moores, 1978, p. 134). In fact, Suppes (1972) argued that deaf people are indeed using a type of language but are using it internally (p. 41). Moreover, Debes and Williams (1978), in a seminal paper on visual literacy, indicated that for a person reading manual communication, no cognition occurs that is separate from or not based originally on signs that have been read (p. 142).

Thus, we see normal performance by hearing-impaired subjects on some cognitive tasks and not on others; we also see controversy among the researchers as well as a number of unanswered questions for further research. It is generally accepted that the hearing-impaired child will have difficulty with English-language-related tasks if that child's native language is not English but American Sign Language. However, Furth made a useful point in regard to the whole area of cognitive development among hearing-impaired children when he hypothesized that deficient cognitive areas may be due not to any language deficiency but to a limited social environment (1964, p. 154). He later elaborated that deaf and culturally disadvantaged hearing groups were "remarkably similar" in overall intellectual development due to a lack of stimulation leading to thinking activities in both home and school (1973, p. 47). The latter statement would apply to the hearing-impaired children of hearing parents because of the frequent lack of regular manual communication by hearing parents with their hearing-impaired children. Furth's remark about school is an indictment of educational programs that have failed to stimulate and maintain high expectations for hearing-impaired children in the cognitive skills domain. The paper by Braden in this volume (see pp. 148–150), however, will be seen to challenge this assumption.

The relationship between language and cognition is both essential and complex. We know, for example, that using language enables us to restructure mental schemata, perceive reality in new ways, and redesign the strategies employed to solve problems (Klein, 1981, p. 449). A major body of research during the past 50 years indicates that language in social interaction is critical to effective cognitive development (Vygotsky, 1962, 1978; Wertsch, 1978). The work of Halliday (1973) and Tough (1977) has reinforced Vygotsky's work and given new insights into the degree of linguistic use by children in attacking cognitive problems.

The linguists' controversy over whether language determines thought or the reverse has been debated also in the field of deafness. Quigley and Kretschmer (1982) provide a highly useful summary of that research. Specifically, they provide a six-part categorization of the abilities of deaf learners to (a) discover principles, (b) transfer knowledge of a principle, (c) associate stimuli, (d) categorize objects, (e) solve Piagetian problems, and (f) think logically and manipulate symbols (p. 57). Thus, it is highly appropriate that cognitive intervention programs for hearing-impaired children should recognize and use language in a systematic manner since the linguistic deficits of hearing-impaired children are considered to be partly responsible for some of their difficulties in cognition.

Intervention Programs

If we accept the fact that certain specific cognitive deficiencies do exist for hearing-impaired children but that no evidence suggests less than the normal range of intellectual potential among the hearing impaired as a general group, then it is apparent that specific programs of activities in an educational setting may have promise for improvement of these skills.

The need for systematic intervention programs to address this cognitive problem has been recognized. Project LIFE, funded through a grant from the Bureau for the Education of the Handicapped of the U.S. Office of Education, is a mediated instructional program aimed at significantly reducing the language and reading problems of hearing-impaired children.

This program consists of several components, one of which focuses on perceptual thinking and is based on the theoretical model of the structure of intellect developed by J.P. Guilford (1966) and later refined for application to education by Mary Meeker (1969). The program uses a series of filmstrips and has been used widely in classes for hearing-impaired children with reported positive outcomes in language development.

Considerable interest is now being expressed in improving thinking skills in the classroom setting. Cognitive skills improvement programs for schools today are varied in form, depth, breadth, media, intent, and degree of required teacher preparation. Such programs have been categorized as follows:

1. Cognitive operations programs

2. Problem-solving or heuristics programs

3. Programs to develop thinking through language and the manipulation of symbols

4. Metacognitive programs

5. Programs to stimulate divergent thinking

A recent issue of the *Volta Review* carried two articles on improving cognitive skills, including one in which the writer called for classroom teachers of hearing-impaired students to develop their own programs and explained some guidelines for so doing (Cole, 1980, p. 344). Furth, after drawing conclusions from research on deaf children's need for practice in thinking and reasoning, developed an entire book of thinking games based on Piagetian theory and tasks (Furth & Wachs, 1974). Other existing school programs, such as the Peninsula Oral School approach, have focused on sequences of cognitive strategies or tasks for the hearing impaired, leading them through concept formation, interpretation, inference, and application of principles (Levine, 1976, p. 54).

The Instrumental Enrichment program (Feuerstein, 1978, 1980) is being used with some hearing-impaired adolescents. The program was developed originally in Israel by Reuven Feuerstein, a student of Piaget's, in response to the need for mediated learning experiences for culturally disadvantaged groups emigrating to Israel. In this program, which is a 3-year supplement to the regular curriculum, students focus on paper-and-pencil exercises of increasing complexity designed to develop and enhance 14 specific cognitive skills at the representational level of thinking. Evaluation data (Martin, Rohr-Redding, & Innes, 1983) indicate measurable gains in reading comprehension, math computation, abstract thinking, and systematic planning in problem-solving situations (see related papers in part 9).

Thus, the case for a wide range of prior research into the cognition of the hearing-impaired learner is clearly established as a means of developing specific methods for systematic intervention in the educational context.

Areas for Investigation

The many current questions in regard to cognition are impossible to answer in totality in any single volume. These questions include the following:

1. What do we mean by cognition?
2. Are cognitive skills generalizable across different domains of knowledge?
3. How can cognitive skills be best measured?
4. What roles do development, learning, and instruction play in the process of cognitive skill acquisition?
5. How can thinking skills be taught most effectively to hearing-impaired learners?
6. How can teachers be best trained to carry out that instruction?

From the review of the literature and the questions listed, the symposium planners proposed the following more specific organizing questions to which investigations were addressed.

1. What differences exist in cognition between hearing-impaired and hearing learners?
2. What variations in cognition for the hearing-impaired person are attributable to the effects of cultural background?
3. What effects on cognition are attributable to the communication modality of the learner (e.g., sign language users vs. oralists)?
4. What fundamental brain processes underlie cognition in hearing-impaired persons?
5. What techniques of cognitive measurement are the most useful in assessing the hearing-impaired learner, and why?
6. What types of interaction occur between cognition and social-emotional or affective factors in hearing-impaired persons?
7. What educational programs and procedures have been found to be successful school-based intervention strategies for improving the cognitive performance of hearing-impaired learners?
8. What effects do various parental activities have on the cognitive development of the hearing-impaired child?
9. What career-choice factors are related to cognitive development in the hearing-impaired person?

This list by no means exhausts the questions related to cognition and deafness, but it represents the major themes that will be seen in the papers that follow.

It is not expected that the papers contained herein will answer all of these critical questions. Yet, they should prove to be stimuli for careful thought and future research.

Readers who are interested in the detailed study behind any of the papers in this volume may (in many cases) obtain a copy of the longer original paper. These papers are available through the ERIC system; the ERIC document number is listed on the opening page of each paper.

A Final Cautionary Note About the State-of-the-Art

It is important to point out that this volume cannot be truly comprehensive in the sense of providing a complete picture of the state-of-the-art in the area of cognition, education, and deafness. The symposium for which these papers were prepared was conducted on the basis of the widely accepted procedure of a call for papers, a blind review and careful screening of all submitted papers, and, finally, a selection and categorization of those papers that met the established standards for addressing the symposium themes. However, no specific papers (except for the keynote address and the four-part synthesis) were specifically solicited; thus, the informed reader may well perceive some gaps in the topical coverage.

It is essential that readers wishing to have a thorough view of this field at this time consider both the breadth of paper topics in this volume and the well-prepared reaction remarks at the end of this volume by Donald F. Moores. The points made by Moores will be of great value in delineating those topics and researchers whose work complements the work in this volume. Thus, this collection together with those suggestions given by Moores should constitute a rather fully developed image of the field of cognition, education, and deafness as of the mid-1980s.

Purpose and Organization of This Book

This volume is designed to be far more than a proceedings of a conference. Rather, it is a summary of presented papers and the issues raised during their discussion, an analysis of groups of papers according to common themes, a synthesis of the overall implications of the symposium and its deliberations, and a challenge to the reader to carry on with further research and educational applications of what we are now learning about cognition and hearing impairment.

Part 2 of this book now continues with a keynote chapter that is a charge to educators and researchers on the importance of this topic as a subject for investigation. The following parts contain brief summaries of all the symposium papers arranged according to seven major themes. Some of the authors have cited papers within this text. These citations appear as (see [Author], pp. 000–000). At the end of each theme grouping is a thoughtful analysis of that group of papers by an objective expert in that theme area, followed by a list of issues raised for further investigation. Finally, a synthesis of the entire group of papers is presented, including the appropriate next steps for increasing our knowledge in this area; two responses to the synthesis are included from the complementary perspectives of an educational practitioner and an educational researcher, and the volume concludes with a more general response on the relationship between the field of psychology and the field of deafness. A list of suggested further readings is attached to some of the reference lists to assist readers who may wish to pursue various facets of this subject in more detail before embarking on their own research or on an educational implementation of the ideas presented.

References

Best, B., & Roberts, G. C. (1975). *Cognitive development in young deaf children* (Grant No. OEG 093321894533 [032]). Minneapolis: University of Minnesota, Research Development and Demonstration Center.

Brewer, L., Caccamise, F., & Siple, P. (1979). Semantic integration in the adult deaf. *Directions, 1*(2), 15–23.

Brown, A. (1978). Knowing when, where, and how to remember: A problem of metacognition. In R. Glaser (Ed.), *Advances in instructional psychology* (pp. 77–165). Hillsdale, NJ: Lawrence Erlbaum Associates.

Bruner, J. S. (1969, July). *Origins of problem-solving strategies in skill acquisition.* Paper presented at the International Congress of Psychology, London, England.

Cole, J. R. (1980). Thinking and curriculum. *Volta Review, 82,* 337–344.

Debes, J. L. & Williams, C. M. (1978). *Visual literacy, language, and learning.* Washington, DC: Gallaudet College, Visual Literacy Center.

Drever, J., & Collins, M. (1928). *Performance tests of intelligence.* Edinburgh: Oliver & Boyd.

Feuerstein, R. (1978). *Instrumental enrichment.* Baltimore: University Park Press.

Feuerstein, R. (1980). *Instrumental enrichment: An intervention program for cognitive modifiability.* Baltimore: University Park Press.

Furth, H. (1964). *Thinking without language.* New York: Free Press.

Furth, H. (1973). *Deafness and learning: A psychological approach.* Belmont, CA: Wadsworth.

Furth, H., & Wachs, H. (1974). *Thinking goes to school.* New York: Oxford University Press.

Guilford, J. P. (1966). *Structure-of-the-intellect factors and their tests.* Columbus, OH: Charles E. Merrill.

Gutentag, M., & Longfellow, C. (1977). Children's social attributions: Development and change. In C. Keasey (Ed.), *Nebraska Symposium on Motivation 1977: Social cognitive development* (pp. 305–334). Lincoln: University of Nebraska Press.

Halliday, M. A. K. (1973). *Explorations in the function of language.* London: Edward Arnold.

Hauptman, A. R. (1980). An investigation of the spatial reasoning abilities of hearing impaired students. *Directions, 1*(3), 43–44.

Henker, B., Whalen, C. K., & Hinshaw, S. P. (1980). The attributional contexts of cognitive intervention strategies. *Exceptional Education Quarterly, 1*(1), 17–30.

Jensema, C. (1975). *The relationship between academic achievement and the demographic characteristics of hearing impaired children and youth.* Washington, DC: Gallaudet College, Office of Demographic Studies.

Johnson, J. (1981, April). *Hearing impaired learner with special needs.* Paper presented at the Symposium on Media and the Hearing-Impaired, Lincoln, NE.

Kagan, J. (1971). *Understanding children: Behavior, motives and thought.* New York: Harcourt Brace Jovanovich.

Karchmer, M. A., & Belmont, J. M. (1976, November). *On assessing and improving deaf performance in the cognitive laboratory*. Paper presented at the meeting of the American Speech and Hearing Association, Houston, TX.

Keogh, B. K., & Glover, A. T. (1980). The generality and durability of cognitive training effects. *Exceptional Education Quarterly, 1*(1), 75–82.

Klein, M. L. (1981). Key generalization about language and children. *Educational Leadership, 38*(6), 446–448.

Levine, E. S. (1976). Psychological contributions. In R. Frisina (Ed.), *A bicentennial monograph on hearing impairment: Trends in the USA* (pp. 23–33). Washington, DC: A. G. Bell Association.

Lloyd, J. (1980). Academic instruction and cognitive behavior modification. *Exceptional Education Quarterly, 1*(1), 53–63.

Loper, A. B. (1980). Metacognitive development: Implications for cognitive training. *Exceptional Education Quarterly, 1*(1), 1–8.

Martin, D. S., Rohr-Redding, C., & Innes, J. (1983). Teaching thinking skills to the hearing-impaired adolescent. *Directions, 3*(4), 9–15.

McKinney, J. D., & Haskins, R. (1980). Cognitive training and the development of problem-solving strategies. *Exceptional Education Quarterly, 1*(1), 41–52.

Meadow, K. (1980). *Deafness and child development*. Berkeley: University of California Press.

Meeker, M. N. (1969). *Structure-of-the-intellect: Its interpretation and uses*. Columbus, OH: Charles E. Merrill.

Meichenbaum, D. (1980). Cognitive behavior modification with exceptional children: A promise yet unfulfilled. *Exceptional Education Quarterly, 1*(1), 83–88.

Moores, D. F. (1978). *Educating the deaf: Psychology, principles, and practices*. Boston: Houghton Mifflin.

Ottem, E. (1980). An analysis of cognitive studies with deaf subjects. *American Annals of the Deaf, 125*, 564–575.

Parasnis, I., & Long, G. L. (1979). Relationships among spatial skills, communication skills, and field dependence in deaf students. *Directions, 1*(2), 26–37.

Pfau, G. S. (1975). *Final report for Project LIFE* (Contract No. OEC 0-73-0608). Washington, DC: U.S. Office of Education.

Quigley, S. P., & Kretschmer, R. E. (1982). *The education of deaf children: Issues, theory and practice*. Baltimore: University Park Press.

Shulman, L. (1984, April). *Acquisition of reasoning skills: Agenda for research in the information age—The psychological perspective*. Paper presented at the annual conference of the American Educational Research Association, New Orleans, LA.

Suppes, P. (1972). *A survey of cognition in handicapped children* (Tech. Rep. No. 197). Stanford, CA: Stanford University, Institute for Mathematical Studies in the Social Sciences.

Tough, J. (1977). *The development of meaning*. New York: John Wiley & Sons.

Vernon, M. (1968). Five years of research on the intelligence of deaf and hard-of-hearing children: A review of literature and discussion of implications. *Journal of Research on Deafness, 1*(4), 1–12.

Vygotsky, L. S. (1962). *Thought and language*. Cambridge: MIT Press.

Vygotsky, L. S. (1978) *Mind in society*. Cambridge: Harvard University Press.

Webster's new world dictionary. (1970). New York: New World Publishing.

Wertsch, J. V. (Ed.). (1978). *Recent trends in Soviet psycho-linguistics*. White Plains, NY: M. E. Sharpe.

2 Cognition, Education, and Deafness: The Challenge

Cognition, Education, and Deafness: The Challenge

Edward E. Corbett, Jr.

We, in the field of deafness, have a great need to start a process by which new knowledge can be created. This process must begin by providing educators and researchers in deafness with the opportunity to probe at increasingly deeper levels into the areas of cognition, education, and deafness. We must go beyond our present efforts and extend research opportunities to more people, thus ensuring contributions from a much broader base.

One way in which we can broaden our knowledge is by studying the *cerebral cortex*. Over the years we have studied the brain's control over the hearing and speech processes. This study has provided us with information about disturbances in hearing and speech caused by the pathology of the ear; the disruption of the eighth cranial nerve; and the pathology of the brain itself, which makes it difficult to analyze or produce sound. In the last few years, researchers have described the mechanism whereby nerve impulses in individual auditory nerve fibers are initiated by receptor organs. Researchers also have been working on hearing aids to regulate the intensity of sound. Recent experiments with cochlear implants that evoke the electrical potential within the cochlea to stimulate hearing are making important progress.

In August 1983, *Time* magazine carried a cover story entitled, "What Do Babies Know?" Most notable in this article was the fact that studies of infant cognition had tripled in the past 5 years. In regard to studies of cognition and hearing, the article reported that

> the baby's ears have been functioning even before birth, and the newborn arrives with a whole set of auditory reactions. As early as the 1960's tests indicated that babies go to sleep faster to the recorded sound of a human heartbeat or any similarly rhythmic sound. More recent studies indicate that by the time they are born, babies already prefer female voices; within a few weeks, they recognize the sound of their mother's speech. (Friedrich, 1983, p. 55)

This is but one example of the numerous research endeavors in the areas of hearing and speech. As for language, just over 120 years ago Paul Broca formalized the notion of cerebral dominance for language (Segalowitz, 1983). Yet, in the last 15 years we have seen an enormous growth in this area stemming from Eric Lenneberg's treatise, *Biological Foundations of Language* (1967).

Segalowitz (1983) studied how language is represented in the human brain and found that each language function can be discussed with respect to its own organization within the brain. It continues to be a source of wonder that the 3-pound convoluted glob of gray tissue that controls life is capable of controlling language, speech, and emotion in humans, and that science has localized the functions of the brain in both hemispheres. Blakes-lee (1980) cites scientific evidence indicating that only the left hemisphere of our brain is capable of expressing its thoughts in words (verbal thoughts). The right hemisphere of the brain has its own separate train of thoughts that are nonverbal. This differentiation may not be as clear-cut as was once believed, and both controversy and research continue in this domain (see Rodda et al., pp. 94–99).

We know that there are four lobes of the brain in each cerebral hemisphere: (a) frontal, which contains the motor cortex; (b) parietal, which receives sensory input from the skin and muscles; (c) temporal, which contains nerve centers that influence speech, hearing, and emotions; and (d) occipital, which serves as the visual center of the brain.

For us in the field of deafness, it is common knowledge that much of what deaf people know about their world comes to them through their eyes. This fact tells us that the occipital lobe is frequently activated. For people with normal hearing, the ability of the brain to connect auditory with visual stimuli in the temporal lobe is evident. But what about the deaf? What evidence do we have that both components—auditory and visual—are less developed in people with sensory impairments?

Lenneberg (1964) stated that

> the ability to learn language is so deeply rooted in man that children learn it even in the face of dramatic handicaps. Congenital blindness has no obvious effect on word acquisition even though there is only a small fraction of words whose referents can be defined tactually. Congenital deafness has a devastating effect on the vocal facilitation for speech, yet presentation of written material enables the child to acquire language through a graphic medium without undue difficulties. Children suffering from gross and criminal parental neglect, or who have parents who have no spoken language whatever, as in the case of adult congenitally deaf parents, may nevertheless learn to speak with only a minimal delay. (p. 67)

Patten (n.d.) reported the case of Albert Einstein as an example of how visually mediated thinking could be effective.

> The eminent physicist Albert Einstein himself. . .indicate(s) that the creative thought process responsible for relativity theory and all the other Einsteinian innovations was completely non-verbal and mediated through the constructive manipulation of mentally visualized images. A biographical review shows that Einstein had a disability in verbal realms that contrasts sharply with his ability in non-verbal

spheres of activity. The scientist's poor school work, childhood misbehavior, and deficient and delayed language skills are explainable by a developmental defect in verbal learning probably due to a dysfunction of the dominant hemisphere. In the same way his extraordinary visual and spatial abilities can be explained by a compensatory increase in function of the non-dominant hemisphere.

At least one scientific genius was able to overcome a handicap by circumventing the verbal modality in which he was deficient and achieve greatness through the use of an unusual way of visual thinking. The suggestion is that other prople might benefit from a similarly applied strategy for solving problems, and that our present verbally oriented educational system may be preventing geniuses in visual thinking from achieving their full potential. (p. 1)

The implications here for deaf learners using a visual communication system are enormous. Medical doctors are finding that positron emission tomography (PET) is a useful tool in the diagnosis of human neurological disorders. Simply put, the PET takes pictures as we think. It takes pictures of the electrical functioning of the brain and isolates those activities that show neurological problems. However, Michael E. Phelps, a UCLA biophysicist, recently went beyond the realm of neurological problems and did a study of people with normal brains. Using PET, Phelps attempted to determine the subjects' ability to think in music and match pairs of musical tones.

To his surprise, some people's brain lit up on the left side, while others did so on the right. Perplexed, he and his colleagues checked the subjects' backgrounds. They found that those who had responded primarily on the right side had no musical background while those who lit up on the left side had been trained in music.

"Now that made sense," says Phelps. Those who used the right side of the brain said they used the bar scale to judge if the musical tones were alike. The left-hand side of the brain is thought to be the more analytical side. (Hale, 1983, p. 1)

Several questions come to mind in light of this information: Does visually mediated thinking apply to deaf people in general or in particular? Do we need a concerted effort to investigate the cerebral cortex involving the workings of the occipital lobe? Should we accentuate the positive—the fact that deaf people's cognitive efforts are enhanced by the use of vision—rather than identify the weaknesses of the auditory mechanism in the temporal lobe? We could call this study the *proficiency* model (vision) rather than the *deficiency* model (hearing and speech).

Another question that comes to mind is, Do deaf people dream? Of course they do, but how do they dream? Do they dream using the language of signs or vocal speech? Some psychiatrists who are interested in dream recall insist that people practice dream recall to improve the flow of information between the right and left hemispheres of the brain (Blakeslee, 1980). In retrospection, I find that I, who am deaf, do not use the language of signs in my dreams; I use vocal speech. Why? Is it because of my early training in the use of speech? I have checked with several of my deaf friends, and they say they communicate by signs in their dreams; so, we have an interesting variation among deaf persons that requires more research.

Some researchers unfortunately have equated speech with language or language with speech; however, as professionals in the field of deafness, we all know deaf people who do not speak intelligibly but who have mastered the English language. Our goals have been to teach speech to deaf children and to help them develop a language system that will enable them to function effectively in society. In the foreword to *Turning Points in the Education of Deaf People* (Scouten, 1984), Davila reiterated this point.

> Throughout the centuries, the men and women who have pioneered developments in the field of education of the deaf have been obsessed with singleness of purpose: teaching deaf children to process spoken and written language accurately, thereby permitting them to master learning and to interact successfully with the world around them. . . .the same basic objectives have guided, and more or less eluded educators of the deaf over the years. (p. vii)

Davila's conclusions echo the findings of a federally sponsored committee that was charged with investigating the state of education of the deaf in the early 1960s. Under the direction of Homer Babbidge, the committee found that success in educating and preparing deaf children for full participation in society was very limited due to two major factors: the failure to use experience and research in addressing the basic problems of language learning and the failure to develop more systematic and adequate programs for the deaf at all age levels (Babbidge, 1967).

This report discouraged many people in the field of deaf education because teaching speech and language to the deaf has been and continues to be an arduous task. In fact, Scouten (1984) pointed out that the Babbidge report had a traumatic effect on the field because of the negative publicity surrounding it. However, the report did list a number of recommendations for improving education in the age groups of 0–5, 6–16, 17–21, and 22. As a result of those recommendations, we have seen an infusion of federal priorities and dollars into this field over the last 20 years. It would be interesting now to have a "Babbidge Report Revisited" to determine the impact of those priorities and funds on the state of education of the deaf.

The International Symposium on Cognition, Education, and Deafness is a beginning step in the process of improving the state of education of the deaf. Perhaps with professionals like those assembled at the symposium contributing to the existing body of knowledge and continuing to help it grow, we may be in a position to find answers to those elusive butterflies— the questions. We may find ourselves doing more investigating now in the area of vision, having already spent considerable time and effort in the areas of hearing and speech. We know that the area of vision will contribute new information that will complement our knowledge in the areas of speech and hearing. This is my challenge to the field: Deaf children will continue to arrive in schools during the years ahead. Their characteristics are changing—from predominantly postlingually deaf to predominantly prelingually deaf. These children will continue to come to us with various sets of problems, so we must continue to apply the knowledge that we have accumulated over the years and develop new knowledge to help them develop language and become full participating members in society.

References

Babbidge, H. D. (1967). *Education of the deaf—The challenge and the charge.* Washington, DC: U.S. Government Printing Office.

Blakeslee, T. R. (1980). *The right brain.* New York: Doubleday, Anchor Press.

Davila, R. (1984). Foreword. In E. L. Scouten, *Turning points in the education of deaf people* (p. vii). Danville, IL: Interstate Printers and Publishers.

Friedrich, O. (1983, August 15). What do babies know? *Time,* pp. 52–59.

Hale, E. (1983, June 24). New scanner takes photos as we think. *USA Today,* p. 1.

Lenneberg, E. H. (Ed.). (1964). *New directions in the study of language.* Cambridge: MIT Press.

Lenneberg, E. H. (1967). *Biological foundations of language.* New York: John Wiley & Sons.

Patten, B. (n.d.). *Visually mediated thinking—A report of the case of Albert Einstein.* Unpublished manuscript.

Scouten, E. L. (1984). *Turning points in the education of deaf people.* Danville, IL: Interstate Printers and Publishers.

Segalowitz, S. J. (1983). *Language functions and brain organization.* New York: Academic Press.

3 Issues in the Growth and Development of Hearing-Impaired Learners

Theories and Models of Human Development: Their Implications for the Education of Deaf Adolescents

Irene Athey

Psychological theorists are by no means agreed on basic assumptions about human nature. Some of the most divisive issues focus upon whether the human organism is inherently reactive or proactive, whether perceptual and cognitive processes are essentially synthetic or analytic, and even upon the nature of the reality we perceive and know. Thus, the practitioner is at liberty to select among the various models, provided that these models do not start from opposite assumptions or lead to contradictory implications.

Theories of human development may be classified in many ways. A complex classification scheme can be used to generate a two-way table or grid that would serve as a framework for a systematic and unbiased review of competing theories. In this grid, theories and models can be categorized in two ways: *by content area* (i.e., physical/motor, cognitive, language, emotional/social, personality, moral, and vocational/career development) and *by type* (i.e., maturational/biological, environmental, and interactionist). Since the focus of this volume is on cognition, this paper will review only the cognitive area.

Children's cognitive abilities progress with age along the following dimensions: simple to complex, concrete to abstract, subjective to objective, and familiar to unfamiliar. All theories must account for these facts, but they do so in very different ways.

Cruickshank (1963) has suggested that phenomenological models are useful for understanding the dynamics of handicapped children because these models help us to see the world as these children construct it in their perception. An underlying assumption of these models is that, at any given time, the person constructs reality out of the past and present experience of the environment by using the cognitive skills acquired up to that time. Hence, the person is conceived as a product of construed experience-to-date interacting with the cognitive/affective modalities available as a product of this construed experience. Since a handicapped child's environment is by definition restricted, the reality that is constructed may be less differentiated (i.e., more simplistic, concrete, subjective, and lacking in distinctions and elaborations).

It is no accident, therefore, that Piaget's is the most useful theory in the cognitive area. We do not normally think of Piaget's theory as phenomenological, but his theory of knowledge bears certain similarities to phenomenological models. Piaget's early interest in biology provided him with the useful concept of *equilibration*, which he thought could be profitably applied to the problems of knowledge. Equilibration may be defined as "the internal regulatory factor underlying a biological organization" (Furth, 1969,

The complete version of this paper is available in microfiche or hard copy from ERIC Document Reproduction Service. Ask for Document No. ED 247 721.

p. 261). It is the process that restores a balance or harmony to an organism perturbed by events in its environment. For example, a jellyfish will respond to a blob of ink dropped in its immediate vicinity by swimming away or taking other evasive action. The maintenance of equilibrium appears to be a functional ingredient in an organism's welfare and in the preservation of the species. Like visual acuity or fleetness of foot, intelligence is also a form of adaptation to the environment and as such, Piaget reasoned, should be capable of explanation by the same principles.

Assimilation and accommodation are complementary aspects of the equilibration process. Assimilation is the process by which "every encounter with an environmental object necessarily involves some kind of cognitive structuring (or restructuring) of the object in accordance with the nature of the organism's existing intellectual organization" (Flavell, 1963, p. 48). Accommodation refers to the changes both in outward behavior and in the internal structures that occur as a result of the assimilation of new information. When both assimilation and accommodation have occurred, the structure is clearer, more sharply defined, and elaborated, and a new level of equilibrium is reached as a consequence. Hence, equilibration is the mechanism by which intellectual development takes place, and it is a conceptual cornerstone of Piaget's theory.

The functions of assimilation and accommodation are invariant through life. What then are the structures that result from the operations of equilibration? The structures are not invariant with age; they are what emerge when the functions operate on the raw data. It is the changes in the structures that give rise to the qualitative differences in thinking at different stages of development.

Growth in intelligence is continuous, but the qualitative differences that emerge are so great that it is possible to discern maturational stages that are rather broadly delineated, subject to wide individual variations in attainment, yet universal in their existence and invariant in sequence. An important feature of stage theories is that each stage builds upon earlier stages, so that lack of success in the tasks peculiar to one stage will have detrimental effects upon later stages. If we think of the skills to be attained at each level as developmental tasks, we may expect to find remnants of unresolved tasks from previous stages still affecting behavior at later stages, especially in the case of handicapped or deprived children.

The stages in Piaget's theory are (a) *sensorimotor period* (0–2 years), (b) *preoperational period* (2–7 years), (c) *concrete-operational period* (7–11 years), and (d) *formal-operational period* (11–adulthood). *Operations*, in Piaget's terminology, refers to the abililty to perform intellectual operations on data and to reason about their relationships. Facility in these operations makes for flexibility in thinking, again a quality that is sometimes lacking in deaf children.

Since growth is dependent on the assimilation of and accommodation to experience, it is necessarily slow. Each stage moves gradually into the next, and the final stage of formal operations may never be reached by some people in certain areas. Growth comes about when new experiences or new information upsets the person's mental equilibrium. If the new information is too alien to the person's experience or beyond comprehension, it will, of course, be ignored and thus will not upset the equilibrium. Typically, however, new information does set up a state of disequilibrium, which persists until, through assimilation and accommodation, a new level of equilibrium is reached (see Figure 1). According to Piaget, a primary stimulus for disequilibrium at all ages is the conversation of other children who are cognitively more advanced and thus able to challenge the learner's current beliefs. If deaf children are excluded from such experiences, or if their conversations are limited to peers who do not challenge their equilibrium, their world is likely to remain undifferentiated. Moreover, knowledge tends to feed upon itself, becoming geometrically self-generating. In this regard, the importance of conceptually and linguistically challenging experiences in early childhood cannot be overemphasized.

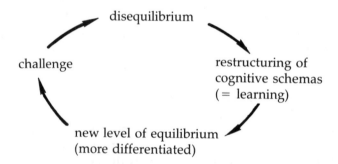

Figure 1. The cyclical causal spiral of intellectual growth.

A deaf child whose early environment contains few stimuli that provoke disequilibrium is unlikely to develop the cognitive structures necessary to proceed to higher levels of intellectual functioning. As noted earlier, the development of operational thinking proceeds from simple to complex, concrete to abstract, subjective to objective, and familiar to unfamiliar. Thinking that remains undifferentiated is thus likely to be simplistic, concrete, subjective, and non-risk-taking. In those areas where the child is *unsocialized* (to use Piaget's term), thinking remains at a lower operational level. If young deaf children remain in an overprotected environment or are exposed to drill rather than dialogue in school, they will be especially vulnerable in this regard. A well-developed communication system is clearly at the heart of the entire process. The medium in which this intellectual exchange takes place is probably less critical than the need for early and persistent efforts to establish and nurture opportunities for stimulating communication.

In his paper on egocentrism in adolescence, Elkind (1974) discussed the unique form that egocentrism takes at each stage of development. Each stage is treated as being primarily concerned with one major cognitive task. The major cognitive task of infancy is the conquest of the object, and the egocentrism of this stage is seen as the difficulty in differentiating between the object itself and the experience of the object. During the preschool period, the major cognitive task is the conquest of the symbol, and the egocentrism of this period consists in a lack of differentiation between symbol and referent. With the emergence of concrete operations, the task is that of mastering classes, relations, and quantities, and here it is the inability to differentiate clearly between mental constructions and perceptual givens that constitutes the egocentrism of middle childhood.

The major cognitive task of early adolescence is the conquest of thought. Formal operational thought not only enables adolescents to conceptualize thought, it also permits them to conceptualize the thought of other people. This is the crux of adolescent egocentrism (Muuss, 1962).

Egocentrism of all types may persist in the operational thought of deaf adolescents. In attempting to determine how well they comprehend academic content, world events, or personal situations, teachers and counselors who deal with deaf students may find Piaget's concepts to be illuminating and helpful.

It is perhaps the preoccupation with self noted by Elkind that leads the young person to question the basic meaning and value of human existence. The capacity for abstract thought leads to idealism and euphoria alternating with periods of despair and cynicism. Concern with national and global problems leads to comparisons of what could be with what is and to an impatience with the imperfections of the social world that adults have created and seem unable or unwilling to change. Political leaders have long recognized the value of harnessing the idealism and energy of youth to particular causes. The challenge to the behavioral scientist is to help develop the forms and means to enable adolescents everywhere to take a leading role in the struggle for the attainment of a world in which peace, freedom, and economic opportunity are omnipresent.

This challenge is particularly severe in dealing with deaf adolescents. Certainly it is desirable that they function to the fullest extent possible as participating citizens of the society, but a judicious appraisal of the forms that this participation may take is necessary. It requires a particular form of sensitivity and intuitive awareness of a deaf person's level of functioning to know how and when to advise bold new ventures or to be content with the consolidation of present achievements. Ultimately, it is deaf people themselves who must determine how they will construct their world, so that a balance between challenge and comfort is achieved. During adolescence, persons who serve as mentors and role models would seem to be of critical importance.

Though the picture painted here appears rather gloomy, it does not apply to all deaf adolescents. It is possible to find young deaf people who are alert, knowledgeable, socially adept, and realistically oriented toward a vocation. Such individuals provide us with an interesting test of the theories and hypotheses delineated here. We can only try to interpret the theories and to discern what they mean for the atypical adolescent. The picture is very complex because, given the nature of cognitive growth, one kind of deficiency is likely to lead to other types of deficiency. A study of those deaf students who *do* adjust to their handicap and cope with the demands and expectations of a frequently unsympathetic world presents a challenge to these theories, as well as a potentially rewarding source of insight.

References

Cruickshank, W. M. (1963). *The psychology of exceptional children and youth* (2nd ed.). Englewood Cliffs, NJ: Prentice-Hall.

Elkind, D. (1974). *Children and adolescents: Interpretive essays on Jean Piaget* (2nd ed.). New York: Oxford University Press.

Flavell, J. H. (1963). *The developmental psychology of Jean Piaget.* New York: Van Nostrand.

Furth, H. J. (1969). *Piaget and knowledge: Theoretical foundations.* Englewood Cliffs, NJ: Prentice-Hall.

Muuss, R. E. (1962). *Theories of adolescence* (2nd ed.). New York: Random House.

Play Behaviors of Deaf and Hearing Children

Lynne F. Mann

Piaget (1962a) maintained that the basic structure of cognitive development belies the necessity of oral language. Interaction and experiences with the environment enable a child to advance to higher levels of cognitive functioning. Although oral language, when it emerges, may enhance cognitive functioning, it is neither necessary nor sufficient for cognitive development to proceed (Furth, 1966). The earliest stages of cognitive development consist of nonverbal, sensorimotor activities. This sensorimotor activity eventually involves activities that require a child to operate upon the environment at a level that is concrete and bound by the child's perception of that environment. As the child grows and continues to interact with the environment, he or she becomes less perception-bound and exhibits abilities that require abstract rather than concrete thought. Cognitive development, from sensorimotor activity to abstract thought processes, is thought to be the result of the child's interaction, exploration, and experimentation in and with the environment (Piaget, 1962b).

Play may be defined as the process through which a child experiments with and interprets the environment. Through manipulation, imitation, and experimentation, the child proceeds from a subjective, egocentric understanding of the world to an objective, decentered interpretation of reality. This gradual shift from subjective to objective reality occurs as the child's cognitive abilities develop through increasingly sophisticated levels. Cognitive growth is therefore manifested in the observable play behaviors of the child. Play, then, is the external behavioral manifestation of cognitive development. Play is considered to be basic to the psychological, social, cognitive, and affective development of the young child (Mann, 1982).

It has been suggested that play may be a primary agent for cognitive change. Available evidence suggests that the development of cognitive abilities in deaf children appears to be unaffected by their deficient linguistic skill. Therefore, an examination of the play of hearing-impaired children could provide additional information regarding the relationship between play and cognitive development.

The present investigation involved observations of the play behaviors of 5 profoundly deaf children and 5 normally hearing children aged 36 to 72 months. The subjects were closely matched on birthdate, sex, socioeconomic status, and race. The deaf subjects knew no formal manual communication systems and had no other handicapping conditions. The hearing subjects had no handicapping conditions. All subjects were observed for four 15-minute periods during the free play portion of their school day. Only the visually observable behaviors were of interest in the study; any verbal-

The complete version of this paper is available in microfiche or hard copy from ERIC Document Reproduction Service. Ask for Document No. ED 247 722.

izations made by the children were masked from the observer, who was wearing an obsolete hearing aid that produced complex noise.

The investigators used three scales for interpreting the observed play behaviors: the Social Play Scale (Parten, 1932), an adaptation of the Socio-Dramatic Play Scale (Smilansky, 1968), and the Lunzer Scale of Organization of Play Behavior (Lunzer, 1959). These scales were chosen because each examined a different aspect of play development and all were consistent with the developmental nature of play.

The observers' objectivity on play descriptions was high (100% agreement on the Social Play Scale and 92% agreement on the Socio-Dramatic Play Scale). Interrater agreement on the coding procedures was also high (83% average across three play scales).

The results of the investigation indicated that play, as measured on these scales, was developmental in nature and that there was no difference in the sequence or rate of development between the two groups of children. Although there were no qualitative differences in the play behaviors between the two groups, the deaf subjects spent measurably less time at each level of play.

Prior research (Furth, 1966, 1971; Oléron, 1953) has indicated that there may be many factors that account for the quantitative differences found in the study. Among these factors are insufficient experience, lack of opportunity or training, and lack of information. All of these factors can be dealt with in the school and home environments of young deaf children.

If it is accepted that cognitive structures change as a result of the individual's manipulation and exploration of the environment, and if play is that very exploration and manipulation, it follows that play is the primary agent for cognitive change. Therefore, home and school environments must encourage play. In the home, parents and older siblings can initiate and participate in pretend or dramatic play with the young child. In the schools, teachers can encourage play by providing toys to play with, time to play, and open-ended play materials that call upon the child's imagination for their use.

In addition, teachers and parents must talk to their children as they play. Language that is related to play experiences will be more meaningful to the child than isolated vocabulary drill. Play, then, in addition to providing a medium for cognitive development, will also provide a medium for language development. Play is what children do because they are children, because they want to learn, and because they want to grow. Deaf children must be given that important chance to play.

References

Furth, H. (1966). *Thinking without language*. New York: Free Press.
Furth, H. (1971). Education for thinking. *Journal of Rehabilitation of the Deaf, 5,* 7–71.
Lunzer, E. A. (1959). Intellectual development in the play of young children. *Educational Review, 11,* 205–217.

Mann, L. F. (1982). Play behaviors of deaf and hearing children. *Dissertation Abstracts International, 42.* (University Microfilms No. 82–05, 458)

Oléron, P. (1953). Conceptual thinking of the deaf. *American Annals of the Deaf, 98,* 304–310.

Parten, M. B. (1932). Social participation among preschool children. *Journal of Abnormal and Social Psychology, 27,* 243–269.

Piaget, J. (1962a). *The language and thought of the child.* New York: Harcourt Brace & World.

Piaget, J. (1962b). *Play, dreams and imitation in childhood.* New York: W. W. Norton.

Smilansky, S. (1968). *The effects of socio-dramatic play on disadvantaged pre-school children.* New York: John Wiley & Sons.

Additional Reading

Bruner, J. S., Jolly, A., & Sylva, K. (Eds.). (1976). *Play: Its role in development and evaluation.* New York: Basic Books.

Furth, H., & Wachs, H. (1974). *Thinking goes to school.* New York: Oxford University Press.

Mann, L. F. (1981, November). *Play and the non-verbal child.* Paper presented at the national conference of the National Association for the Education of Young Children, Detroit, MI. (ERIC Document Reproduction Service No. ED 212 381)

Sutton-Smith, B. (1975, February). The useless made useful: Play as variability training. *School Review,* pp. 197–214.

Wolfgang, C. H., Mackender, B., & Wolfgang, M. E. (1981). *Growing and learning through play.* New York: Instructo/McGraw-Hill.

The Development of Communication Functions in Deaf Infants of Hearing Parents

Diana Pien

The development of effective communication skills is one of the primary goals of educational intervention programs for deaf children. One very important aspect of communication competence involves learning to use language for a variety of functions, including requesting actions, asking information-seeking questions, describing events, promising, and making jokes. Halliday (1975a, 1975b, 1978) proposed that language learning begins as soon as the child systematically uses actions and vocalizations to achieve a specific goal. Initially, a given vocalization and/or gesture is used exclusively for a single function so that function equals use. The transition to the adult linguistic system occurs as the child begins to develop more generalized functional categories, first through the acquisition of grammar and later through the adoption of linguistic roles such as questioner, narrator, and respondent/informer.

Halliday argued that prelinguistic acts are first used for the following four communicative functions:

1. *Instrumental:* "I want." The child expresses his or her demands and desires (e.g., points and reaches toward a cookie).

2. *Regulatory:* "Do as I tell you." The child explicitly tries to control the actions of others (e.g., pats a chair and wants mother to sit down).

3. *Interactional:* "You and me." The child uses speech or gestures for primarily social or affective communication (e.g., says "Hi").

' *Personal:* "Here I come." The child expresses his or her feelings, interests, and actions (e.g., says "Cat!" while looking at a cat).

These functions can be expressed nonlinguistically by using gestures, pointing, or uttering systematic vocalizations, as well as through conventional words. Later in the one-word stage, the following two functions appear:

1. *Heuristic:* "Tell me why." The child demands and learns names for objects (e.g., asks "Da?" while pointing to an object).

2. *Imaginative:* "Let's pretend." The child creates a world of his or her own through sound play, make-believe (e.g., sings "la-la-la").

In Halliday's model the most sophisticated and final linguistic function to develop is the *informative* function whereby the speaker imparts new information that is unknown to the listener. This function involves the

The complete version of this paper is available in microfiche or hard copy from ERIC Document Reproduction Service. Ask for Document No. ED 247 723.

narration of past and future events and does not include requests for absent objects or persons. All the earlier functions represent the use of language in contexts that exist independently of the linguistic system. But the informative function has no existence independent of language itself (Halliday, 1975a, p. 31). The informative function requires both the ability to create a mental representation of an event and also skill in role taking; the speaker must adopt the linguistic role of narrator or exchanger of information, as in asking-and-telling. Thus, Halliday not only provides a detailed model of the development of linguistic functions, but he also provides a framework for placing language in its social-cognitive context.

The present paper applied Halliday's model in analyzing the development of communication functions in 5 deaf infants having hearing parents. The 5 deaf children were enrolled in a parent-infant intervention program using total communication with children between the ages of 16 and 29 months. Three 20–40-minute videotapes of each child in a free-play situation with his or her parents were analyzed for this study. The first videotaped session occurred at program-entry and the last two videotapes were made at program-exit at age 3 years. The functions of all the children's gestures, pointing responses, communicative vocalizations, and signs were coded using adaptations of Halliday's categories of language functions.

The data from the present study in general support Halliday's order of functional development. For all five children, the instrumental, regulatory, interactional, and personal functions seemed to develop prior to the heuristic, imaginative, and informative functions as predicted by Halliday's model. The present data, however, differed from his theory in that the development of the latter three functions was not necessarily concurrent with the development of syntax (i.e., combination of signs and/or gestures to form multisign utterances; Hoffmeister, Moores, & Ellenburger, 1975). Syntax did not appear to be sufficient for the use of language for the imaginative, heuristic, and informative functions because all five children produced multisign/gesture utterances in the last two videotapes, but only one child productively used these three functions. The late appearance of the heuristic function was consistent with other studies that have found that deaf children of hearing parents infrequently ask information-seeking questions (Day, 1981; Meadow, Greenberg, Erting, & Carmichael, 1981).

For the one child who productively used all of Halliday's functions, imaginary pretend-play episodes appeared to facilitate the use of both the imaginative and informative functions. This unexpected finding that the informative function appeared frequently in imaginary pretend-play episodes was interpreted in terms of the shared role-taking skills involved in imaginary pretend-play. This play may have been a highly motivating situation for using language to convey new information unknown to the audience, especially because of the immediate communicative pressure to tell the parents about the imaginary play so they could join in.

One of the specific implications of this research for language programming in parent-infant and preschool programs for hearing-impaired children is the need for a greater focus on the functions of language that deaf children see and use. These functions include not only Halliday's categories but also speech acts used for directives, settling disputes, persuasion, promising, etc. (Ervin-Tripp, 1977; Searle, 1975). While the informative and imaginative functions of language can be facilitated through the encouragement of pretend-play, using imaginary or dissimilar objects, the acquisition of the wider range of direct and indirect speech acts requires exposure to sign language as a first language. Such exposure cannot be given by hearing parents who are learning sign language as a second language. Innovative ideas for giving deaf children exposure to deaf native signers include using deaf adults as "big brothers" or "sisters" for weekend social interactions in nonschool environments as well as employing deaf adults as aides or teachers in classroom settings.

References

Day, P. S. (1981). The expression of communicative intention. In H. Hoemann & R. Wilbur (Eds.), *Interpersonal communication and deaf people* (Working Paper No. 5, pp. 1–22). Washington, DC: Gallaudet College.

Ervin-Tripp, S. (1977). Wait for me, rollerskate! In S. Ervin-Tripp & C. Mitchell-Kernan (Eds.), *Child discourse* (pp. 165–189). New York: Academic Press.

Halliday, M. A. K. (1975a). *Learning how to mean: Explorations in the development of language.* London: Edward Arnold.

Halliday, M. A. K. (1975b). *Learning how to mean.* In E. H. Lenneberg & E. Lenneberg (Eds.), *Foundations of language development* (pp. 239–265). New York: Academic Press.

Halliday, M. A. K. (1978). Meaning and the construction of reality in early childhood. In H. Pick & E. Saltzman (Eds.), *Modes of perceiving and processing information* (pp.67–96). Hillsdale, NJ: Lawrence Erlbaum Associates.

Hoffmeister, R., Moores, D., & Ellenburger, R. (1975). Some procedural guidelines for analyzing ASL. *Sign Language Studies, 7,* 121–137.

Meadow, K., Greenberg, M., Erting, C., & Carmichael, H. (1981). Interactions of deaf mothers and deaf preschool children. *American Annals of the Deaf, 126,* 454–468.

Searle, J. (1975). Indirect speech acts. In P. Cole & J. Morgan (Eds.), *Syntax and semantics* (pp. 59–81). New York: Academic Press.

Additional Reading

Curtiss, S., Prutting, C., & Lowell, E. (1979). Pragmatic and semantic development in young children with impaired hearing. *Journal of Speech and Hearing Research, 22,* 534–552.

Dore, J. (1975). Holophrases, speech acts and language universals. *Journal of Child Language, 2,* 21–39.

Jackowitz, E., & Watson, M. (1980). Development of object transformations in early pretend play. *Developmental Psychology, 16,* 543–549.

McCune-Nicolich, L. (1981). Toward symbolic functioning: Structure of early pretend games and potential parallels with language. *Child Development, 52,* 785–797.

Nelson, K. (1978). Early speech and its communicative context. In F. Minifie & L.
Lloyd (Eds.), *Communicative and cognitive abilities* (pp. 443–473). Baltimore: University Park Press.

Shatz, M., Shulman, M. A., & Bernstein, D. K. (1980). The responses of language
disordered children to indirect directives in varying contexts. *Applied Psycholinguistics, 1,* 295–306.

Analysis

Pat Spencer Day
Kathryn P. Meadow-Orlans

The three papers in part 3 are concerned with both cognitive and linguistic development of deaf children in three different age groups: 1–3-year-olds (Pien), 3–6-year-olds (Mann), and adolescents (Athey). Profound and difficult issues are raised about (a) the relationship of language to thought, and cognitive to linguistic development and (b) the effect of environmental differences in deaf children's development of language and cognitive skills.

Pien studied the pragmatics (functional use) of language of deaf toddlers with hearing parents, all of whom were learning a signed language. Pragmatics is an aspect of language development felt to be heavily related to both symbolic abilities (cognition) and social interaction (Bates, 1976a, 1976b; Halliday, 1975). Discussion of Pien's study focused on the relative lack of the children's use of the informative function as compared to hearing children's productions at the one- and two-word stage of expressive language. This finding corroborates earlier work with preschool-age hearing-impaired children by Curtiss, Prutting, and Lowell (1979), and Day (1981). Of special interest, however, was Pien's apparently serendipitous finding that the one subject who engaged most frequently in symbolic or imaginary play was also most proficient in using language for the informative function and that that function was expressed primarily during symbolic play. Pien proposed that this apparent relationship could have implications for pragmatic assessment procedures and for parent-infant or toddler educational programs. She suggested that the child's participation in imaginary play could encourage the development and use of the informative function in language.

Pien also pointed out that her signing deaf subjects might develop a different pragmatic system than that of hearing children due to the more restricted use of signing by persons in the deaf subjects' environment. In addition to the often noted restriction in the number of people that those children can observe and "oversee" using language (Liben, 1978; Schlesinger, 1978), studies have reported that hearing parents of deaf children tend to give more directive or instructive messages and fewer explanatory or informative messages to their children than do parent-child dyads who share hearing status (Hyde, Power, & Elias, 1980; Meadow, Greenberg, Erting, & Carmichael, 1981; Schlesinger & Meadow, 1972). The functional language system that is modeled for deaf children of hearing parents therefore may be structurally different from that to which hearing children are exposed.

Some modifications in procedure would strengthen and simplify the interpretation of Pien's important work. These modifications would be aimed toward more standardization of the context in which the communicative behaviors are observed. First, instructions to parents should be uniform. Pien noted in her discussion that the parent of the child who demonstrated symbolic play during the taping session was asked to engage in some pretend play; other parents were not. This procedure was done because the parent had apparently originally misinterpreted the purpose of the session and seemed to be limiting the kind of activity that was occurring. After this child's symbolic play was observed, Pien asked the children's teachers which of the children frequently engaged in such play in the classroom. The response was that the subject who became involved in such play during the taping session was the only child reported to do so in the classroom. This anecdotal evidence seems to support Pien's interpretation of her data, but her findings would be strengthened by having the instructions uniform for all participants in the activities.

Another variation in the context of Pien's communication samples is the sex of the participating parent. Some of her subjects were taped while interacting with their mothers; at least one subject was interacting with her father. Literature regarding interaction between hearing children and their parents suggests that there are some interactive differences related to the sex of the parent (Lamb, 1978). Interaction studies of hearing-impaired children and their parents should, therefore, attempt to control for this factor.

Mann carefully avoided including language behaviors in her study of preschool orally trained deaf children's play skills. Discussion of her findings and interpretations, however, focused on the same topics of communication and interaction that are so salient in the Pien paper. In comparison with a matched group of hearing children, the deaf children engaged in the same types of play but spent less time in each activity. In addition, one of Mann's older deaf subjects engaged in considerably more isolated, but symbolically advanced, play than did any of the other deaf or hearing children. Mann interpreted the deaf children's different pattern of time spent in each play category as reflecting a lack of general information plus a lack of opportunities for and experiences with play. She assumed these deficiencies were due in part to the emphasis on parents' roles as teachers of their deaf children, which leaves little time or energy for play, as well as to the children's delay in language skills. Both parents and teachers, she stressed, should recognize the importance of play as a major vehicle deserving a significant place in school and at home.

Mann's data presentation seems to indicate individual differences among her subjects that may not be related to hearing status. Her oldest hearing-impaired subject, for example, seems to have presented a different pattern of time spent in the various play categories compared to either hearing subjects or the younger hearing-impaired subjects. These differences between subjects affect the confidence with which interpretation of the hearing-impaired children's play behaviors can be made.

Athey's theoretical paper reviewed the implications of phenomenological models of development for understanding deaf adolescents' cognitive skills. She concluded that Piaget's stage theory of development, which is similar to phenomenological models, was most helpful. Piaget (1954) described development as an invariant sequence of qualitatively different stages resulting from interaction between maturation, or biological factors, and experience.

A discussion of Athey's paper was prepared for the Symposium on Cognition, Education, and Deafness by Barry Culhane of the National Technical Institute for the Deaf. He noted that Piaget's concept of disequilibration-equilibration implies a need to challenge the deaf child, giving him or her the means for questioning ideas, opinions, and beliefs. In addition to how one communicates with deaf children and adolescents, what is communicated is critical for cognitive growth beyond the stage of an egocentric or subjective view of events and feelings toward a stage of flexibility in perspective.

Although Athey's paper most directly addressed the application of Piaget's developmental model to descriptions of deaf children's cognitive skills, all three papers rely to some degree on assumptions from that model. The most evident common assumption is that the role of interaction with persons in the environment is a critical element in the process of cognitive and linguistic development. Piaget, although he did not emphasize affective or social development in his studies, did point out that communication and interaction with people and objects is an important source of new information, which can result in modification of existing concepts and ideas as exemplified in the equilibration model (Piaget, 1968). It is clear that the interactions between deaf children and parents who do not share a functional communication system are different from those reported for parent-child dyads who do share the same system (Meadow, Greenberg, & Erting, 1983; Wedell-Monnig & Lumley, 1980).

Similarly, the deaf child's interactive experiences with other children and adults (providing they do not share a system of fluent communication) differ from those described for hearing children who were used as a basis of existing developmental models such as Piaget's. All three of the papers presented are concerned with the deaf child's verbal or nonverbal interactive experiences, and each author seems to propose that specific environmental modifications be undertaken in order to make the deaf child's interactive experiences more like those described for hearing children or for deaf children with deaf parents. Those modifications would involve teaching parents how to play with their children, increasing the role of play in the classroom, and structuring deaf students' educational environments to maximize possibilities for disequilibration.

A second assumption shared by all three authors, which can be traced to Piaget's work, is that despite the value of verbal skills and interaction for cognitive development, cognitive development can and does occur separately from linguistic development. Language is seen as one specialized form of a more general symbolic or representational ability (Bates, 1976a; Piaget, 1962). Based on this assumption, both Pien and Mann propose that development of this symbolic ability through play will promote and advance cognitive growth as well as provide a context for language experience.

Related to this issue of the relationship between linguistic and cognitive development is the work of Hans Furth, who has been an important interpreter of Piaget's work in the United States. Furth based much of his Piagetian research on work with deaf children, particularly his book *Thinking Without Language* (1966). His basic conclusion was summarized in the title of his book: Logical, intelligent thinking does not need the support of a language, but language is dependent on the structure of intelligence (p. 228). One questionable aspect of Furth's conclusion is his definition of language as an *oral and spoken medium.* At the time his research was done, sign language was not considered a real language, and researchers did not collect data on deaf children's proficiency in a sign language system. More recently, of course, sign language has come of age, and deaf children may well be considered to have language proficiency even though their English proficiency is sometimes minimal.

A third assumption inherent in these papers is the acceptance of a stage theory of development in which successful accomplishment of tasks in one stage is a necessary base for subsequent accomplishments. Thus, incomplete or very uneven development at an early stage may alter the organization of future development and result in its becoming more and more different from the expected sequence as the child matures. Such an assumption can result in a disproportionate emphasis on preschool development and in desperate efforts to compensate for differences resulting from hearing loss.

Although the assumptions just described are commonly accepted in the field of special education and have been supported in studies of exceptional development, their uncritical acceptance may lead to overdependence upon untried interventions before they are experimentally validated and may also lead to limiting the scope of instructional interventions. The idea of encouraging play between parent and child, or teacher and child, is positive. Discussants of these papers were eager to obtain curricula to build play skills. However, this approach to structuring adult-child interaction, despite being called play, does not necessarily justify that label. Play encompasses characteristics of playfulness, spontaneity, and joy (Lieberman, 1977), which are difficult to reproduce in a structured situation. It is interesting that Pien's subject who demonstrated elaborate symbolic play had not been in such a training program. It is important to provide opportunities at home and at school for all kinds of play. It may be necessary to show teachers and parents that play is a valuable mechanism for learning and to officially give permission for play if adults have been previously convinced that they must constantly teach the deaf child. But the affective component of play and interaction, which is most likely to be lost in a structured approach, should not be forgotten. This aspect of play was not addressed in these papers.

Suggestions that participating in symbolic play will affect language development should also receive critical attention. While there is general agreement that language skills do not develop without underlying cognitive abilities and that symbolic play and language tend to emerge closely in time (Bates, Camioni, & Volterra, 1975), those relationships are not sufficient to indicate any causal effect between the two functions. In fact, the very assumption that at least early cognitive development can proceed beyond language skill level seems to indicate that no such causal relationship exists. This is not to say that there is not a large role for play in school or home; however, expectations that specific play activities will improve language skills may be dashed when exposed to experimental validation procedures.

There is a similar need for controlled research on the validity of the stage concept of development for hearing-impaired children. Piaget's work, despite the abstraction of qualitative stages, has frequently referred to the existence of horizontal *décalage,* or varied levels of development across cognitive areas at one point in time (Inhelder & Piaget, 1958; Piaget, 1960). By stretching that concept, a deaf child's different levels of verbal and nonverbal functioning at one time might be considered to be a very special kind of décalage. The question remains as to whether such a décalage in the early years has consistent effects on later functioning, or whether compensatory instruction or intensive experiences at later ages can fill those gaps and result in normal functioning. Projects currently underway with hearing-impaired adolescents (see Jonas & Martin, pp. 172–175) may provide some answers to that question. The fact that such work is being undertaken demonstrates that educators expect to be able to effect significant change in deaf adolescents' logical thinking, conceptualizing, and learning skills despite earlier deficiencies. If methodologies for producing such change during the school years could be identified, some of the intense pressure might be removed from parents and teachers of younger deaf children. Then perhaps more spontaneous play and interaction could occur without structured programming.

Any such spontaneity will be dependent upon the factor central to all considerations of development in hearing-impaired children: communication. A review of the differences and deficits in deaf children and adolescents reported or presumed in these papers, suggests that most might be resolved if ways could be found to help all hearing parents acquire and use a manual method of communicating with their deaf infants and children.

Schlesinger contends (1972) that both meaning and enjoyment are necessary components of successful mother-child interaction. Thus, shared symbol systems of one kind or another must exist if participants in an interaction are to share meaning. That sharing of meaning—

> reciprocity, appropriateness, playfulness—appears to be prerequisite for optimal cognitive development, particularly in the area of linguistic meaning and competency. A warm and positive mother-child relationship does not appear to be enough to insure linguistic competence if these other characteristics are not present. But a warm, mutually gratifying learning environment does seem to be a necessary if not sufficient condition in cognitive growth (p. 99) . . . Meaning has been studied microscopically; enjoyment has barely been touched upon. (p. 100)

Enjoyment, meaning, symbolization, interaction, language, and disequilibration—all are necessary to the optimal development of a child. There are important gaps in our knowledge about the interplay among these factors in the growth of hearing-impaired children, particularly in the first 2 years of life. Many questions remain to be researched. Meanwhile, educators must read widely, critically evaluate findings and suggestions made by researchers, and synthesize ideas offering promise of facilitating students' development. Research reports should be considered with several questions in mind: Is the research based on current knowledge about deaf children's needs and on special characteristics of language acquisition and use? Does the researcher perceive deaf children as potentially competent rather than as necessarily deficient? Do suggested interventions consider the total child, including affective and social aspects of development? Do the ideas make sense in relation to the practitioner's experiential knowledge of deaf children's learning and development?

Because we lack a cohesive body of descriptive information, it is especially important for researchers and educators to work together with deaf students and their parents to facilitate optimal development for each individual deaf child.

References

Bates, E. (1976a). *Language and context: The acquisition of pragmatics.* New York: Academic Press.

Bates, E. (1976b). Pragmatics and sociolinguistics in child language. In D. Morehead & A. Morehead (Eds.), *Normal and deficient child language* (pp. 411–463). Baltimore: University Park Press.

Bates, E., Camioni, L., & Volterra, V. (1975). The acquisition of performatives prior to speech. *Merrill-Palmer Quarterly, 21,* 205–226.

Curtiss, S., Prutting, C., & Lowell, E. (1979). Pragmatic and semantic development in young children with impaired hearing. *Journal of Speech and Hearing Research, 22,* 534–552.

Day, P. (1981). The expression of communicative intention: Deaf children and hearing mothers. In H. Hoemann & R. Wilbur (Eds.), *Interpersonal communication and deaf people* (Working Paper No. 5, pp. 1–22). Washington, DC: Gallaudet College.

Furth, H. (1966). *Thinking without language: Psychological implications of deafness.* New York: Free Press.

Halliday, M. A. K. (1975). *Learning how to mean: Explorations in the development of language.* London: Edward Arnold.

Hyde, M. B., Power, D. J., & Elias, G. C. (1980). *The use of the verbal and non-verbal control techniques by mothers of hearing-impaired infants* (Research Report No. 5). Australia: Mt. Gravatt College of Advanced Education, Centre for Human Development Studies.

Inhelder, B., & Piaget, J. (1958). *The growth of logical thinking from childhood to adolescence.* New York: Basic Books.

Lamb, M. E. (1978). The father's role in the infant's social world. In J. H. Stevens, Jr., & M. Mathews (Eds.). *Mother/child father/child relationships* (pp. 87–108). Washington, DC: National Association for the Education of Young Children.

Liben, L. S. (1978). Developmental perspectives on the experiential deficiencies of deaf children. In L. S. Liben (Ed.), *Deaf children: Developmental perspectives* (pp. 195–215). New York: Academic Press.

Lieberman, J. N. (1977). *Playfulness: Its relationship to imagination and creativity.* New York: Academic Press.

Meadow, K. P., Greenberg, M. T., & Erting, C. (1983). Attachment behavior of deaf children with deaf parents. *Journal of the American Academy of Child Psychiatry, 22,* 23–28.

Meadow, K. P., Greenberg, M. T., Erting, C., & Carmichael, H. (1981). Interactions of deaf mothers and deaf preschool children: Comparisons with three other groups of deaf and hearing dyads. *American Annals of the Deaf, 126,* 454–468.

Piaget, J. (1954). *The construction of reality in the child.* New York: Ballantine Books.

Piaget, J. (1960). The general problems of the psychobiological development of the child. In J. M. Tanner & B. Inhelder (Eds.), *Discussion on child development* (Vol. 4, pp. 3–27). *The fourth meeting of the World Health Organization Study Group on the Psychobiological Development of the Child.* London: Tavistock Publications.

Piaget, J. (1962). *Play, dreams and imitation in childhood.* New York: W. W. Norton.

Piaget, J. (1968). *The psychology of intelligence.* Totowa, NJ: Littlefield, Adams.

Schlesinger, H. S. (1972). Meaning and enjoyment: Language acquisition of deaf children. In T. J. O'Rourke (Ed.), *Psycholinguistics and total communication: The state of the art* (pp. 92–102). Silver Spring, MD: American Annals of the Deaf.

Schlesinger, H. S. (1978). The effects of deafness on childhood development: An Eriksonian perspective. In L. S. Liben (Ed.), *Deaf children: Developmental perspectives* (pp. 157–169). New York: Academic Press.

Schlesinger, H. S., & Meadow, K. P. (1972). *Sound and sign: Childhood deafness and mental health.* Berkeley: University of California Press.

Wedell-Monnig, J., & Lumley, J. (1980). Child deafness and mother-child interaction. *Child Development, 51*(3), 766–774.

Related Educational and Research Issues

1. To what extent is parent mediation essential in the play of hearing-impaired children as a facilitator of language development?

2. What differences in ultimate language development are brought about by parent use of ASL versus English, versus gestures?

3. What are the positive and negative effects of mainstreamed classrooms on the cognitive development of hearing-impaired learners in relation to the interaction between hearing and hearing-impaired children?

4. What is the role of hearing siblings in the cognitive development of the hearing-impaired child, particularly in relation to play situations?

5. What active role, if any, should teachers and parents take in the stimulation and mediation of play among hearing-impaired children?

4 Cognitive Styles and Problem-Solving Strategies

The Development of Perceptual Processes and Problem-Solving Activities in Normal, Hearing-Impaired, and Language-Disturbed Children

Felicie Affolter

Developmental skills appear and improve in a regular sequence in normal children. Severely hearing-impaired children develop similarly to normal children (Furth, 1966); performances that do not require auditory information-processing show the same sequence of stages. Gaps can be accounted for by the auditory impairment and are predictable. Current theories of development account for such observations. They assume the existence of a direct relationship between skills and stages; complex skills develop out of simple skills in a regular manner (Mussen, 1970). For some theories, such development occurs continuously, for others it occurs in stages.

However, such a model does not account for the results of our observational study conducted with a group of children with language and learning problems. One subgroup of children had additional severe hearing losses, the other subgroup did not (Affolter & Stricker, 1980). Longitudinal findings underlined that the sequences of skill acquisition of these children differed substantially from normal controls. Investigations of perceptual performances and of problem-solving activities of these children revealed two other important differences. First, hearing-impaired children were like normals in successive pattern and form recognition in different modality conditions and in problem-solving activities. Second, children with severe language and learning problems, with or without a hearing loss, differed from the normal and hearing-impaired children (a) in successive pattern recognition in all modality conditions; (b) in the recognition of tactile but not of visual forms (Affolter & Stricker, 1980); and (c) in the evaluative but not in the hypothetic or feedback aspects of problem-solving activities.

The investigators inferred that severely language-disabled and learning-disturbed children with or without hearing loss exhibit perceptual disturbances not of a visual but of a tactile-kinesthetic or intermodal kind. Such disturbances seem to inhibit adequate evaluation of information when solving problems in daily life situations. Observations of problem-solving activities of normal children (Bower, 1977) and hearing-impaired children over the years suggest that tactile-kinesthetic experiences arising out of such activities are basic to development. Since language-disturbed children fail in such experiences, their development is therefore disturbed.

To account for such longitudinal and cross-sectional findings, another model of development must be described, one that assumes no direct rela-

Preparation of this article was supported in part by Swiss National Science Foundation Grants 3.237.69, 3.448.70, 3.902.72, 3.2050.73, 3.504.75, 3.711.76, and 3.929-0.78.

The complete version of this paper is available in microfiche or hard copy from ERIC Document Reproduction Service. Ask for Document No. ED 247 708.

tionship among skills or stages. Complex skills do not develop out of simple skills in a direct manner. Skills develop out of tactile-kinesthetic interactions with reality in the form of problem-solving activities. Experience of this kind allows for the acquisition of limited sets of tactile-kinesthetic-visual and/or tactile-kinesthetic-auditory rules. A given set of such rules permits an infinite number of performances. These rules, which gain increasing complexity, at first permit performances that are characteristic of lower levels of development, while later performances are characteristic of higher developmental levels.

The results of the investigations described here have direct implications for teaching and research. Teachers must now

1. Focus on the acquisition of a limited set of tactile-kinesthetic-visual rules and not on the acquisition of a list of numerous skills.

2. Provide an environment of reality that confronts the child continually with problems of daily life and permits active tactile-kinesthetic exploration (Affolter, 1981).

3. Ascertain that children extract adequate tactile-kinesthetic information when interacting with the environment (Affolter, 1974).

Researchers must consider the possibility that tactile-kinesthetic interaction with the environment is necessary for development. There is a lack of information about tactile-kinesthetic information processing and its relationship to cognitive development (Pick, 1980) and existing disturbances. Further research in this area must be conducted.

Interaction with the environment gives the child the required experience for extracting basic sets of tactile-kinesthetic rules. There is little knowledge yet about which sets of tactile-kinesthetic rules underlie developmental performances. How these rules are acquired and what kinds of disturbances are possible are important areas to investigate.

References

Affolter, F. (1974). Einsatz und Beschränkung der audio-visuellen Methode im Sprachaufbau des schwer hörbehinderten Kindes. In Verein Desterreichischer Taubstummenlehrer (Eds.), *Audio-visuelle Mittel und Medien im Unterricht Hörgeschädigter*. Linz: Trauner.

Affolter, F. (1981). Perceptual processes as prerequisites for complex human behavior. *International Rehabilitation Medicine, 3*, 3–10.

Affolter, F., & Stricker, E. (1980). *Perceptual processes as prerequisites for complex human behavior*. Bern: Hans Huber.

Bower T. G. R. (1977). *A primer of infant development*. San Francisco: Freeman.

Furth, H. (1966). *Thinking without language*. New York: Free Press.

Mussen, P. H. (Ed.). (1970). *Carmichael's manual of child psychology*. New York: John Wiley & Sons.

Pick, H. L. (1980). Tactual and haptic perception. In B. Blasch & R. L. Welsh (Eds.), *Foundations of orientation and mobility* (pp. 89–114). New York: American Foundation for the Blind.

Hearing-Impaired Students' Performance on the Piagetian Liquid Horizontality Test

Virginia Murphy-Berman
Lee Witters
Richard Harding

Numerous studies have been conducted to assess patterns of cognitive development in children. One skill considered important by Piaget and Inhelder (1956) in the developmental sequence is the child's ability to understand the principle of liquid horizontality—the idea that still water remains invariantly level regardless of the angle of the container. Comprehension of this principle taps the child's ability to utilize external frames of reference to accurately represent objects in space.

Studies with hearing subjects have indicated that females appear to have considerably more difficulty with the horizontality principle than males (Kelly & Kelly, 1977; Kelly & Witters, 1981; Morris, 1971; Rebelsky, 1964; Williamson & Reynolds, 1973). Hearing subjects, in general, have also been found to perform better on the horizontality task if the water containers are depicted with curved rather than more perceptually distracting straight sides (Walker & Krasnoff, 1978; Williamson & Reynolds, 1973).

Several investigators have studied acquisition of the horizontality principle among secondary-level hearing-impaired students (Murphy-Berman, Witters, & Harding, 1983; Witters-Churchill, Kelly, & Witters, 1983). These studies indicated that container shape had a similar impact on students' task performance in both the hearing and hearing-impaired samples. Unlike results with hearing subjects, however, consistent patterns of sex differences have not been reported among the hearing-impaired students.

The present study assessed the effect of students' gender and the shape of the water container (curved versus straight-sided) on primary-aged hearing-impaired students' performance on the horizontality task. This age group is important to study because during this developmental period, comprehension of horizontality should just begin to emerge.

Study Design

The subjects consisted of 7 male and 8 female hearing-impaired children from a residential school. The children's ages ranged from 9 to 12 years, with a mean age of 10.73. The subjects were selected from among students with a pure-tone hearing loss of 92 dB or greater. The students had been previously identified by school records as being within the normal range of intelligence, and their reading levels ranged from second to fourth grades.

The measure for assessing the subjects' perception of liquid horizontality was a paper-and-pencil test with a series of sketches of 24 bottle shapes (12 rectangular and 12 curved) drawn analogous to hourly clock positions.

The 12 different bottle orientations were categorized into *vertical/horizontal* positions (12, 3, 6, and 9 o'clock) and *oblique* positions (1, 2, 4, 5, 7, 8, 10, and 11 o'clock). *Oblique* referred to those positions that were neither vertical nor horizontal but rather had an inclined or diagonal plane. The liquid horizontality test modification and the scoring criteria were identical to those described in detail elsewhere (Kelly & Kelly, 1977). To minimize misunderstanding, the assessment tool was administered by a teacher of the hearing impaired who was fluent in American Sign Language.

Findings and Implications

Separate mixed-model analyses of variance were performed for the summed scores for the oblique and horizontal/vertical bottle positions. For the oblique items, a 2 (male/female) x 2 (bottle shape) x 8 (bottle position) analysis was performed. For the horizontal/vertical items, a 2 (male/female) x 2 (bottle shape) x 4 (bottle position) analysis was computed. The last two factors in both analyses were repeated factors, and the first variable was a grouping factor. The results of the analysis yielded significant main effects for bottle shape (straight-sided containers induced more errors than curved-sided containers) and bottle position (early items were more difficult than later items). Also, males were found to perform better than females on some item subsets.

Several conclusions can be drawn from the data. The pattern of findings for bottle shape was quite similar to that found with populations of secondary-level hearing-impaired students, suggesting that primary- and intermediate-level deaf youngsters may process this type of spatial transformation in a manner quite similar to their older peers. Bottle shape had also been found to affect hearing students' performance on this type of task in a similar manner (Walker & Krasnoff, 1978; Williamson & Reynolds, 1973) suggesting that the cue value of the container shape operates in the same way for hearing and hearing-impaired youngsters.

The pattern of sex differences found in this investigation also lends support to findings from previous studies with hearing-impaired subjects. Although in this study males were found to perform slightly better than females on some question subsets, on the majority of items no significant sex differences were reported. Perhaps hearing-impaired students' reduced linguistic sophistication shields them from assimilating some of the subtle sex biases present in the auditory language that may depress hearing females' performance on spatial tasks. These data also suggest that the consistent pattern of sex differences found with hearing students may have more of a social/experiential than a biological basis.

The findings have several further instructional implications. Organizing the relationship of objects in space is essential to the study of a variety of academic subjects, such as geography and mathematics, and requires an ability to utilize spatial reference cues. Our data suggest that hearing-impaired children can begin to appropriately represent spatial relationships at an early age, but they need practice in learning to disregard distracting spatial cues.

Provision of an environment in which learners can solve problems and self-regulate their own learning would appear to be desirable (Copeland,

1979). This self-paced instruction suggests the need for more inductive approaches to teaching and learning in which students can acquire understanding of concepts through personal discovery and through working with concrete objects and materials. Such an approach may lay the groundwork that would help hearing-impaired students comprehend the more abstract spatial principles that are encountered later in academic subjects such as physics, geography, and geometry.

References

Copeland, R. W. (1979). *How children learn mathematics*. New York: Macmillan.

Kelly, J. T., & Kelly, G. N. (1977). Perception of horizontality by male and female college students. *Perceptual and Motor Skills, 44,* 724–726.

Kelly, R., & Witters, L. (1981). Developmental and sex differences of gifted children's perception of liquid horizontality. *The Journal for the Education of the Gifted, 4*(2), 85–96.

Morris, B. B. (1971). Effects of angle, sex and cue on adults' perception of horizontal. *Perceptual and Motor Skills,* 827–830.

Murphy-Berman, V., Witters, L., & Harding, R. (1983). *The effect of giftedness, sex, and bottle shape on hearing impaired students' performance on the water line task*. Unpublished manuscript.

Piaget, J., & Inhelder, B. (1956). *The child's conception of space*. London: Routledge & Kegan Paul.

Rebelsky, F. (1964). Adult perception of the horizontal. *Perceptual and Motor Skills, 19,* 371–374.

Walker, J. T., & Krasnoff, A. G. (1978). The horizontality principle in young men and women. *Perceptual and Motor Skills, 46,* 1055–1061.

Williamson, E., & Reynolds, B. (1973). Sex differences in adults' judgments of the horizontal. *Developmental Psychology, 8,* 309.

Witters-Churchill, L., Kelly, R., & Witters, L. (1983). Deaf students' perception of liquid horizontality: An examination of effects of gender, development and training. *Volta Review, 85,* 211–229.

Additional Reading

DeLisi, R. (1983). Developmental and individual differences in children's representation of the horizontal coordinate. *Merrill-Palmer Quarterly, 29,* 179–197.

Piaget, J. (1977). Problems of equilibration. In M. H. Appel & L. S. Goldberg (Eds.), *Topics in cognitive development* (Vol. 1, pp. 3–13). New York: Plenum Press.

Field Dependence of Deaf Students: Implications for Education

Joan M. Gibson

The perceptual component of the larger cognitive dimension of differentiation is termed *field dependence*. Psychological differentiation, as proposed by Witkin, Dyk, Faterson, Goodenough, and Karp (1962), serves as a construct for conceptualizing one's degree of articulation of experience of the world and of the self. It also serves as a construct in intellectual functioning. The construct of field dependence (with no hyphen) is often referred to as the field-dependence/independence dimension involving field-dependence (with hyphen) at one end of the continuum and field-independence at the other end.

Field-dependence is a cognitive style that describes the tendency to give greater credit to external referents in a self-consistent way, to experience surroundings in a relatively global fashion, and to passively conform to the influence of the prevailing field or context.

Field-independence is a cognitive style that describes the tendency to rely primarily on internal referents in a self-consistent way and to perceive one's surroundings analytically, with objects experienced as discrete from their backgrounds.

A recent study conducted with students from St. Mary's School for the Deaf, Buffalo, New York, examined the pattern of field dependence among the deaf according to age, sex, age of onset of hearing loss, and degree of loss. The investigators looked at the relationship between degree of differentiation as reflected in field dependence and results on certain language measures in deaf persons. Since the Embedded Figures Test is a timed visual perception test requiring visual-motor skills, any handicapping condition that would bias these test results was eliminated. The conditions eliminated included legal blindness, partial sightedness, perceptual-motor disorders, educable mental retardation, and some upper-body orthopedic disabilities. The Embedded Figures Test (EFT) was devised by Witkin (1950) as a measure of field dependence. This test involved embedding simple figures into complex figures. A score on the EFT is the mean time in seconds for the completion of the disembedding task. A high score indicates a field-dependent perceptual style, while a low score indicates a field-independent style. A shortened form (Form A) of the EFT, which was devised by Jackson (1956) and revised by Witkin, Oltman, Raskin, and Karp (1971), was used for this study.

The complete version of this paper is available in microfiche or hard copy from ERIC Document Reproduction Service. Ask for Document No. ED 247 709.

Summary of Results

The investigators reported three specific findings from this study.

1. A significant relationship between field dependence and sex was found only at age 15; however, the low number of subjects at each age level limited the study. EFT performance exhibited a moderately linear and significant relationship to age for males, with age accounting for 23% of the variance. The relationship for females, however, was curvilinear. Males, especially, exhibit an age-regressive pattern in adolescence. A strong but not significant interaction effect was found between age and sex in EFT performance, with females being more field-independent at ages 10, 11, and 12 and males being more field-independent at ages 13, 15, and 17.

2. No significant relationship was found between degree of hearing loss and field dependence. No significant relationship was found between age of onset and field dependence, given the limited range tested.

3. A significant relationship was found between field dependence and verbal ability when measured by the California Achievement Test Reading and Language subtests. When both age and IQ were controlled, only the Reading subtest remained a significant predictor of field dependence for females.

Discussion

Age and Sex

The mean differences by sex and age obtained in this study were rarely greater than the deviation within each group. Certainly, the sex differences in field-dependence/independence are not inherent features of the development of differentiation. Witkin (1979) states that child-rearing practices, social organization, and the role of ecological factors carry congruent consequences in extent of differentiation.

Kohlberg (1966), in a study with hearing children, found that cross-sex interests (associated with field-independence) in girls first increases during the preschool period and then decreases. For boys, same-sex interests and preferences increase during the same period. A similar pattern of results was found in this present study with deaf children, but at much later age periods.

The results of this study in part contradict previous research (Best, 1974/1975; Blanton & Nunnally, 1964; Fiebert, 1967; Naiman, 1969/1970; Parasnis & Long, 1979) in the sense that the only significant difference favoring males here occurred at age 15. The finding that females in this sample tended to be more field-independent through the age range of 10 to 13 was not supported in the prior literature.

The pattern of development of field-independence for the deaf subjects in this study was compared to the hearing norm group. The patterns illustrated at earlier ages (10 to 13) showed no significant differences in extent of differentiation. The deviant pattern for the deaf subjects that becomes evident during adolescence is perplexing, and explanation must now be sought outside the physiological dimension involving hearing impairment.

Degree of Loss and Age of Onset

The results of this study also indicated no significant relationship between age of onset and field dependence, nor between degree of loss and field dependence for the ranges tested. Parasnis and Long (1979), by contrast, had found that degree of loss was the second best predictor of field dependence (measured by the Group Embedded Figures Test) for males only.

Age of onset is not discussed as a variable in any of the previous studies and is addressed only as a descriptor of the samples. In the present study, the majority of subjects were deaf at birth (78%) and the resultant mean age at onset was 4 years, 4 months. Age of onset was negligibly correlated with EFT performance at a nonsignificant level.

Even with the very early age of onset and the severe dB loss, comparison to hearing norms shows that in several instances, these deaf subjects performed as well as or better on the EFT than their hearing counterparts. Other factors that are side effects of the hearing loss, rather than the loss itself, would seem to be the hindrances to the development of field-independence.

Verbal Ability Variable

In this study, when sex differences were taken into account and IQ was controlled, reading level was a significant predictor for female field-independence, while language level was a significant predictor for male field-independence. When age was added, reading was still a significant predictor variable for females only. This finding supports Fiebert's (1967) results for females and also supports Parasnis and Long's (1979) findings with the Simultaneous Reception Test. For hearing students, however, field dependence was not significantly correlated with verbal ability for either sex (Witkin, Dyk, Faterson, Goodenough, & Karp, 1962). The nonlinear, non-age-dependent pattern of EFT scores for the deaf females in this study makes interpretation of the reading results tenuous at best.

Although the males and females in this study followed the national trend of linguistic deficiency for deaf students, this deficiency did not actually hinder performance on EFT. These females' EFT scores were above the norm group means for ages 10, 11, and 12. The conclusion is that linguistic deficiencies themselves for these subjects do not retard the development of field-independence.

Conclusion

The results of this investigation demonstrated that the differences in the developmental pattern of differentiation for a deaf person are not attributable to the relatively fixed and unchangeable factors of degree of loss or age of onset. The comparison of EFT performance of deaf subjects to the hearing norm group also indicated that up to age 13, deaf and hearing individuals have rather similar field-dependence/independence developmental patterns. Only at adolescence do sex differences become significant; deaf subjects significantly vary from the hearing group. Factors other than the hearing loss itself are apparently operative. If the hearing impairment itself does not prevent the beginning of normal development of differentiation, then with appropriate life circumstances, deaf persons potentially may acquire access to cognitive restructuring skills and to interpersonal competencies, whatever their standing on the field-dependence/independence continuum. The results of this investigation encourage the shifting of research attention to communication patterns within the family, to attitudinal and cognitive aspects surrounding the disability, and to other psychosocial factors that influence the development of this differentiation.

References

Best, P. K. (1975). *Psychological differentiation in the deaf* (Doctoral dissertation, Wayne State University, 1974). *Dissertation Abstracts International, 35*, 4239A.

Blanton, R., & Nunnally, J. (1964). Semantic habits and cognitive style processes in the deaf. *Journal of Abnormal and Social Psychology, 68*, 397–402.

Fiebert, M. (1967). Cognitive styles in the deaf. *Perceptual and Motor Skills, 24*, 319–329.

Jackson, D. N. (1956). A short form of Witkin's Embedded-Figures Test. *Journal of Abnormal and Social Psychology, 53*, 254–255.

Kohlberg, L. (1966). A cognitive-developmental analysis of children's sex-role concepts and attitudes. In E. E. Maccoby (Ed.), *The development of sex differences* (pp. 82–173). Stanford, CA: Stanford University Press.

Naiman, B. (1970). *The relation of verbal language ability to psychological differentiation in the adult deaf* (Doctoral dissertation, New York University, 1969). *Dissertation Abstracts International, 31*, 2261B.

Parasnis, I., & Long, G. (1979). Relationships among spatial skills, communication skills, and field dependence in deaf students. *Perceptual and Motor Skills, 49*, 879–887.

Witkin, H.A. (1950). Individual differences in ease of perception of embedded figures. *Journal of Personality, 19*, 1–15.

Witkin, H. A. (1979). Socialization, culture and ecology in the development of group and sex differences in cognitive style. *Human Development, 22*, 358–372.

Witkin, H. A., Dyk, R., Faterson, H., Goodenough, D., & Karp, S. (1962). *Psychological differentiation*. New York: John Wiley & Sons.

Witkin, H. A., Oltman, P., Raskin, E., & Karp, S. (1971). *Embedded Figures Test manual*. Palo Alto, CA: Consulting Psychologists Press.

Additional Reading

Coates, S., Lord, M., & Jakabovics, E. (1975). Field dependence-independence, social-nonsocial play and sex differences in preschool children. *Perceptual and Motor Skills, 40,* 195–202.

Hulfish, S. (1978). Relationship of role identification, self-esteem, and intelligence to sex differences in field independence. *Perceptual and Motor Skills, 47,* 835–842.

Jensema, C., & Trybus, R. J. (1978). *Communication patterns and educational achievement of hearing-impaired students.* Washington, DC: Gallaudet College, Office of Demographic Studies.

Kagan, J., & Kogan, N. (1970). In P. H. Mussen (Ed.), *Carmichael's manual of child psychology* (Vol. 1, p. 1334). New York: John Wiley & Sons.

Ruesch, J. (1957). *Disturbed communication.* New York: W. W. Norton.

Schildroth, A. (1976). *The relationship of nonverbal intelligence test scores to selected characteristics of hearing-impaired students.* Washington, DC: Gallaudet College, Office of Demographic Studies.

Schlesinger, H. S. (1978). The effects of deafness on childhood development: An Eriksonian perspective. In L. S. Liben (Ed.), *Deaf children: Developmental perspectives* (pp. 69–85). New York: Academic Press.

Sherman, J. A. (1967). Problems of sex differences in space perception and aspects of intellectual functioning. *Psychological Review, 74,* 290.

Sisco, F. H., & Anderson, R. (1980). Deaf children's performance on the WISC-R relative to hearing status of parents and child-rearing practices. *American Annals of the Deaf, 125,* 923–930.

Trybus, R. J., & Karchmer, M. A. (1977). School achievement scores of hearing-impaired children: National data on achievement status and growth patterns. *American Annals of the Deaf, 122,* 62–69.

Vaught, G. M. (1965). The relationship of role identification and ego strength to sex differences in the rod and frame test. *Journal of Personality, 33,* 271–283.

Cognitive Style as a Mediator in Reading Comprehension Test Performance for Deaf Students

Beth Davey
Carol LaSasso

The valid assessment of deaf students' educational achievements and cognitive processes remains a challenge for practitioners and researchers. This challenge is particularly apparent in the case of reading comprehension. As has been frequently noted, decisions concerning optimal measurement in reading comprehension should be based upon careful consideration of interactions between reader characteristics and testing-task characteristics (Benson & Crocker, 1979; Johnston, 1981; Kendall, Mason, & Hunter, 1980; Traub & Fisher, 1977). This paper summarizes relevant research that implicates cognitive style in the reading comprehension performance of deaf students under particular testing conditions.

Many alternatives are available for describing aspects of comprehension processes, such as retelling activities, cloze procedures, maze techniques, and strategies requiring direct demonstration of comprehension (e.g., putting together a model car after reading its written directions). However, the most commonly used approach for assessing reading comprehension in both formal (e.g., standardized tests) and informal classroom settings is the *wh-* question form (Durkin, 1978). Evidence is accumulating that points to potential bias in reading comprehension questions related to such features as item format, type of information assessed, and task conditions (e.g., timing and reinspection-of-text options). Results from several recent studies have suggested that the reading performance of deaf students may be particularly affected by these task features (Davey, LaSasso, & Macready, 1983; LaSasso, 1979; McKee & Lang, 1982). One factor that appears to interact with such features of question tasks and thus to mediate comprehension performance is cognitive style (Dunn, Gould, & Singer, 1981; Pitts & Thompson, 1984; Witkin, Moore, Goodenough, & Cox, 1977).

Cognitive style is a general term describing rather self-consistent stable ways of perceiving, remembering, information processing, and problem solving. These process-oriented individual differences (Wittrock, 1979) appear to reflect overlapping facets of cognitive, perceptual, and personality systems. Many of the dimensions of cognitive style researched over the years appear to relate to a variety of educationally relevant behaviors (Messick, 1983).

Field dependence is one cognitive style dimension implicated in many reading performance tasks (Annis, 1979; Davey, 1983; Spiro & Tirre, 1980). Field dependence was originally described by Witkin (1950) using a variety of spatial tasks. In some of the group-administered paper-pencil embedded figures tests, subjects are required to identify a target form embedded within

The complete version of this paper is available in microfiche or hard copy from ERIC Document Reproduction Service. Ask for Document No. Ed 247 710.

a complex design. Subjects with high scores on this task are termed *field-independent*. They appear to employ highly articulated analytical strategies and are capable of disembedding salient information from irrelevant, competing events. Subjects with low scores are identified as *field-dependent*. They react more globally to the total field and demonstrate greater dependence on external referents for structure. Several recent investigations have suggested a rather consistent relationship of field dependence to tasks involving memory efficiency and general cognitive restructuring (Bennink & Spoelstra, 1979; Berger & Goldberger, 1979; Davis & Frank, 1979; Goodenough, 1976; Robinson & Bennink, 1978).

The limited number of studies involving cognitive styles and deafness (Blanton & Nunnally, 1964; Fiebert, 1967; Parasnis, in press; Parasnis & Long, 1979) suggest that field dependence may be a particularly relevant variable for study in explicating the roles of visual and spatial systems in verbal information-processing tasks for deaf students. Deafness may "place demands on the visual system which may alter both the functioning of the visual system and the selection and processing of information in the conceptual/memory system" (Parasnis & Samar, 1982, p. 54).

A recent study (Davey & LaSasso, 1985) examined the relations of cognitive style to reading-comprehension-question performance for 48 prelingually, profoundly deaf adolescents. Three facets of assessment were considered: *question format* (multiple-choice, free-response), *lookback condition* (looking back, not looking back), and *information type* (literal questions, inferential questions). Analyses conducted for composite test scores and separate test facets revealed significant interactions between cognitive style and several reading comprehension test components. Relatively field-independent students scored higher than field-dependent students when not permitted to refer back to the passages for answering questions and when responding to inferential-type items in a multiple-choice format. These two interactions are consistent with theory (i.e., notions of the memory and restructuring components of field dependence) and with research utilizing hearing subjects (Witkin, Moore, Goodenough, & Cox, 1977; Witkin, 1978).

From this study and its supporting research and theory, then, it appears that practitioners and researchers would do well to consider carefully the cognitive styles of their deaf students as well as particular test facets when making decisions concerning optimal measurements of reading comprehension processes. The use of multiple measures (varying task features) should enhance assessment accuracy. In addition, caution should be exercised when generalizing findings from tests with certain item features to students with different cognitive styles and to outcomes using different item features. Further research should focus on the particular question-answering strategies used by students differing in cognitive styles (perhaps using error analysis procedures suggested by Glaser, 1981), and on the effects of training students in more appropriate test-taking strategies.

References

Annis, L. F. (1979). Effect of cognitive style and learning passage organization on study technique effectiveness. *Journal of Educational Psychology, 71*, 620–626.

Bennink, C. D., & Spoelstra, T. (1979). Individual differences in field articulation as a factor in language comprehension. *Journal of Research in Personality, 13*, 480–489.

Benson, J., & Crocker, L. (1979). The effects of item format and reading ability on objective test performance: A question of validity. *Educational and Psychological Measurement, 39*, 381–387.

Berger, E., & Goldberger, L. (1979). Field dependence and short-term memory. *Perceptual and Motor Skills, 49*, 87–96.

Blanton, R. L., & Nunnally, J. (1964). Semantic habits and cognitive style processes in the deaf. *Journal of Abnormal and Social Psychology, 68*, 397–402.

Davey, B. (1983). Cognitive styles and reading research: Some methodological concerns and future directions. *Reading Psychology, 4*, 65–78.

Davey, B., & LaSasso, C. (1985). Relations of cognitive style to assessment components of reading comprehension for deaf adolescents. *Volta Review, 87*, 17–27.

Davey, B., LaSasso, C., & Macready, G. (1983). A comparison of reading comprehension task performance for deaf and hearing subjects. *Journal of Speech and Hearing Research, 26*, 622–628.

Davis, J. K., & Frank, B. M. (1979). Learning and memory of field independent-dependent individuals. *Journal of Research in Personality, 13*, 469–479.

Dunn, B. R., Gould, J. E., & Singer, M. (1981). *Cognitive style differences in expository phrase recall* (Tech. Rep. No. 210). Urbana: University of Illinois, Center for the Study of Reading.

Durkin, D. (1978). What classroom observations reveal about reading comprehension instruction. *Reading Research Quarterly, 14*, 481–533.

Fiebert, M. (1967). Cognitive styles in the deaf. *Perceptual and Motor Skills, 24*, 319–329.

Glaser, R. (1981). The future of testing. *American Psychologist, 36*, 923–936.

Goodenough, D. R. (1976). The role of individual differences in field dependence as a factor in learning and memory. *Psychological Bulletin, 83*, 675–694.

Johnston, P. H. (1981). *Implications of basic research for the assessment of reading comprehension* (Tech. Rep. No. 206). Urbana: University of Illinois, Center for the Study of Reading.

Kendall, J. R., Mason, J. M., & Hunter, W. (1980). Which comprehension? Artifacts in the measurement of reading comprehension. *Journal of Educational Research, 73*, 233–236.

LaSasso, C. (1979). The effect of WH question format versus incomplete statement format on deaf subjects' demonstration of comprehension of text-explicit information. *American Annals of the Deaf, 124*, 833–837.

McKee, B., & Lang, H. G. (1982). A comparison of deaf students' performance on true-false and multiple-choice items. *American Annals of the Deaf, 127*, 49–54.

Messick, S. (1983, January). *Developing abilities and knowledge: Style in the interplay of structure and process* (Research Report). Princeton, NJ: Educational Testing Service.

Parasnis, I. (1983). The effects of parental deafness and early exposure to manual communication on the cognitive skills, English language skill and field-independence of young deaf adults. *Journal of Speech and Hearing Research, 26*, 588–594.

Parasnis, I., & Long, G. (1979). Relationships among spatial skills, communication skills, and field independence in deaf students. *Perceptual and Motor Skills, 49*, 879–887.

Parasnis, I., & Samar, V. (1982). Visual perception of verbal information by deaf people. In D. Sims, G. Walter, & R. Whitehead (Eds.), *Deafness and communication: Assessment and training* (pp. 53–71). Baltimore: Williams & Wilkins.

Pitts, M. C., & Thompson, B. (1984). Cognitive styles as mediating variables in inferential comprehension. *Reading Research Quarterly, 19,* 426–435.

Robinson, J. A., & Bennink, C. (1978). Field articulation and working memory. *Journal of Research in Personality, 12,* 439–449.

Spiro, R., & Tirre, W. (1980). Individual differences in schema utilization during discourse processing. *Journal of Educational Psychology, 72,* 204–208.

Traub, R., & Fisher, C. (1977). On the equivalence of constructed-response and multiple-choice tests. *Applied Psychological Measurement, 1,* 355–369.

Witkin, H. (1950). Perception of the upright when the direction of the force acting on the body is changed. *Journal of Experimental Psychology, 40,* 93–106.

Witkin, H. (1978). *Cognitive styles in personal and cultural adaptation.* Worcester, MA: Clark University Press.

Witkin, H., Moore, C., Goodenough, D., & Cox, P. (1977). Field-dependent and field-independent cognitive styles and their educational implications. *Review of Educational Research, 47,* 1–64.

Wittrock, M. C. (1979). The cognitive movement in instruction. *Educational Researcher, 8,* 5–11.

Analysis

Robert Lee Williams

The papers presented in part 4 all relate to the general area of the development of information processing in deaf children. They have interesting theoretical implications as well as practical applications, and in a sense they are all paeans to individual differences. Three of the papers deal specifically with the topic of field independence-dependence while the fourth investigates some of the possible perceptual precursors of language in children.

Affolter's paper on the development of perceptual processes and problem-solving activities concerns some of the possible perceptual precursors of language development.

In the general area of language precursors, at least four skill areas are necessary before children can begin learning and using language. First, a child must be able to represent things from memory. Second, there must be some degree of object permanence and, therefore, perceptual stability in the child's world, which enables the child to begin labeling things. Third, the child must also be able to use and understand the nature of tools. In a sense, words are tools; the fact that a high proportion of children's early speech acts are requests attests to this. The fourth precondition for language development is what Piaget (1951) referred to as the semiotic function—the ability to represent something that is not present.

On a different level, Affolter has examined a constellation of perceptual-motor skills that appear to be learned with relative ease by both hearing and deaf children but not by language-disabled children. Previous cross-sectional studies (Affolter, 1974) had seemed to indicate that these were prerequisites for language development. In this study, Affolter examined the relative development and performance of three groups of children: hearing impaired without any specific learning problems, hearing impaired with language problems, and hearing with learning and language problems. These children were tested on a variety of perceptual-motor tasks in longitudinal and cross-sectional designs. Results showed that while the language-disturbed group did not perform as well as the non-language-disturbed group, the pattern of development did not seem to indicate that the perceptual-motor skills are prerequisites for language development. Rather, Affolter believes that it was these children's inability to interact effectively with their environment that limited their skills in both the development of complex perceptual-motor areas as well as language. This interaction with the environment was limited by the child's perceptual deficiencies as described in the paper. Further, in a somewhat revolutionary result, Affolter found that the pattern of development did not follow a strict stage process as is common in Piaget's theories, but rather was one, smooth, continuous developmental progression.

Affolter's applications of her work are congruent with the ideas of Piaget and Feuerstein. Piaget suggested, and he has been supported in research by

Bower (1974), that equilibration is crucial to cognitive development. Equilibration was Piaget's concept of returning to a state of dynamic equilibrium. According to Piaget (Ginsburg & Opper, 1979), children develop cognitively through resolutions of conflicts. A conflict sets up a state of disequilibrium (disharmony) within the child's cognitive system and motivates him or her to attempt to restore the balance. The child moves to a higher level of cognitive functioning by restoring the system to a state of equilibrium.

According to Piaget, two of the important characteristics of equilibration are the field of application (usually the perceptual field of the child) and the quality of perceptual mobility. That these are truly intrinsic to cognitive development is further supported by Affolter's research. As mentioned previously, this equilibration occurs only through interactions with the environment. Obviously language-disabled children have not been raised in "black boxes" all their lives; they have had interactions with the environment, but it is important to distinguish between the quantity of interaction and the quality of that interaction. Their perceptual deficiencies have reduced the usefulness and therefore the quality of their interactions.

Affolter suggests that interactions must therefore be guided; although she is somewhat sketchy in her descriptions of the guided exploratory activities, they appear to be somewhat reminiscent of Feuerstein's Instrumental Enrichment program (1980). Instrumental Enrichment was designed to teach children problem-solving skills leading to more effective interactions with the environment. Affolter, however, as distinct from Feuerstein and Piaget, believes that "teaching . . . cognitive skills must be embedded in daily life activities" (1984, p. 31). She also emphasizes the importance of early identification of language-disabled children and early intervention programs. Obviously the longer these children languish, the further behind they will fall.

Murphy-Berman, Witters, and Harding's paper on the Piagetian horizontality task is related to the broader area of field-dependence/independence, a topic examined more specifically by Gibson and Davey and LaSasso. Field-dependence/independence is a dimension that represents the degree to which people rely on external frames of reference. Two methods are typically used to measure this dimension. One is to embed an abstract figure in a complex design and ask subjects to find or disembed it. Field-dependent people typically have difficulty in extricating the figure from the background. A second way of measuring where a person lies on the continuum is with a rod-and-frame apparatus where both the rod and its surrounding frame are tilted, and the subject must decide if the rod is vertical. Field-independent people rely on their own inner senses and judgments to decide more easily than do field-dependent people, who depend more on the frame than on their inner sense of what is vertical. In their investigations, Murphy-Berman et al. used a standard Piagetian horizontality task.

The horizontality task (knowing that the imaginary water line remains horizontal regardless of the tilt or the shape of the bottle) is obviously related to the rod-and-frame test. Previous research on normally hearing subjects shows that males tend to be more field-independent and they perform better on this task than females. Research has also shown that straight-sided bottles induce more errors than curved ones. Although the sample of hearing-impaired children was small (7 males and 8 females), the authors found no consistent advantage for males, even though males were found to perform slightly better on some particular question subsets. Other results such as the effect of bottle shape and position are similar to the results with hearing samples.

Interestingly, Murphy-Berman et al. report that other research has also found no sex differences among hearing-impaired subjects. The suggestion that the somewhat sheltered and English-languge-deprived environment may have shielded the deaf females from the ravages of society's sexism is of course a possibility, although as the authors suggest, there are no data here to support that conclusion. A more likely possibility is that the small sample, together with the inherent heterogeneity of deaf samples in general, has washed out any main effect due to sex.

These coauthors also found that the subjects improved with practice, but they do not mention whether the subjects received feedback—an important consideration. The authors go on to suggest that children be allowed to figure things out for themselves, proceed at their own pace, and work with concrete objects and materials. These recommendations are acceptable but seem to bear little specific relationship to their findings as reported in this paper. These are all general axioms found in many educational texts. More appropriately, it might be interesting to see if children are distributed along a dimension in this task as are adults in other measures of field-dependence/ independence. The answer to this question would go a long way toward finding out when and how people sort themselves out on this continuum. Further, if a child were at this young age already identified as being at one end of the continuum, one could then design methods of instruction specifically geared for field-independent or -dependent people, a possibility that will be discussed later.

The study by Gibson on field independence used a standard embedded figures task with deaf students aged 9 to 19 years old. Results showed that males improved with age, while a curvilinear effect was seen with females. Comparing males with females, males were significantly more field-independent only at age 15. There was no significant relationship between field-independence and either age at onset or degree of hearing loss. For males, significant positive correlations were found between field-independence and language levels, while females showed positive correlations between field-independence and both reading and language levels.

As mentioned in reference to Murphy-Berman et al.'s paper, the lack of consistently significant differences between the males and females in the Gibson study may be hidden by the heterogeneity and the smallness of the sample, although Gibson suggests that an increase in heterogeneity may be required to tease out a relationship between degree of hearing loss and field-dependence/independence (if indeed, one exists).

The study by Davey and LaSasso on relations between cognitive style and assessments of reading comprehension also examined the relationship between reading and field-dependence/independence. The authors considered the relationship of field dependence to three facets of assessment: question format, lookback condition, and information type. The principal finding was that under certain conditions, field dependence (as a measure of cognitive style) "made significant contributions to the reading comprehension test score variance" (Davey & LaSasso, 1984, p. 78).

The authors suggest that similar abilities are used in disembedding figures and in restructuring deep linguistic processing. This phenomenon may account for the relationship between female subjects' scores on the embedded figures task and their reading ability. However, in this explanation Davey and LaSasso may have raised more questions than they have answered. The chief dilemma here is that while males typically are more field-independent (that is, they do better at disembedding figures from grounds), females tend to do better on an assortment of linguistic tasks (Parlee, 1972). This interesting quandary deserves more study. It may suggest, for example, the degree to which reading processes in deaf readers are fundamentally and qualitatively different from those processes in hearing readers.

The real strength of this study, however, is its explication of the effect of individual differences. For example, field-independent readers do better in no-lookback conditions. If this finding holds up under the scrutiny of further research, it should be possible to design assessment techniques to fit the cognitive style of the individual. By looking at the relative performance of a child under both conditions and by taking into account the child's particular cognitive style, one could obtain a much clearer picture of his or her level of functioning. Field-independent readers also scored higher with objective tests of implicit information. The authors believe that this finding may be due in part to the fact that field-independent individuals tend to be more reflective.

If it is true that one can teach impulsive children to be more reflective, might it not also be possible to teach field-dependent children to become more field-independent? Before we travel down that road, however, it might be worthwhile to consider just how desirable that change would be. At least one researcher (Levy, 1981) has suggested that by simply changing the name of the continuum from field-dependence/independence to context-sensitive/context-insensitive, one's whole value outlook is also changed. Imagining the continuum in this way would make it easier to explain why females are more field-dependent (context-sensitive) and also why they do better at linguistic tasks. Although the area of field-dependence may be in danger of becoming overextrapolated, as has the left hemisphere/right hemisphere cerebral dominance topic, it does seem that field dependence has been found to be related to a very wide variety of social and cognitive traits (Goodenough, 1976; Witkin, 1979). This fact should cause educators and researchers to think twice about trying to change children from one style to the other.

Regardless of the label for the continuum, it has had multiple effects on a wide variety of tasks (as explained in the papers in part 4). Combined with the known heterogeneity that deafness superimposes on the individual (etiology, age at onset, degree of loss, method of communication, etc.), the importance of individual differences can hardly be overemphasized. As admirably summarized by Davey and LaSasso, "sensitivity to these salient individual differences should inform practitioners, researchers, and test design specialists, [and educators] in their efforts toward enhancing optimal measurement [and instruction] of cognitive and linguistic competencies for deaf students" (1984, p. 81).

References

Affolter, F. (1984). Development of perceptual processes and problem-solving activities in normal, hearing-impaired, and language-disturbed children: A comparison study based on Piaget's conceptual framework. In D. S. Martin (Ed.), *International Symposium on Cognition, Education, and Deafness: Working Papers* (Vol. 1, pp. 19–33). Washington, DC: Gallaudet College.

Affolter, F. (1974). Einsatz und Beschränkung der audiovisuellen Methode im Sprachaufbau des schwer hörbehinderten Kindes. In Verein Desterreichescher Taubstummenlehrer (Eds.), *Audio-visuelle Mittel und Medien im Unterricht Hörgeschädigter*. Linz: Trauner.

Bower, T. G. R. (1974). *Development in infancy*. San Francisco: W. H. Freeman.

Davey, B., & LaSasso, C. (1984). Relations of cognitive style to assessment components of reading comprehension for deaf adolescents. In D. S. Martin (Ed.), *International Symposium on Cognition, Education, and Deafness: Working Papers* (Vol. 1, pp. 67–84). Washington, DC: Gallaudet College.

Feuerstein, R. (1980). *Instrumental enrichment: An intervention program for cognitive modifiability*. Baltimore: University Park Press.

Ginsburg, H., & Opper, S. (1979). *Piaget's theory of intellectual development* (2nd ed.). Englewood Cliffs, NJ: Prentice-Hall.

Goodenough, D. R. (1976). The role of individual differences in field dependence as a factor in learning and memory. *Psychological Bulletin, 83*, 675–694.

Levy, J. (1981, Fall). Yes Virginia, there is a difference: Sex differences in human brain asymmetry and in psychology. *The L. S. B. Leaky Foundation News*, No. 20.

Parlee, M. B. (1972). Comments on "Roles of activation and inhibition in sex differences in cognitive abilities," by Donald M. Broverman, Edward L. Klaiber, Yutaka Kobayashi, & William Vogel. *Psychological Review, 79*, 180–184.

Piaget, J. (1951). *Play, dreams and imitation in childhood* (C. Gattegno & F. M. Hodgson, Trans.). New York: W. W. Norton.

Witken, H. A. (1979). Socialization, culture and ecology in the development of group and sex differences in cognitive style. *Human Development, 22*, 358–379.

Related Educational and Research Issues

1. What is the role of tactile/kinesthetic perceptual processes in the cognitive development of the hearing-impaired child?

2. How can tactile/kinesthetic perceptions be integrated in the hearing-impaired learner?

3. In what ways can educators easily determine field-dependence vs. field-independence in hearing-impaired learners?

4. How does the field-dependence vs. field-independence factor affect the learning of hearing-impaired children?

5. To what degree is field-dependence/independence based on hereditary/biological versus environmental factors in the hearing-impaired learner?

6. To what extent is the field-dependence trait modifiable in the hearing-impaired learner?

7. What actual techniques can be used to modify field dependence?

5 Cognitive Strategies and Processes

The Development and Use of Memory Strategies by Deaf Children and Adults

Lynn S. Liben

The cognitive and occupational achievements of deaf individuals often compare unfavorably with the accomplishments of their hearing peers (Liben, 1978). An important goal of research is to understand why these deficits arise and how they may be prevented or remediated. One important cognitive skill focused on here is the ability to memorize. Memory is of importance for learning material in school and for succeeding in everyday living and occupational tasks. Furthermore, memory skills may be especially important for deaf people; information acquired incidentally by hearing people (e.g., linguistic information) must be memorized intentionally by deaf people.

A Developmental Approach to Teaching Memory Skills

The overriding question from the perspective of basic research, as well as from the perspective of educational intervention, is whether deaf people have the same memory skills as hearing people. It is not sufficient, however, simply to compare absolute levels of memory performance by deaf and hearing individuals. Too many factors (e.g., different knowledge of stimulus materials) vary simultaneously between the two groups to allow interpretable comparisons. For the same reasons, developmental psychologists recognize that simple comparisons of absolute levels of performance in older and younger children are flawed, so they increasingly have turned to approaches that examine children's strategy use rather than their absolute performance.

One such approach is to use tasks that externalize the competencies being examined. A second approach is to manipulate various features of the task materials, while a third approach is to instruct subjects to use particular strategies. Whenever strategies that are not normally used are elicited by simple stimulus variations or instructional manipulations, we can infer that the strategies of interest were available and needed only to be activated (Overton & Newman, 1982).

These approaches, used in developmental work, provided a model for the design of the studies described in this paper. That is, rather than designing studies to catalog deaf and hearing subjects' absolute levels of performance on particular memory tasks, these studies were designed to provide data on the processes used by subjects in approaching memory tasks. Each study contained a stimulus or instructional manipulation designed to determine whether some situations would be differentially conducive to the application of potentially available strategies.

The complete version of this paper is available in microfiche or hard copy from ERIC Document Reproduction Service. Ask for Document No. Ed 247 717.

Rehearsal

Perhaps the most frequently studied process in the literature on the development of memory is rehearsal. During rehearsal, the individual repeats the items to be remembered in order to prevent their loss from working memory and to permit the transfer of items into long-term memory. Evidence from research on hearing children indicates that older children are more likely than younger children to use rehearsal strategies and to use more elaborate forms of rehearsal (Flavell, 1970; Ornstein, 1978).

To examine the use of rehearsal strategies in deaf children, we gave serial probe tasks to 6- and 8-year-old deaf children (Liben & Drury, 1977). Of interest were both direct and indirect indices of rehearsal. Direct evidence for rehearsal was obtained by observing the children during the testing itself. Indirect evidence was obtained by examining the serial learning curves for primacy effects; that is, how well subjects recalled items presented at the beginning of the list.

Given our interest in the issue of competence/performance, we were also interested in exploring whether deaf children's tendency to use rehearsal strategies might vary as a function of the stimulus materials. Thus, stimuli used for the serial probe tasks varied with respect to how familiar and labelable they were (common animals vs. novel nonsense shapes) and the extent to which stimuli were expected to be conducive to kinesthetic rehearsal (fingerspelled letters vs. printed letters). Interestingly, all four types of stimuli elicited strong primacy effects in the serial learning curve, as well as in overt labeling and gesturing during stimulus presentation. These findings suggest that the children were using appropriate rehearsal strategies.

Free Recall: Semantic Clustering

A second process that has attracted considerable attention in the literature on memory development is semantic clustering. Subjects are given randomly presented lists of items, which they are then asked to recall in any order (a free-recall task). Of interest is whether subjects organize their recall by grouping or clustering the items that they recall into the conceptual categories that have been built into the list.

To examine developmental changes in clustering in deaf children, a free-recall task was given to third-, fifth-, and seventh-grade deaf children (Liben, 1979). To determine whether any apparent failure to use semantic categorization was simply a problem of activating or utilizing underlying competence, instructions were manipulated in this study. Some children were given the study and test trials without being explicitly told of the categorical nature of the list, while others were specifically informed of the categorical structure and told of its potential utility for memory. As in the study on rehearsal, both direct and indirect indices of clustering were used. A direct indication of clustering was provided by observing whether children grouped cards into categories during the study period. The indirect measure was the extent to which items were recalled in categorical clusters during recall.

As predicted, older children showed more spontaneous clustering than younger children on both direct and indirect measures. The instructional manipulation increased categorical clustering in all grades. Thus, results showed that deaf children used semantic clustering and were able to enhance recall from instruction in categorization.

Free Recall: Formational Versus Semantic Clustering

The research just described addressed children's tendencies to make use of semantic or conceptual features of lists to organize study and recall. In a third study (Liben, Nowell, & Posnansky, 1978), deaf adults' use of categorization was examined when two bases for categorization were available in the list: categories based on semantic meaning (e.g., foods, occupations) and categories based on formational similarity of signs (e.g., *train, egg, chair, name*). While subjects were able to group items according to formational similarity when specifically asked to do so, their spontaneous preference was to cluster by semantic meaning. This finding is parallel to the finding that hearing people virtually always favor semantic meaning over surface features (e.g., rhyming words) as the basis of organization.

Summary and Conclusions

Although it must be considered premature to attempt any firm conclusions on the basis of so few studies, our research suggests considerable competence in the memory strategies used by deaf children and adults. The kinds of strategies available and their spontaneous use in laboratory settings appear to be comparable to those of the hearing population.

Despite the apparent similarity of processes, however, the success of these processes is often reduced among deaf subjects. For example, in both the free-recall studies with children and adults described earlier, the absolute levels of recall of items were lower in deaf than hearing subjects. Since these deficits do not appear to be accounted for by different kinds of strategies, it is important to direct future research and educational curricula to understanding and facilitating the application of strategies to learning tasks in an efficient and consistent manner. It may not be necessary to provide instruction in memory strategies per se or in the cognitive underpinnings of such strategies. However, it may well be useful to provide instruction that increases deaf learners' conscious knowledge of strategies already available to them and the circumstances under which these available strategies may be applied. In addition, it would be useful to focus curriculum development on methods that will enhance the optimal application of strategies already available to the deaf learner.

References

Flavell, J. (1970). Developmental studies of mediated memory. In L. P. Lipsitt & H. W. Reese (Eds.), *Advances in child development and behavior* (Vol. 5). New York: Academic Press.

Liben, L. S. (1978). The development of deaf children: An overview of issues. In L. S. Liben (Ed.), *Deaf children: Developmental perspectives* (pp. 3–20). New York: Academic Press.

Liben, L. S. (1979). Free recall by deaf and hearing children: Semantic clustering and recall in trained and untrained groups. *Journal of Experimental Child Psychology, 27,* 105–119.

Liben, L. S., & Drury, A. (1977). Short-term memory in deaf and hearing children in relation to stimulus characteristics. *Journal of Experimental Child Psychology, 24,* 60–73.

Liben, L. S., Nowell, R. C., & Posnansky, C. J. (1978). Semantic and formational clustering in deaf and hearing subjects' free recall of signs. *Memory and Cognition, 6,* 599–606.

Ornstein, P. A. (Ed.). (1978). *Memory development in children.* Hillsdale, NJ: Lawrence Erlbaum Associates.

Overton, W. F., & Newman, J. L. (1982). Cognitive development: A competence-activation/utilization approach. In T. Field, A. Huston, H. Quay, L. Troll, & G. Finley (Eds.), *Review of human development* (pp. 217–241). New York: John Wiley & Sons.

Classification Skills in Normally Hearing and Oral Deaf Preschoolers: A Study in Language and Conceptual Thought

Jenny Friedman

The issue of the role of language in thought has been of theoretical interest to philosophers and psychologists for many years. A variety of methodologies have been used for the empirical study of this issue, including the use of atypical populations as control groups (Furth, 1966; Oléron, 1977). The deaf have been most widely studied because the lack of oral language is the most significant deficit resulting from profound congenital deafness (Kretschmer & Kretschmer, 1978; Meadow, 1980). For deaf children trained exclusively by the oral method of education, there is a generalized language deficiency because signing is not used to compensate for their limited oral abilities. Understanding the cognitive skills of these hearing-impaired children has implications for the role which language plays in various aspects of cognition. The research reported here focuses specifically on the area of concept development.

The author's study matched 20 normally hearing and 20 deaf preschool children on age, performance/intelligence, and socioeconomic status. The deaf children met the criteria of (a) exclusively oral educational training, (b) no use of signing in their homes, and (c) below-average performance on an oral receptive vocabulary measure. All the normally hearing children had at least average oral receptive skills. These criteria ensured that the two groups of children, though closely matched on factors that might affect cognitive performance, were significantly discrepant in their language skills.

There is some evidence that the role that language plays in concept acquisition varies as a function of the level of abstraction at which categories are formed (Horton & Markman, 1980; Rosch, Mervis, Gray, Johnson, & Boynes-Braem, 1976). Three levels of classification were explored in this author's study. The first, the *perceptual level*, involves sorting by visually perceptible, nonsymbolic attributes such as color and shape. The *basic level* of abstraction (e.g., dogs, chairs) is defined as the most inclusive level at which there are attributes common to all or most members of the category (Rosch et al., 1976). At the *superordinate level* (e.g., animals, furniture) members share fewer attributes.

Two free-sorting trials separated by a structured-sorting procedure were administered for two separate tasks at each of the three levels of classification. In the first free-sorting trial (Trial 1), the child was given an array of nine items and was encouraged to sort them appropriately into three baskets. During the structured-sorting task, the examiner placed one examplar from each class in each of the three baskets. The child then received the remaining objects, one at a time, and decided in which baskets the items should be placed. If the child chose the incorrect basket, the examiner nonverbally corrected the selection by placing the object in the correct basket. In the second free-sorting trial (Trial 2), the child was given the objects to sort in a manner identical to Trial 1. Finally, receptive and expressive knowledge of the category labels was tested.

Results indicated that the difference in categorization skills between the deaf and normally hearing children on Trial 1 was not significant at the perceptual or basic levels, but it was significant at the superordinate level. This finding implies that language is an important factor in the acquisition of superordinate level concepts, while it is not essential to the formation of perceptual and basic level categories. This result is further supported by a significant correlation between performance on superordinate level classification and labeling. No correlation was found at the basic level.

The scores of the deaf and normally hearing groups were not significantly different at any level of classification for either structured sorting or Trial 2 free sorting. The fact that their performances did not differ at the perceptual or basic levels is further evidence that language competence is not necessary for acquisition of these concepts. The similar superordinate level performance of the two groups, however, indicates a strong improvement by the deaf children following Trial 1. It was hypothesized that the additional structure of the task allowed the deaf children to use alternative strategies, such as the similarity in the location (e.g., food is found in the kitchen) and function of the items (e.g., clothes are to wear), in order to classify the superordinate categories. Although this hypothesis suggests that superordinate categories can be formed without knowledge of the labels, it is clear that language is the most direct and useful method for acquiring these concepts, particularly when the task demands are more complex, as they are during free sorting.

Several important implications of these data are indicated for the diagnosis and education of deaf children. There is evidence that children with receptive language impairments have more difficulty with perceptual and basic level sorting than do oral deaf children (Friedman, 1984). In addition, these language-impaired children profit to a lesser degree from the structured sorting and additional trial steps. This finding means that a diagnostic evaluation that includes perceptual and basic level categorization as well as the teaching of superordinates can help to determine whether a deaf preschooler has deficits in language learning or in concept development in addition to the hearing impairment.

In the classroom setting, the teacher should use a structured approach to emphasize the similarity of certain elements when deaf children cannot readily learn new concepts by simply viewing exemplars and abstracting shared features. Perhaps orally trained deaf children can be taught the superordinate category and its associated label at the same time. The teacher may also have to use nonverbal means of emphasizing shared features such as the functional and locational ways in which the items are related.

References

Friedman, J. (1984). *Classification skills in normally hearing/achieving, oral deaf, and language impaired preschoolers: A study in language and conceptual thought.* Unpublished doctoral dissertation, Northwestern University.

Furth, H. (1966). *Thinking without language.* New York: Free Press.

Horton, M. S., & Markman, E. (1980). Developmental differences in the acquisition of basic and superordinate categories. *Child Development, 51,* 708–719.

Kretschmer, R. R., & Kretschmer, L. W. (1978). *Language development and intervention with the hearing-impaired.* Baltimore: University Park Press.

Meadow, K. (1980). *Deafness and child development.* Berkeley: University of California Press.

Oléron, P. (1977). *Language and mental development.* Hillsdale, NJ: Lawrence Erlbaum Associates.

Rosch, E., Mervis, C., Gray, W. D., Johnson, D. M., & Boynes-Braem, P. (1976). Basic objects in natural categories. *Cognitive Psychology, 8,* 382–439.

The Role of Inference in Effective Communication

Paula M. Brown
Gary S. Dell

Theoretical models of effective communication have emphasized the co-operative nature of a speaker–listener interaction. Various attempts have been made to delineate the rules governing this cooperation, mainly in terms of sociocultural conventions for language use. However, some rules may have evolved out of cognitive processing considerations. For example, rules might ensure that information will be produced in accordance with the way that it is comprehended. A variety of features influencing comprehension have been identified; however, few studies have looked at whether speakers produce messages accordingly.

One comprehension process that has been extensively studied is the drawing of inferences to fill in or embellish a text. Results show that if listeners hear about an action, they can infer what tool or object (i.e., instrument) was used to accomplish it. If an action has a strongly associated instrument and if that instrument is left implicit, the listener will infer that the most likely object was used (McKoon & Ratcliff, 1981). For example, if listeners hear that someone pounded a nail, they assume it was with a hammer. Do speakers present information in accordance with this inferential strategy? That is, do they leave that information implicit which is likely to be inferred by the listener?

In our study, a speaker's explicitness was examined in terms of instrumental inferences. The first hypothesis being tested was that atypical instruments would be mentioned more often than typical. The second hypothesis was that speakers would explicitly mention important instruments more frequently than unimportant ones. It would be more crucial for the listener to know which instrument was used when the instrument was important to the progress of the story than when it was irrelevant.

In addition to examining this behavior in general, this study compared the performance of hearing and hearing-impaired speakers on the task. While the communication difficulties of the latter group have been studied extensively, little is known about the cognitive bases for communication difficulties. If speakers adapt the explicitness of their messages to the inferential needs of their listeners, violations of this adaptation may impair communication. Listeners may have difficulty in comprehending a message when their expectations about the presentation of information are not met.

Forty college students, 20 hearing and 20 hearing-impaired, were asked to read a series of stories that depicted characters performing different actions. Each story had four versions, derived by crossing the two experimental factors: (a) whether the instrument utilized was frequently or infrequently associated with the action and (b) whether the instrument was

The complete version of this paper is available in microfiche or hard copy from ERIC Document Reproduction Service. Ask for Document No. ED 249 742.

important in the story. Four lists of stories were assembled so that each list contained 20 stories, with 5 stories in each condition. Each subject received a single list of 20 randomized stories. The subjects were instructed to read a story and then retell it as clearly and completely as possible. At the end of the 20 stories, the students performed an instrument recall task.

Each story was transcribed and then analyzed using a four-category coding scheme to characterize the explicitness of an instrument's mention. A rating of 1 indicated that the target instrument was named explicitly when the action was mentioned. An analysis of variance on the number of 1s was performed with hearing status as a between-subject factor and frequency and importance as within-subject factors. This analysis was performed on the means for each condition for each subject (F_1 statistic) and on the means for each condition for each story (F_2 statistic). The analysis yielded significant main effects for frequency, F_1 $(1,32) = 21.36$, $p < .01$; F_2 $(1,16) = 7.77$, $p < .01$; and importance, F_1 $(1,32) = 11.52$, $p < .01$; F_2 $(1,16) = 10.27$, $p < .01$. The effect of hearing status was not significant and there were no significant interaction effects.

The probability that an instrument could be associated with an action was a significant factor in whether or not it was mentioned. Speakers explicitly stated the instrument in an action 39% of the time when the instrument was less frequently associated with that action, versus 24% of the time when the instrument was that which is most frequently associated with the action. The mentioning of an instrument was also influenced by the instrument's importance in the story. Important instruments were specified more often (37%) than unimportant instruments (27%).

The lack of a main effect for hearing status shows that the two groups were equally likely to state instruments explicitly. The lack of any interaction between hearing status and the other two variables indicates that hearing-impaired subjects are influenced by instrument frequency and importance in the same way that hearing subjects are. Both hearing and hearing-impaired speakers explicitly mentioned instruments when the instruments were atypical or important.

On the instrument recall tasks, the hearing subjects were more accurate (99%) than the hearing-impaired subjects (85%). Interestingly, 85% of the errors were on infrequent instruments. Subjects either forgot what happened and thus inferred the most likely instrument at recall, or they immediately inferred the most likely instrument during reading and did not revise that inference when it was contraindicated by subsequent information. This latter explanation is supported by two observations: (a) only two (0.3%) of the instruments missed at recall were mentioned explicitly as 1s during the communication task, and (b) 74% of the errors occurred on the version when the instrument was unimportant later on in the passage. In this version, information contradicting a wrong inference is less salient than in the important version.

The results of this study suggest that the explicit mentioning of an instrument serves a special purpose. It either informs the listener that the instrument is atypical and is not the one expected through prior knowledge, or it signals to the listener that the instrument is to have some significance later on in the discourse and should be noted.

The findings indicated that hearing-impaired students as well as hearing students were cooperative communicators. In modifying what they told their listener, they considered what their listener already knew via world knowledge. The hearing-impaired subjects were thus demonstrating competencies in two skill areas frequently considered to be deficient in deaf communicators: (a) they adjusted to their listener's needs, and (b) they accessed world knowledge to constrain their productions.

Perhaps hearing-impaired speakers would be less competent with more complex inferences or when explicitness required more sophisticated linguistic strategies than demanded by this task. This possibility requires further investigation. Investigators should also explore the effectiveness of an internal monitor in checking and evaluating effectiveness and consistency.

References

McKoon, G., & Ratcliff, R. (1981). The comprehension processes and memory structures involved in instrumental inference. *Journal of Verbal Learning and Verbal Behavior, 20,* 671–682.

Additional Reading

Clark, H. H. (1978). Inferring what is meant. In W. J. M. Levelt & G. B. Flores d'Arcais (Eds.), *Studies in the perception of language* (pp. 295–322). New York: John Wiley & Sons.

Corbett, A., & Dosher, B. (1978). Instrument inferences in sentence encoding. *Journal of Verbal Learning and Verbal Behavior, 17,* 479–491.

Grice, H. (1975). Logic and conversation. In P. Cole & J. L. Morgan (Eds.), *Syntax and semantics: Vol. 3. Speech acts* (pp. 41–58). New York: Academic Press.

Kintsch, W., & Vipond, D. (1979). Reading comprehension and readability in educational practice and psychological theory. In L. G. Nilsson (Ed.), *Perspectives on memory research* (pp. 329–365). Hillsdale, NJ: Lawrence Erlbaum Associates.

McKoon, G., & Ratcliff, R. (1980). The comprehension processes and memory structures involved in anaphoric reference. *Journal of Verbal Learning and Verbal Behavior, 19,* 668–682.

Searle, J. (1971). What is a speech act? In J. F. Rosenberg & C. Travis (Eds.), *Readings in the philosophy of language.* Englewood Cliffs, NJ: Prentice-Hall.

Singer, M. (1980). The role of case-filling inferences in the coherence of brief passage. *Discourse Processes, 3,* 185–201.

Developing Symbolic Thinking in Hearing-Impaired Children

Anna Knobloch-Gala
Irmina Kaiser-Grodecka

The tight conjunction of thinking and language seems to be evident. In the majority of studies on deafness, difficulties in the development of symbolic and abstract operations are treated as resulting from the lack of oral/aural language. Normally hearing children acquire language through direct interaction with the speaking environment, which enables them to benefit from social experience. Deaf children grow up to a large extent without such ready-made systems of symbols and are, therefore, mostly dependent on their own inventiveness for mental activity. Some studies dealing with abstract thinking have demonstrated that the abstraction level of deaf children was in these respects inferior to that of normal children; generally, authors of these studies (Myklebust, 1964; Oléron, 1951; Pettifor, 1968; Vincent, 1957) have been inclined to explain the data by referring to language deficits in the deaf as the main responsible factor.

These well-known theories not only interested teachers of disabled children, but inspired them to create an "adequate" school curriculum. The main point of that curriculum was the intensive teaching of oral language. However, if this project had been successful, we need not have carried out our investigations.

The main goal of our study was to discover a classification principle used by 11- to 13-year-old deaf children. The method involved demonstration or display of labels containing relevant words or iconic signs. Each introductory label with verbal or iconic signs considerably facilitated the discovery of classificatory principles. However, a learning procedure based on verbal signs demonstrated poorer results than did the procedure based on iconic signs. The kind of errors indicated the most probable reason for that significant worsening: the series of errors resulted from the poor processing of information that is inherent in verbal symbols.

In the present study, which employed three methods of teaching classificatory principles (demonstration, verbal labels, or iconic labels in different sequences), it was possible to compare three different learning strategies. The best strategy was hypothesized to be that which facilitated the grasping of classificatory principles and provided a nearly error-free solution. Our findings indicated that the procedure containing iconic signs at the beginning, verbal signs in the second trial, and demonstration of a task at the end produced optimal results.

Our last demonstrations were most pertinent to school practice. Classification of experimental colored blocks was replaced by the classification of animals and plants. In previous studies, iconic signs did not constitute a

The complete version of this paper is available in microfiche or hard copy from ERIC Document Reproduction Service. Ask for Document No. ED 247 718.

uniform system; they were only labels that denoted group qualities of objects, and denotation was the only role they played. In our most recent studies we introduced iconic signs that, when combined, created new relationships, thus changing the range of meaning of the basic sign. For example, a double sign of a tree denoted a forest, whereas a sign of a deciduous tree added to a sign of a coniferous tree denoted a mixed forest.

Apart from such simple combinations, we also used labels with symbols of species and of their various subspecies. A species label contained a graphic sign referring to the characteristic traits of a given species (e.g., wings, the number of limbs), whereas a subspecies label contained the symbol of the species plus an index of a subspecies (e.g., domestic animals were represented by a sign of a house, wild animals by a sign of a forest).

An analysis of errors made by the deaf children during the experiments shows that, in each case, the use of iconic signs guarantees better results. The use of iconic signs allows for a more precise definition and a better separation of a part from a larger whole. Iconic descriptions are also both richer and more adequate than verbal ones.

In the natural development of a hearing child, the development of speech overlaps with the development of intellectual operations. According to Piaget (1967), the period of the first 2 years of life, at the end of which the process of shaping speech takes place, is characterized by constructing the categories of object and space as well as of causality and time. For the time being, they remain practical categories and refer to actions without being intellectual notions. An ability to perform operations in each of the spheres previously mentioned in a different way contributes to the development of the language system. What is extremely important is the achievement of an appropriate level in the sphere of *time* operations, since they enable us to project the sequential qualities of language. On the other hand, *spatial* operations form the basis of a simultaneous organization. For a majority of the deaf, spatial operations are not a problem, whereas time operations seem to be closely connected with aural perception, and the deaf are obviously deficient in this respect. Even material perceived visually but presented successively is remembered less well than the identical material presented simultaneously. It is worth adding that the perception of cause-and-effect relationships, which at least in the phase of concrete operations are closely connected with time operations, is impaired in the deaf as well.

An iconic sign system, however, allows teachers to do either simultaneous or successive presentations according to their teaching needs. We believe that such a system may help to counteract a mental set in the deaf to rely mainly on perceptual data that leads to rigidity and schematism in thinking.

References

Myklebust, H. R. (1964). *The psychology of deafness.* New York: Grune & Stratton.

Oléron. P. (1951). Pensée conceptuelle et langage. Performances comparées de sourd-muets et d'entendants dans des épreuves de classement multiple. *Année Psychol., 51.*

Pettifor, J. L. (1968). The role of language in the development of abstract thinking: A comparison of hard-of-hearing and normal-hearing children on levels of conceptual thinking. *Canadian Journal of Psychology Rev., 22, 3.*

Piaget, J. (1967). *Six psychological studies.* New York: Random House.

Vincent, M. (1957). Sur le rôle du langage à un niveau élémentaire de pensée abstraite. Comparaison d'enfants entendants et sourd-muets dans une épreuve de groupement par ressemblances. *Enfance, 4.*

Additional Reading

Furth, H. G. (1966). *Thinking without language: Psychological implications of deafness.* New York: Free Press.

Kaiser-Grodecka, I., & Knobloch-Gala A. (1978). Signs as modifiers of classifying in deaf children. *Polish Psychological Bulletin, 9.*

Kaiser-Grodecka, I., & Knobloch-Gala, A. (1981). The formation of categorical thinking in deaf children. *Proceedings of the VIII World Congress of the World Federation of the Deaf.* Varna, Poland.

Analysis

Anthony B. Wolff

The traditional literature on deafness is replete with studies that ostensibly demonstrate cognitive deficits among deaf subjects (e.g., Pintner & Paterson, 1917). With few exceptions, however, more recent analyses have found that these deficits are generally attributable to such factors as certain linguistic competencies and secondary handicaps. Contemporary scholarship does not predict a difference between the basic cognitive apparatus of deaf and hearing individuals on a neural or structural level.

Nevertheless, the studies reported in part 5 all attempt to shed light on the manner in which deaf subjects process information, either implicitly or explicitly, in comparison to hearing subjects. Happily, these papers avoid, to some extent, simple deaf/hearing comparisons and focus instead on analyses of strategies. Each paper in its own way attempts to explore the ability of deaf subjects to infer, classify, conceptualize, or generalize. Two of the papers also examine recall. Despite wide differences among subject groups, these papers on the whole demonstrate a resounding lack of difference between deaf and hearing people.

Brown and Dell found that in paraphrasing experimental anecdotes, deaf and hearing college students showed similar patterns of reference to objects that had previously been mentioned. Their recall for such objects was also rather similar. The small reported deficit in recall of these objects by deaf subjects may have been an artifact of communication differences or a result of the very small (possibly unrepresentative) size of the comparison subgroup of hearing subjects.

In several studies of memory strategies, Liben found that deaf children of various ages displayed the usual rehearsal strategies in a sequential-learning paradigm. They also showed semantic clustering in a free-recall paradigm, similar to what has been demonstrated in the past for hearing children. Liben also found that deaf adults tended to categorize both English words and ASL signs based on meaning rather than on formational similarity. This finding is again analogous to previous data for hearing subjects.

Friedman's comparison of classification skills ostensibly compares deaf and hearing preschoolers. In attempting to classify concrete objects on both superficial (perceptual) and specific categorical (basic) principles, the two groups performed similarly. This result was not replicated when a more general, abstract (superordinate) principle was suggested to the subjects; but this difference may have related more to Friedman's subject selection practices than to any inherent differences between deaf and hearing children. Specifically, deaf subjects were chosen in such a way that a linguistic deficit was assured, while hearing subjects were chosen for at least average oral receptive skills. This contrast suggests that the obtained group difference was not necessarily attributable to hearing status, but rather to communication skills and their concomitants. Moreover, the results of Liben's similar sorting task yielded no differences between deaf and hearing children, thus suggesting subjects' adequate mastery of a small set of superordinate categories.

The work reported by Knobloch-Gala and Kaiser-Grodecka again examined classification or concept formation behavior in deaf children. Rather than compare their deaf subjects to hearing controls, these authors compared three modes of presentation: verbal (written form), iconic (graphic/visual), and demonstration of task. Not surprisingly, the more visually graphic stimuli proved more conducive to learning classificatory principles than the written stimuli. This result is especially interesting in light of the heavy oral emphasis in Polish deaf education today.

Synthesizing the various findings in part 5 leads us to the conclusion that, after controlling for mode of presentation or communication system, deaf subjects generally resemble hearing subjects insofar as their capacity for abstraction, categorization, and serial recall are concerned. As with hearing people, deaf people have at their disposal a range of processing strategies and a constructive hierarchy of concepts that allow them to make sense of the world. However, several questions now arise from these papers.

Deafness is not a unitary phenomenon. Nearly one third of the prelingually hearing-impaired U.S. population manifests some form of additional handicap. Liben is unfortunately silent on the presence or absence of such conditions in her subjects. If multihandicapped individuals were included, it would have been interesting to know how task performance was related to condition. If such people were excluded from the subject pool, a replication with, for example, deaf children who were also diagnosed as learning disabled would be of value. In contrast, Friedman's subjects represent a narrow band of deaf children. Although her study therefore lacks some generalizability, her work does seem to say something significant about the cognitive deprivation inherent in an educational strategy that results in poor communication skills. Here, a replication with deaf preschoolers who are immersed in a total communication environment, or with those whose oral skills are stronger, would now shed light on possible reasons for the reported pattern of results.

Knobloch-Gala and Kaiser-Grodecka are scrupulous in their subject inclusion procedures in eliminating children with any significant abnormality. The reader is thus reasonably assured that their findings are generalizable, within the limits of their experimental procedures. Again, however, one would like to know more of how task performance varies with subject characteristics. Brown and Dell's deaf subjects were all college students, which clearly constituted an unrepresentative sample with respect to the larger deaf population. Replication now with a broader spectrum of subjects would help to determine if their findings are valid in general.

For the diagnostician, the procedures described by these authors may eventually hold some promise. For example, as Friedman indicates, her task may have some value in differentiating deaf children with learning deficits from those without such problems. This point may also apply to some of the other authors' procedures. However, a great deal of additional development is required before practitioners will have useful assessment instruments.

The classroom teacher can perhaps take some encouragement from the results reported here, as well as some important guidance. It is heartening to have additional confirmation that the theoretician need not invoke arcane models in order to account for the cognitive processes of deaf students. But there also must be sensitivity to linguistic and modality-specific considerations in deaf students. For example, American Sign Language lacks specific lexical items for certain superordinate categories. The failure of an individual student to sort items into a superordinate category could thus, in some instances, reflect a linguistic-conceptual difference, not a cognitive deficit. The teacher's burden would then be to explain to a child with this orientation the value of learning a particular concept. Any difficulty encountered therein may be better thought of as a product of linguistic incompatibility, rather than as an inherent problem with abstract thought.

It is essential that deaf education now take aim at helping deaf children utilize their intact cognitive machinery to adapt to the general academic and vocational world. The papers presented here suggest that there is no inherent impediment to this goal, notwithstanding the substantial problems of the multihandicapped, which have not been addressed in these works. The greater challenge is to accomplish this goal without discounting deaf persons' abilities and without otherwise dehumanizing the very people who are the subjects of these educational efforts.

References

Pintner, R., & Paterson, D. G. (1917). A comparison of deaf and hearing children in visual memory for digits. *Journal of Experimental Psychology, 2*, 76–88.

Related Educational and Research Issues

1. Are rehearsal strategies internal or external in the hearing-impaired learner?

2. How is it possible to account for relatively poorer performance by hearing-impaired learners on the identification of superordinate categories in classification tasks?

3. To what extent are nonverbal, as opposed to verbal, strategies used by the deaf learner in carrying out classification tasks?

4. What kinds of materials should teachers use to enhance memory, concept development, classification, and symbolic thought in deaf students?

5. How can the findings of these papers be communicated most beneficially to the parents of deaf children so that the parents reinforce these skills in the home?

6 Issues in Cognition and Language Development

Application of Ausubel's Theory of Meaningful Verbal Learning to Curriculum, Teaching, and Learning of Deaf Students

Eileen Biser

Currently, if teachers advocate presentational methods of instruction (i.e., lectures and reading), they are often challenged by educational theorists who claim that discovery methods, open education, and experience-based learning are far superior in enhancing student learning and retention. But many teachers cannot dismiss mastery of an academic discipline as an educational goal for deaf students, especially at the college level. So they continue to struggle with how to help students learn large bodies of information more effectively and efficiently.

Sometimes teachers look to educational, psychological, and/or cognitive theories for guidance. But, unfortunately, there are few occasions when teachers can actually bridge the gap between theory and practice because researchers often fail to offer practical application of their theories or findings. In addition, traditional teacher-preparation courses have been sparse in cognitive psychology, basic statistics, and research interpretation; and sometimes teaching schedules or commitments allow little time for study and reflection. Despite these obstacles, the work of educational psychologist David P. Ausubel provides a bridge between theory and practice for many teachers. He stands out as one of the few theorists who simultaneously addresses curriculum, teaching, and learning issues (Weil & Joyce, 1978). He, like many teachers, believes that the acquisition of information is valid and essential, and he rejects the idea that such expository learning is in any way passive (Ausubel, 1968). Ausubel is one of the few educational theorists who has been concerned with helping teachers to convey large amounts of information as meaningfully as possible.

Ausubel (1963b) described the mind's information-storage and processing system (cognitive structure) as being parallel to the conceptual structure of academic disciplines. That is, at the top of each discipline are a number of broad concepts, under which are subsumed less inclusive subconcepts. From this basic premise, Ausubel developed his theory of meaningful verbal learning.

Ausubel (1968) contended that a parallel exists between cognitive structure and the way that curriculum should be organized to help students process new information meaningfully. Meaningful learning occurs, according to Ausubel, only when new ideas are anchored in or linked to what is already in the cognitive structure of a learner (1967, p. 222). This knowledge can also greatly influence teachers when they present new material to students (Ausubel, 1963a).

The complete version of this paper is available in microfiche or hard copy from ERIC Document Reproduction Service. Ask for Document No. ED 247 712.

Some general implications of adopting Ausubel's theory include the following:

1. The task to be learned becomes more important than exploring the circumstances and conditions that previously have influenced learners. For example, finding out if a student is oral or manual, if a student has much usable hearing, or how the student became deaf are all secondary to the teaching/learning task.

2. By focusing on what the student already knows and can learn, developmental approaches to teaching/learning emerge. This contrasts with remediation, which traditionally has evoked a negative response from students because of an emphasis on what is not known.

3. As a result of implementing Ausubel's theory, the importance of sound diagnostic tools for assessing what is known and what a student can do become high priorities in the teaching task.

Specifically in curriculum development, several implications are embedded in two principles of the theory: progressive differentiation and integrative reconciliation (Ausubel, 1963a). According to these principles, the teacher establishes the hierarchy of knowledge and makes decisions about definitions and meanings based on the discipline. Then, the most highly inclusive concepts of that discipline are presented first. Subsequent ideas of the discipline are presented downward on the hierarchy (Ausubel, 1968, p. 153). Also, the sequence of the curriculum is organized so that each successive learning task is carefully related to what has been presented before. In curriculum development there is a great deal of emphasis on exploring relationships between ideas within the hierarchy (both similarities and differences), as well as on making a conscious effort to help students reconcile inconsistencies between ideas both within the hierarchy and among hierarchies (Ausubel, 1968, p. 155).

Within the realm of direct teaching application, we find a derivative of Ausubel's theory: the concept of the *advance organizer*. Advance organizers are previews or introductions that the student sees or reads before studying the main body of new material (Anderson & Faust, 1973). The principal function of the organizer is described as "bridging the gap between what the learner already knows and what he needs to know so that he can learn the task at hand more expeditiously" (Ausubel, Novak, & Hanesian, 1978, p. 148, 628). The teacher develops advance organizers by (a) translating new concepts into a frame of reference that has personal meaning for the student and (b) comparing and contrasting new material with what the student already knows.

The implications for the learner (both hearing and hearing-impaired) who works under an Ausubel-designed curriculum and classroom include both affective and performance benefits. One of the most important occurrences is that students sense that the learning task is not amorphous and unmanageable, and that there is structure and finiteness to the task. This confidence instills motivation to continue learning and builds pride in subsequent accomplishments. In addition, a student's cognitive structure is strengthened and information processing is fine tuned because learning becomes meaningful. A stable and clear organization eliminates the need for rote memorization, thus making the newly learned information more readily available in memory and more useful in real-life situations (Ausubel, 1963b, 1968). A cyclical process then evolves as the student's self-image and motivation are again positively affected.

Clearly, the theory of meaningful verbal learning simultaneously addresses curriculum, learning, and teaching by considering (a) how knowledge is organized (curriculum), (b) how one processes new information (learning), and (c) how teachers can apply these curriculum and learning ideas when presenting new material to students (instruction).

Teachers who attempt to incorporate cognitive theory into classroom reality undoubtedly discover that it is a valuable and worthwhile endeavor. Although Ausubel's work stands as a beacon to practitioners who strive to base their curriculum and classroom activities on a strong theoretical foundation, one point remains clear: Teachers cannot assume sole responsibility for bridging the gap between theory and practice. Researchers, teacher-training programs, and school administrators must also recognize that they have an obligation to foster and enhance teacher knowledge in cognitive psychology, statistics, and research. Discovering the relevancy and applicability of an intricate cognitive psychological theory, such as Ausubel's, should be the rule, not the exception in every teacher's experience. Deaf learners will be the beneficiaries.

References

Anderson, R. C., & Faust, G. W. (1973). *Educational psychology: The science of instruction and learning.* New York: Harper & Row.

Ausubel, D. P. (1963a). Cognitive structure and the facilitation of meaningful verbal learning. *Journal of Teacher Education, 14,* 217–222.

Ausubel, D. P. (1963b). *The psychology of meaningful verbal learning.* New York: Grune & Stratton.

Ausubel, D. P. (1967). A cognitive structure theory of school learning. In L. Siegel (Ed.), *Instruction: Some contemporary viewpoints* (pp. 207–257). San Francisco: Chandler.

Ausubel, D. P. (1968). *Educational psychology: A cognitive view.* New York: Holt, Rinehart & Winston.

Ausubel, D. P., Novak, J. D., & Hanesian, H. (1978). *Educational psychology: A cognitive view.* New York: Holt, Rinehart & Winston.

Weil, M., & Joyce, B. (1978). *Information-processing models of teaching.* Englewood Cliffs, NJ: Prentice-Hall.

Additional Reading

Anderson, R. C., Spiro, R. J., & Anderson, M. C. (1978). Schemata as scaffolding for the representation of information in connected discourse. *American Educational Research Journal, 15,* 433–440.

Ausubel, D. P. (1960). The use of advance organizers in the learning and retention of meaningful verbal material. *Journal of Educational Psychology, 51,* 267–272.

Ausubel, D. P. (1961). In defense of verbal learning. *Educational Theory, 11,* 15–25.

Ausubel, D. P. (1962). A subsumption theory of meaningful verbal learning and retention. *Journal of General Psychology, 66,* 213–224.

Ausubel, D. P. (1965). A cognitive structure view of word and concept meaning. In R. C. Anderson & D. P. Ausubel (Eds.), *Readings in the psychology of cognition* (pp. 58–75). New York: Holt, Rinehart & Winston.

Ausubel, D. P. (1978). In defense of advance organizers: A reply to critics. *Review of Educational Research, 48,*251–257.

Ausubel, D. P. (1980). Schemata, cognitive structure, and advance organizers: A reply to Anderson, Spiro, and Anderson. *American Educational Research Journal, 17,* 400–404.

Ausubel, D. P., & Fitzgerald, D. (1962). Organizer, general background, and antecedent learning variables in sequential verbal learning. *Journal of Educational Psychology, 53,* 243–249.

A Contextualist Perspective of Language Processing by Prelingually Deaf Students

Janis Morariu
Roger Bruning

The often heated controversy in deaf education concerning language acquisition continues to pervade the literature on cognition, education, and deafness. Two major questions have emerged: Which language system will best prepare deaf individuals to communicate effectively in society? and Which language system will best allow for normal cognitive development within prelingually deaf individuals' unique information-processing system? Although the most widely accepted solution to the first question is to provide deaf learners with proficient English-language skills, nearly half of the deaf students age 20 and younger read at less than a 4.5 grade-equivalent level (Trybus & Karchmer, 1977). This paper focuses on the second question through an examination of the influence of language mode (print or sign) and syntax (English or American Sign Language [ASL]) on prelingually deaf individuals' access to meaning, which is an essential component of effective communication.

Some theorists purport that the prelingually deaf child's lack of auditory input leads to the development of a visual information-encoding system that is vastly different from that developed in normally hearing individuals (Goldin-Meadow & Mylander, 1983; Kretschmer & Kretschmer, 1978). In support of this theory, the majority of encoding studies suggest that the encoding and retrieving of information from a print medium by deaf individuals may actually be a multiple-step process in which they first transform a typically verbal code (printed English) into a visual mode (a sign language system) for processing, and then they recode the stored visual code back into a verbal code to communicate in what is normally a spoken language system (Frumkin & Anisfeld, 1977; Hanson, 1982; Shand, 1982; Treiman & Hirsh-Pasek, 1983).

In an attempt to use the sign-based encoding orientation of deaf children to facilitate English-language acquisition, many educational programs for deaf learners adopt a system of signed English in which signs are borrowed and modified from ASL while the syntax of English is held intact (Kretschmer & Kretschmer, 1978). Although signed English appears to be similar to ASL in that the two share much of their sign vocabulary, they are actually two distinct language systems. ASL is a visual and conceptual language system, whereas signed English is based on an auditory and temporal orientation (Bellugi & Klima, 1975; Kretschmer & Kretschmer, 1978).

American Sign Language is acquired by many deaf individuals through an informal, and often sporadic, exposure to other deaf individuals who use ASL outside of the family and the formal classroom environment (Hoemann, 1975; Kretschmer & Kretschmer, 1978). Although most deaf children

The complete version of this paper is available in mircofiche or hard copy from ERIC Document Reproduction Service. Ask for Document No. ED 247 714.

receive exclusive formal instruction in the use of the English-language system, often through a variety of modes and methods, most are likely to choose to use a form of ASL as adults (Hoemann, 1975; Kretschmer & Kretschmer, 1978). The main question that arises at this point is why most prelingually deaf individuals adopt ASL, which is so radically different from English, as their primary language when they have been formally trained in and reinforced for acquiring standard English (signed, spoken, and/or written). Perhaps visual and conceptual languages such as ASL are better suited than English to deaf individuals' information-processing capabilities.

The contextualist perspective of information processing suggests that the total language encounter will exert a significant influence on an individual's processing of a language experience (Jenkins, 1974; Watkins & Tulving, 1975). When this view of information processing is applied to the deaf individual's experience, the language encounter may include any combination of printed or signed modes of information presented in either English or ASL syntax.

In a study by Morariu and Bruning (1984), two experiments were conducted on the influence of language mode (print or sign) and syntax (English or ASL) on a free-recall task. Experiment 1 tested the effects of reading meaningful print passages in ASL or English on deaf and hearing high school subjects. The results supported an effort toward comprehension interpretation by only the hearing subjects. Deaf subjects (not trained in ASL) exhibited a familiarity with ASL syntax that was not exhibited by the hearing subjects. In Experiment 2, meaningful passages were presented to prelingually deaf subjects in four language contexts (signed English, signed ASL, printed English, and printed ASL). Results showed greater recall from ASL than from English contexts, irrespective of mode of presentation. These experiments indicated that the visual orientation of prelingually deaf individuals, regardless of their training in ASL, leads to the development of a sign-based encoding system that responds to ASL as a familiar language.

Language context, as described in the Morariu and Bruning study, appears to play a major role in facilitating the prelingually deaf individual's access to meaning, which is the foundation of effective communciation. The fact that ASL provides a greater capacity for the encoding and retrieving of information than does the typical language of instruction (English) suggests that ASL should be encouraged as a first language among prelingually deaf individuals.

Providing prelingually deaf children with a comfortable, yet linguistically rich, language such as ASL as their first language may furnish them with the necessary tools for understanding the nature and utility of language for the purposes of successful communication, thinking, and manipulation of the environment. Without such an early established language base, the proven difficulties that many prelingually deaf individuals experience in developing a sophisticated grasp of English may never be overcome.

References

Bellugi, U., & Klima, E. S. (1975). Aspects of sign language and its structure. In J. F. Kavanagh & J. E. Cutting (Eds.), *The role of speech in language* (pp. 171–203). Cambridge: MIT Press.

Frumkin, B., & Anisfeld, M. (1977). Semantic and surface codes in the memory of deaf children. *Cognitive Psychology, 9,* 475–493.

Goldin-Meadow, S., & Mylander, C. (1983). Gestural communication in deaf children: Noneffect of parental input on language development. *Science, 221,* 372–374.

Hanson, V. (1982). Short-term recall by deaf signers of American Sign Language: Implications of encoding strategy for order recall. *Journal of Experimental Psychology: Learning, Memory, and Cognition, 8,* 572–583.

Hoemann, H. W. (1975). *American Sign Language: Lexical and grammatical notes with translation exercises.* Silver Spring, MD: National Association of the Deaf.

Jenkins, J. J. (1974). Remember the old theory of memory? Well, forget it. *American Psychologist, 29,* 785–795.

Kretschmer, R. R., & Kretschmer, L. W. (1978). *Language development and intervention with the hearing impaired.* Baltimore: University Park Press.

Morariu, J. A., & Bruning, R. H. (1984). Cognitive processing by prelingual deaf students as a function of language context. *Journal of Educational Psychology, 76,* 844–856.

Shand, M. A. (1982). Sign-based short-term coding of American Sign Language signs and printed English words by congenitally deaf signers. *Cognitive Psychology, 14,* 1–12.

Treiman, R., & Hirsh-Pasek, K. (1983). Silent reading: Insights from second-generation deaf readers. *Cognitive Psychology, 15,* 39–65.

Trybus, R. J., & Karchmer, M. A. (1977). National data on achievement status and growth patterns. *American Annals of the Deaf, Directory of Programs and Services, 122,* 62–69.

Watkins, M. J., & Tulving, E. (1975). Episodic memory: When recognition fails. *Journal of Experimental Psychology: General, 104,* 5–29.

Linguistic Encoding and Adult-Child Communication

Harley Hamilton

During interpersonal communication, short-term memory appears to function as a central or on-line processor for information received or expressed by an individual. Of particular interest are the linguistic encoding bases used in short-term memory by deaf subjects; these bases appear to be cherologically or sign-based for signs and printed information. Studies of recall performance (Bellugi & Siple, 1974; Klima & Bellugi, 1979; Hamilton, 1984b; Shand, 1982), perception of signs (Grosjean, Teuber, & Lane, 1979; Hamilton, 1984a; Shand, 1982), and intrusion errors made in the experimental setting and during spontaneous conversation (Bellugi & Siple, 1974; Hamilton, 1984b; Newkirk, Klima, Pederson, & Bellugi, 1980) have been used as the bases for this claim. The intrusion error data are perhaps most important for educators of deaf students. These intrusion errors, termed *slips of the hand* when they are expressive and *slips of the eye* when they are receptive, are commonplace occurrences in human communications. They are also a source of some teacher-child miscommunication.

When a slip occurs, information has been erroneously expressed or received. For example, upon seeing a carrot, an 11-year-old responded by signing, "Butterfly eat carrot." This response appears to be odd until one considers that the local signs for *butterfly* and *rabbit* differ only in handshape. They are considered a *minimal pair* because they differ in only one aspect. This error can then be readily explained as a slip of the hand. A slip of the eye also causes confusion; for instance, a teacher asked a child, "Who sleeps in your room?" using signs for each word spoken. The child answered, "blue," which again appears to be a rather odd response. However, if this response is analyzed from a perceptual point of view, a slip of the eye readily explains it. By combining the location and movement of the sign for *who* (mouth/wiggle) and the initial handshape of the sign for *sleep* (5-hand) the sign *color* is formed. The question asked by the teacher then becomes "Colors in your room?" to which blue is an appropriate answer.

Young deaf children are confronted with many similarly produced signs in their everyday activities. For example, in a preschool classroom or at home there is usually an abundance of cooking and play activities. The children, who are new to signs, are exposed during a cooking activity to such signs as *egg, knife, salt, spoon, soup, butter,* and *sit,* which are all minimal pairs. While some misunderstandings may be due to the child's lack of vocabulary knowledge, others may be due to a misreading or misproduction of a sign. For example, the adult asks the child to get *butter,* and the child returns with *soup* or a *spoon.* By realizing that signs are perceived and encoded based on sign parameters rather than on spoken parameters, teachers will be able to recognize more quickly a possible source for a child's

The complete version of this paper is available in microfiche or hard copy from ERIC Document Reproduction Service. Ask for Document No. ED 247 713.

misunderstanding and then correct it. Children are more likely to confuse signs such as *egg* and *knife*, which differ only in movement, than they are to confuse *egg* and *leg* where the spoken English is similar but the signs differ greatly.

By accepting that signs are perceived and produced based on sign parameters, educators can then address the development of sign language perception. A great deal of research has been done on auditory perceptual skills (Ling, 1976; Sanders, 1971), yet the sign perceptual skills of young deaf children have not been studied until recently (Hamilton, 1984a). It is first necessary for research to delineate this area of language development so that education will have developmental data on which to base any program designed to help children develop their sign perceptual skills.

An immediate implication for teaching methodology is that teachers may wish to either maximize or minimize the differences between signs for items they present. For example, when working on color recognition with the children, the teacher may wish to contrast items that are blue and red (these color signs differ greatly), or blue and yellow (these color signs differ minimally). Research must then address the question, Is planned presentation or planned avoidance of minimal pairs of signs the better teaching strategy? Also, if one strategy is better, is it better for all learners at all times, or is it related to the learner's age or experience with the language?

Earlier it was mentioned that linguistic slips occur in normal human communication. Research with hearing speakers has indicated that slips of the tongue and auditory perceptual miscues are more common with some language-disabled individuals, such as aphasics (Talo, 1980) and language-delayed individuals (Tallal & Stark, 1980), than they are with normal speakers. Also, such mistakes go unnoticed more often by the language-disabled person. From preliminary observations of signers, this author suggests that there is also a group of deaf children for whom mistakes go unnoticed. Several students who have been labeled as low-language children have shown a greater tendency to make slips of the hand and eye than other deaf children. As research investigates this area more thoroughly, these children can be more accurately identified, and programs can be developed and implemented to help them eliminate such mis-signings and mis-seeings in communication.

The encoding of signs and some implications for education have been discussed. Equally important for deaf education are the perception and encoding of simultaneous and oral communication. Several questions must now be addressed in these areas.

1. How is simultaneous communication encoded? Is it as signs alone or speech alone, or both as separate codes or as a unitary whole? Also, does this feature change with age, linguistic experience, or amount of hearing?

2. Will simultaneous communication ever overload the working memory space of young children? Or, does it always enhance reception of communication? Also, are either of these possibilities a function of age, linguistic experience, or amount of hearing?

3. How is oral communication encoded? Is it recoded into signs by younger signers or is it dealt with as a separate speech code? Also, what implications do either of these possibilities have for the development of the child's oral skills?

Perhaps it will be most important to investigate how individuals of different ages, linguistic backgrounds, and hearing losses encode information under different presentation conditions. It is important for educators who present information to deaf students via various modes of communication to be aware of how the students are processing that information. Teachers may then better understand how to present information, why a student may have made a particular error in communicating or receiving information, and how they may then help the student to correct the error.

References

Bellugi, U., & Siple P. (1974). Remembering with and without words. In F. Bressen (Ed.), *Current problems in psycholinguistics* (pp. 215–236). Paris: CNRS.

Grosjean, F., Teuber, H., & Lane, H. (1979). *When is a sign a sign? The on-line processing of gated signs in American Sign Language* (Working Paper). Boston: Northeastern University.

Hamilton. H. (1984a). Cheremic perception by deaf children. *Sign Language Studies, 42,* 23–30.

Hamilton, H. (1984b). *Linguistic encoding in short-term memory.* Unpublished doctoral dissertation, Georgia State University, Atlanta.

Klima, E. S. & Bellugi, U. (1979). *The signs of language.* Cambridge: Harvard University Press.

Ling, D. (1976). *Speech and the hearing-impaired child.* Washington, DC: A. G. Bell Association.

Newkirk, D., Klima, E. S., Pederson, C., & Bellugi, U. (1980). Linguistic evidence from slips of the hand. In V. A. Fromkin (Ed.), *Errors in linguistic performance: Slips of the tongue, ear, pen, and hand* (pp. 165–198). New York: Academic Press.

Sanders, D. A. (1971). *Aural rehabilitation.* Englewood Cliffs, NJ: Prentice-Hall.

Shand, M. (1982). Sign-based short-term coding of American Sign Language signs and printed English words by congenitally deaf signers. *Cognitive Psychology, 14,* 1–12.

Tallal, P., & Stark, R. E. (1980). Speech perception of language delayed children. In G. H. Yeni-Komishian, J. F. Kavanagh, & C. A. Ferguson (Eds.), *Child phonology: Perception* (pp. 155–169). New York: Academic Press.

Talo, E. S. (1980). Slips of the tongue in normal and pathological speech. In V. A. Fromkin (Ed.), *Errors in linguistic performance: Slips of the tongue, ear, pen, and hand* (pp. 81–86). New York: Academic Press.

Cognitive Processing and Language in Deaf Students: A Decade of Research

Michael Rodda
George Buranyi
Ceinwen Cumming
Beverly Muendel-Atherstone

Despite intensive educational efforts, it is not uncommon for deaf students to lag behind hearing peers in the acquisition of verbal language and academic skills. Available neuropsychological research provides conclusive evidence for the reasons for this phenomenon. One problem is that variables such as age of onset of deafness, etiology, degree of hearing loss, amount of language before hearing loss occurred, and educational treatment are not usually controlled, and they exert a significant effect on the results obtained (Kelly & Tomlinson-Keasey, 1978). Nevertheless, a number of suggestions are possible, and these will be considered in some detail in the remainder of this paper.

Differential Hemispheric Specialization and Memory Strategies

Studies of commissurotomized patients (i.e., patients who have surgically divided forebrain commissures), despite being open to criticism, have provided valuable information on hemispheric specialization in the brain and have produced some fairly consistent findings. Research with these patients indicates that, in addition to left-hemispheric dominance in language skills and right-hemispheric dominance in visual-spatial skills, the left hemisphere may be more specialized for analytical processing and the right hemisphere for gestalt processing (Bogen, 1969; Nebes, 1974; Sperry, 1973). In particular, studies of this type appear to demonstrate that the right hemisphere of commissurotomized patients is superior in generating a complete stimulus configuration from partial or fragmentary information (Nebes, 1971, 1972, 1973, 1974). However, the right hemisphere is not totally nonverbal, and it does play a vital role in the recovery of speech and language functioning in cases where the left hemisphere has been damaged or is malfunctioning (Searleman, 1977; see Kusché, pp. 115–120).

Evidence concerning cerebral specialization has also been obtained from neurologically abnormal deaf subjects. Not surprisingly, lateralization of language functions has been the focus of much of this research. Kimura (1976), in examining seven cases of deaf aphasia cited in the literature, noted an association of manual communication disorder (sign language) with left-hemisphere control of complex motor behavior rather than of language. The analysis of McKeever, Hoemann, Florian, and Van Deuenter (1976) supports this hypothesis; they conclude that such patients may be demonstrating motor skill deficits rather than aphasia. Kimura, Battison, and Lubert (1976)

The complete version of this paper is available in microfiche or hard copy from ERIC Document Reproduction Service. Ask for Document No. ED 170 066.

provided additional support for such an explanation when they stated: "It is quite possible that the degree of impairment seen in our subject on the linguistic hand movements parallels that of the nonlinguistic—that is, his defect is primarily one of motor sequencing" (p. 571).

Recent research involving neurologically normal hearing-impaired subjects has been illuminating on hemispheric specialization in such individuals. Employing tachistoscopic presentation of verbal and nonverbal stimuli to the visual hemifields (left or right half of the visual field), Phippard (1977) found that a group of deaf subjects taught by oral methods had a right-hemisphere advantage in perceiving both verbal and nonverbal material. A group of subjects taught by a combination of oral and manual techniques showed no evidence of lateralization. The results of McKeever, Hoemann, Florian, and Van Deuenter (1976) indicated that when stimuli are bilaterally presented, deaf subjects show minimal hemifield asymmetry for both English words and ASL stimuli. With unilateral presentation, deaf subjects showed a left-hemisphere advantage for the recognition of words. In discussing their results, these authors suggested that as the task becomes more complicated, there is less dominance in one hemisphere in deaf subjects. However, Wilson (1977) suggested that this finding is a strategy effect unrelated to cerebral dominance and that subjects presented with bilateral stimuli decide to either shadow the right or left channel. Wilson, using unilateral presentation of stimuli to the visual hemifields, found no cerebral asymmetry effects in deaf subjects for the processing of words, letters, or signs. These findings tend to substantiate the view that left-hemisphere superiority for language in hearing subjects results from auditory input to the left auditory association cortex of the brain. Wilson also found that signed stimuli are easier to identify than printed stimuli when the exposure time is brief (20 msec). She attributed this result to the slower decay of spatial information, when compared to the decay of figural information.

The possibility that deaf subjects rely on visual codes is also supported by studies of short-term memory. Research has shown that deaf subjects make more formational errors, while hearing subjects make semantic errors (Bellugi, Klima, & Siple, 1975; Wallace, 1972). The study by Wallace (1972) does, however, suggest that the deaf make use of other codes. Wallace found that orally trained subjects showed some evidence of using an articulatory code, while manually taught subjects used a code based partly on fingerspelling. He also noted that the deaf performed better than the hearing on a facial recognition task, again stressing the importance of the visual channel. The use of different encoding strategies has been explored by Boshoven, McNeil, and Harvey (1982). They related these differences to hemispheric specialization for various functions, and suggested that in processing drawings, deaf subjects may use nonverbal referents while hearing subjects use verbal referents. Overall, they suggested that the deaf subjects may have adopted holistic/gestalt processing strategies, whereas hearing subjects may use more analytical strategies.

Experimental Studies

The authors of this paper have been involved in a number of studies of various aspects of language and cognition (Grove, O'Sullivan, & Rodda, 1979; Rodda & Grove, 1982). These studies are summarized in the following section.

Studies of Information Transmission

Response latency. The time taken to respond to a stimulus (including transmission time) is a useful way of measuring overall differences in cognitive-processing strategy. In one study by Rodda and Grove (1982), the overall average latency of response (t) to signed and orally communicated sentences was calculated. The regression functions for the two groups of subjects (when r is the coefficient of correlation) were clearly different.

Total: TS $= 0.871 - 0.0044t$ $\quad r = -0.31$ n.s. (A)

Oral: TS $= 1.04 - 0.023t$ $\quad r = -0.61$ n.s. (B)

With so few degrees of freedom, two-tailed t-tests fail to reach significance, but the trend seems to be fairly clearly established.

1. Total communicators show total scores (TS) that are virtually independent of latency. Also, a very slow responder achieves about the same total score as a fast responder.

2. Oral communicators have total scores that indicate a moderately strong negative relationship between the two variables.

Rate of information transfer. The differential relationship just described led to the development of an estimated rate at which information is transmitted during testing (Rodda & Grove, 1982).

An arbitrary metric was employed to assess different coding systems (reading, total, oral, and manual). Table 1 shows the mean information transfer rate (ITR) as a function of two age groups (9–13 years and 14–20 years) and method of communication. The overall superiority of reading and the relative weakness of the oral method are emphasized when the transmission rate is taken into account, but the mean ITR rates for total and manual methods of communication were almost identical.

Laterality Studies

In a study by Muendel-Atherstone and Rodda (1983), signed and unsigned stimuli were visually presented to 20 hearing and 20 prelingually deaf

Table 1
Information Transfer Rate (ITR)[a] As a Function of Age and Method
of Communication

Communication Method	Subjects 9–13 Years Old		Subjects 14–20 Years Old		All Subjects
	Group Size	ITR	Group Size	ITR	ITR
Reading	9	2.10	12	2.61	2.39
Total	14	1.77	11	2.45	2.07
Oral	8	0.95	9	1.72	1.36
Manual	8	1.74	13	2.27	2.07

[a]ITR = messages correctly received per minute.

adults. Materials were presented unilaterally in a randomized sequence to both right and left visual hemifields through a two-field tachistoscope. Hearing and deaf subjects differed significantly in the number of correctly identified stimuli, with hearing subjects scoring higher on all six types of materials presented. Four factors were found in the hearing subjects' responses and three factors in the deaf subjects' responses. The factors for hearing subjects were signed presentations, unsigned materials, right hemispheric presentation of road signs, and right hemispheric presentation of letters. In deaf subjects, the factors were signed presentations, road signs, and letters; these factors showed no laterality effects.

Because no difference was found between the materials presented to the left and right visual hemifields, the data substantiated the hypotheses that (a) the deaf sign subjects would show an overall reduced laterality effect, and (b) hearing signing subjects would show bilateral effects. Interestingly, and predictably, more road signs were perceived in the left hemisphere in both groups, and both groups tended to more correctly identify materials presented to the left hemisphere.

Discussion and Conclusions

While previous research into cerebral lateralization of language with hearing-impaired populations has provided some conflicting results and has been open to criticism, it does indicate that the field has promising potential for increasing our understanding of cognitive processing in both hearing and deaf individuals. If deaf individuals acquire a different cerebral organization for language as compared to hearing populations, then such differences could have a considerable impact on the intervention methods used with young children.

Even if language is not lateralized differently in deaf children, adolescents, and/or adults, a number of important questions remain to be answered. For example, Does the acoustic code have unique properties or can the signs of a visually based language (such as American Sign Language) fulfill the same tasks? If such signs can be utilized equally well in the acquisition of language structures, will this acquisition occur in the same way as it does with an acoustic code? How is a language such as ASL processed by both deaf and hearing populations? Are signs mediated equally well by both hemispheres? If so, this mediation could have significance for intervention not only with deaf children but with hearing aphasics who could learn sign language as a means of communication.

However, it may be that educational experiences result in patterns of atypical lateralization in deaf subjects. Since atypical lateralization has been associated with cognitive and perceptual deficits in hearing populations (Levy & Reid, 1978), it is also possible that the language problem associated with early prelingual deafness may be a consequence of educational deficits rather than neurological differences.

References

Bellugi, U., Klima, E. S., & Siple, P. (1975). Remembering in signs. *International Journal of Cognitive Psychology, 3,* 93–125.

Bogen, J. E. (1969). The other side of the brain: An appositional mind. *Bulletin of the Los Angeles Neurological Society, 34,* 135–162.

Boshoven, M. M., McNeil, M. R., & Harvey, L. O. (1982). Hemispheric specialization for the processing of linguistic and non-linguistic stimuli in congenitally deaf and hearing adults. *Audiology, 21,* 509–530.

Grove, C., O'Sullivan, F. D., & Rodda, M. (1979). Communication and language in severely deaf adolescents. *British Journal of Psychology, 70,* 531–540.

Kelly, R. R., & Tomlinson-Keasey, C. (1978, June). *A comparison of deaf and hearing children's hemispheric lateralization for processing visually presented words and pictures.* Paper presented at the 1978 meeting of the American Educational Research Associaton, Toronto, Canada.

Kimura, D. (1976). The neural basis of language and gesture. In H. Avakian-Whitaker & H. A. Whitaker (Eds.), *Studies in neurolinguistics* (Vol. 2, pp. 145–156). New York: Academic Press.

Kimura, D., Battison, R., & Lubert, B. (1976). Impairment of nonlinguistic hand movements in a deaf aphasic. *Brain and Language, 3,* 566–571.

Levy, J., & Reid, M. (1978). Variations in cerebral organization as a function of handness, hand posture, writing and sex. *Journal of Experimental Psychology, 10,* 119–144.

McKeever, W. F., Hoemann, H. W., Florian, V. A., & Van Deuenter, A. D. (1976). Evidence of minimal cerebral asymmetries for processing of English words and American Sign Language in the congenitally deaf. *Neuropsychologia, 14,* 413–423.

Muendel-Atherstone, B., & Rodda, M. (1983). *Differences in hemispheric processing of linguistic material presented visually to deaf and hearing adults.* Unpublished manuscript, University of Alberta, Department of Educational Psychology.

Nebes, R. D. (1971). Superiority of the minor hemisphere in a commissurotomized man for perception of part-whole relations. *Cortex, 7,* 333–347.

Nebes, R. D. (1972). Dominance of the minor hemisphere in a commissurotomized man in a test of figural unifications. *Brain, 95,* 633–638.

Nebes, R. D. (1973). Perception of dot patterns by the disconnected right and left hemisphere in a commissurotomized man. *Neuropsychologia, 11,* 285–296.

Nebes, R. D. (1974). Hemispheric specialization in a commissurotomized man. *Psychological Bulletin, 81,* 1–14.

Phippard, D. (1977). Hemifield differences in visual perception in deaf and hearing subjects. *Neuropsychologia, 15,* 555–561.

Rodda, M., & Grove, C. (1982). A pilot study of language structures in the receptive language of deaf subjects. *Journal Association of Canadian Educators of the Hearing Impaired, 8,* 168–181.

Searleman, A. (1977). A review of right hemispheric linguistic capabilities. *Psychological Bulletin, 84,* 503–528.

Sperry, R. W. (1973). Lateralization of function in the surgically separated hemispheres. In F. J. McGuigan & R. Schoonover (Eds.), *The psychophysiology of thinking.* New York: Academic Press.

Wallace, G. (1972). *Short-term memory and coding strategies of the deaf.* Unpublished doctoral dissertation, McGill University, Montreal.

Wilson, B. (1977). *Lateralization of sign language.* Unpublished doctoral dissertation, University of London.

Analysis

David F. Armstrong

If we were to search for the one word that would best sum up the papers in part 6, we would probably settle on the word *context*. These papers reflect a theoretical trend in teaching language arts to deaf children that is moving away from mechanistic approaches based on the analysis of syntax and morphology, and toward more naturalistic approaches based upon sociolinguistic and psycholinguistic notions. These notions relate to the significance of cognitive and social contexts in the comprehension and production of words (or signs) and utterances (i.e., speech acts; see Searle, 1969). This shift is evident also in papers presented at the International Symposium on Cognition, Education, and Deafness.

This contextual framework will orient the points in this analysis related to the symposium sessions that discussed these papers, the broader areas of language development, and the facilitation of language development in deaf children. Before proceeding, however, we must first clarify what is meant by language. The term *language* will be understood broadly to encompass human communication via oral or gestural signs (Peirce, 1955) when such signs have a rule-governed system of organization (syntax) and are used in ordinary discourse and social interaction. This definition would, in the current context, include such oral/aural languages as English and Spanish as well as visual languages such as ASL and written English (as distinct from spoken). It is recognized explicitly in these papers that an American deaf child may have very poor skills in written or spoken English and yet not be language deficient if a rich background in a signed language exists.

Let us now proceed to examine the first question of context. This first area broadly encompasses the cognitive texturing that accompanies the use of a particular language. The paper by Morariu and Bruning examined the question of how the mode of presentation (print or sign) and the syntax (ASL or English) affect the ability of prelingually deaf students to recall propositions. The conclusion here was somewhat unexpected from these authors' point of view, in that despite a complete lack of formal instruction in ASL, prelingually deafened students showed better recall for propositions when ASL syntax (word order) was used, even when the medium was print. This conclusion led to extensive discussion of issues surrounding the potential usefulness and desirability of bilingual (i.e., signed/spoken) approaches to deaf education. A paucity of research in this area was noted. We will return to this issue later and present it as a major area in which further research should be focused.

The paper by Biser considered the cognitive features behind language development from a more general perspective, that of Ausubel's theory of meaningful verbal learning.

The paper by Hamilton investigated a second contextual level in regard to some ways in which aural vs. visual perceptual context (one level down from the cognitive) may have significant influence on cognitive outcomes, particularly, in this case, on the ways in which errors may be manifested. This paper and the final paper by Rodda and his associates represent an important trend in deafness-related research toward increasing attention to the neurobiological bases of communicating and learning by deaf students. Rodda's paper in fact represents a third contextual level, that of brain processing. In particular, although it appears that signed and spoken languages may share strong similarities in the ways they are encoded into short-term memory by signers and speakers, we see increasing evidence that deaf signers and hearing speakers may develop brains that are organized differently at the cerebral hemispheric level. This sort of research represents an important part of the process that is needed to define how signed communication can be better employed in the education of deaf children. In other words, if there are important differences in the ways in which brain processing occurs for alternative communication modes, and if these differences have ramifications for the information-carrying characteristics of these modes, we must be aware of and exploit these differences rather than be exploited by them.

Discussion surrounding the papers by Rodda and Hamilton reiterated the belief that contextual support for deaf language learners may be as important as syntactic support or vocabulary building in isolation. In particular, discussants at the symposium expressed opposition to the notion that English-language texts should be simplified syntactically or semantically before being presented to deaf students. The view was expressed that it is much more important to expose deaf children to the real material they will have to read but also to give them the background and world view necessary to comprehend written materials. Further support was expressed for the development of bilingual or English-as-a-second-language approaches to instruction.

The most important question raised by these papers and their discussants is, What should be a first or native language for deaf children? This question is not new, and it has provoked a remarkable amount of controversy and rancor through the years. Leaving aside the controversies concerning oral versus manual education methods, we can ask two more questions: Is it possible to identify current approaches to deaf education that employ truly bilingual methods? and, What is known about the efficacy of bilingual approaches to education in general?

With respect to the question of how much research has been conducted on bilingual approaches to deaf education, a search through the last 10 years of the *American Annals of the Deaf* and *Sign Language Studies* reveals fewer than 10 articles dealing with this subject. The paucity of research in this area reflects a lack of even experimental programs using a truly bilingual approach. By bilingual we mean approaches that include at least some instruction in ASL and some instruction in English—whether oral, written, or signed in some fashion. A recent attempt has been made by Luetke-Stahlman (1983) at least to categorize the types of bilingual or English-as-a-second-language programs that might be possible.

Merely enumerating methods that have been attempted with hearing children will not be enough, however. The literature on bilingual approaches to education with hearing children (e.g., Rotberg, 1982) is not positive enough to suggest that this approach will prove to be a panacea in the education of deaf children. That it should be tried and evaluated conscientiously seems self-evident for both ethical and theoretical reasons because most deaf adults (including many who are orally trained) accept and promote their own visually based languages. It would behoove educators of the deaf to pay close attention to the characteristics of this mode of communication under naturalistic conditions. It would be particularly useful in this regard to have cross-cultural studies of the sign languages of the deaf in different countries. Commonalities among such languages might suggest optimal linguistic and cognitive strategies that deaf people have discovered through natural evolutionary processes. These strategies may remain hidden from us if we rely exclusively on experimental techniques for discovering them.

Another question that arises is whether or not reading and writing can be taught in the absence of oral communication, either with or without the use of a general bilingual approach. (To understand the controversy surrounding this question, see part 7, pp. 108–132.) There are now approaches to teaching second-language-reading that suggest that reading is possible without first learning the language's sound system (e.g., Bar-Lev, 1983; and dialogue journal writing methods). In such cases, the target language is treated as a visual-symbolic system that is independent of its sound system, which may or may not be represented by its writing system (e.g., as in Chinese logographic writing or Japanese Kana and Kanji symbols).

This sort of speculation has obvious implications for the teaching of reading and writing to deaf children, especially since it appears that users of nonphonemically based writing systems may have brains that are organized similarly to those of deaf native signers (see Armstrong & Katz, 1981, for a discussion of this possible similarity). According to this line of thinking, it may be possible to take greater advantage of the visual context of writing in the education of children whose primary sensory modality is vision.

A related question not discussed in the research efforts represented by these papers concerns the cognitive and neurolinguistic effects of communication systems that are designed to visually enhance phonemically based spoken language (i.e., Cued Speech). The efficacy of such approaches remains controversial (Mohay, 1983; Nicholls, 1979), and more research is needed to clarify whether and under what circumstances they may be effective. This issue is embedded in a larger one that was left relatively untreated in the papers in part 6. The larger issue concerns the effects of varying degrees of deafness and ages of onset of deafness in the selection of an appropriate instructional mode and setting.

It is well known that the ease of acquisition of spoken languages varies with the extent of residual hearing, but the assignment of hearing-impaired children to various modes and educational settings still seems to be relatively haphazard. Freeman, Carbin, and Boese (1981) have presented systematically what is known on this topic. For our purposes here, there appears to be relatively little systematized knowledge of the cognitive consequences of the interaction among educational methods, educational settings, degrees of hearing loss, and ages of onset of deafness. This area is another in which a body of knowledge needs to be developed, systematized, and disseminated.

Two interrelated questions remain to be raised: What are the neurolinguistic effects of early language experience in the mode of total communication (i.e., simultaneous communication-amplification)? and What are the information-carrying characteristics of signed as opposed to spoken languages? The first question has to do with whether speech and sign together augment or conflict in their neurolinguistic effects (i.e., do they produce a net gain when used together or do they interfere with each other and, therefore, should they be kept separate? The second question is seldom asked, and we need serious work on the relative complexities of the semantic domains of signs and words. For more detail on the extent to which these domains can diverge for words and signs that usually receive the same gloss, the reader should examine a recent article by Wilcox (1984).

The philosophical underpinnings of simultaneous communication are shaky for the simple reason that we have almost no information about how deaf people use particular signs that are glossed with particular words, not to mention the syntactic barbarisms that sometimes arise through the simultaneous use of potentially incompatible codes. (For a discussion of some of the problems involved in the use of simultaneous communication, see Kluwin & Kluwin, 1983.) We now need a serious examination of these and related questions.

This analysis has raised more new questions than it has answered old ones. This situation probably reflects the larger fact that many of the most important questions facing educators of the deaf have not yet received objective investigation through the use of sophisticated research methods. This point is especially true in the areas of language development and linguistics. It is hoped that some of the questions raised in this volume and in discussions of it will soon have satisfactory answers.

References

Armstrong, D. F., & Katz, S. H. (1981). Brain laterality in signed and spoken language: A synthetic theory of language use. *Sign Language Studies, 33*, 319–350.

Bar-Lev, Z. (1983). Hebrew hieroglyphics. *Visual Language, 17*, 365–379.

Freeman, R. D., Carbin, C. F., & Boese, R. J. (1981). *Can't your child hear?* Baltimore: University Park Press.

Kluwin, T. N., & Kluwin, B. (1983). Microteaching as a tool for improving simultaneous communication in classrooms for hearing-impaired students. *American Annals of the Deaf, 128*, 820–825.

Luetke-Stahlman, B. (1983). Using bilingual instructional models in teaching hearing-impaired students. *American Annals of the Deaf, 128*, 873–877.

Mohay, H. (1983). The effects of cued speech on the language development of three deaf children. *Sign Language Studies, 38*, 25–49.

Nicholls, G. H. (1979). *Cued speech and the reception of spoken language.* Unpublished doctoral dissertation, McGill University, Montreal.

Peirce, C. S. (1955). *The philosophical writings of Peirce.* New York: Dover Publications.

Rotberg, I. (1982). Some legal and research considerations in establishing federal policy in bilingual education. *Harvard Educational Review, 52*, 149–168.

Searle, J. (1969). *Speech acts.* London: Cambridge University Press.

Wilcox, S. (1984). STUCK in school: A study of semantics and culture in a deaf education class. *Sign Language Studies, 43*, 141–164.

Related Educational and Research Issues

1. How do children perceive signs?

2. How are signs encoded and in what sequences?

3. What is the relationship between the encoding of simultaneous communication and variables such as age, degree of hearing loss, and age of onset?

4. What is the relationship between the encoding of oral language and speech learning?

5. What is the effect on cognitive development of using a spatial/visual language?

6. What is the appropriate base language for school instruction for hearing-impaired children—ASL or English?

7. To what extent are bilingual educational methods appropriate for teaching English as a second language to deaf learners?

8. Do the signs of a visually based language perform the same functions as an acoustic code in language acquisition?

9. In what ways, if any, does communication modality (auditory, oral, manual, or simultaneous) affect cerebral lateralization of language functions?

10. Should linguistic stimuli be presented both orally and manually to deaf learners on the assumption that encoding style may involve both phonological and cherological bases?

11. What is the distinction between linguistic competence and communication competence?

12. To what extent are student signing errors truly visual acuity errors, as opposed to linguistic mistakes?

13. If ASL is taught in schools, how would articulatory cues be taught?

14. To what extent is it necessary to actively teach students some code-switching strategies in order to facilitate their moving between ASL and English?

7 Issues in Reading and Reading Methodology

Cognitive Processes in Reading: Where Deaf Readers Succeed and Where They Have Difficulty

Vicki L. Hanson

The act of reading involves the recognition of individual words and the integration of the meanings of those words for text comprehension. The present paper reports on studies with deaf college students, focusing first on their word recognition processes and then on their short-term memory representation of the words processed.

The approach here is to focus on analytic reading, in which the reader takes advantage of the linguistic information reflected in orthography and performs a grammatical analysis on the words of a sentence, thus leading to comprehension (Mattingly, 1980). While some have taken the position that reading need not involve linguistic mediation, there is a great deal of evidence in the literature indicating that such analytic processing promotes acquisition of reading among beginning readers and facilitates reading (especially of difficult material) for more advanced readers (Gleitman & Rozin, 1973; Liberman, 1983). This evidence provides the motivation for focusing on analytic reading in the present paper.

The orthography of English is an alphabetic writing system that reflects the morphophonemic structure of the language (Chomsky & Halle, 1968; Klima, 1972; Venezky, 1970). Hearing college students exploit this structure in the reading of words, even in the reading of those words that are familiar (Brooks, 1977; Massaro, Taylor, Venezky, Jastrzembski, & Lucas, 1980). Similarly, deaf college students are sensitive to orthographic structure (Hanson, 1983; Hanson, Shankweiler, & Fischer, 1983), and they take advantage of this structure to facilitate word recognition (Hanson, 1982b, 1983). In a study of letter recall, deaf students were presented with letter strings that were orthographically regular (e.g., *remond, siflet*) and orthographically irregular (e.g., *rdemno, eflsti*). These students recalled letters of the orthographically regular strings more accurately than those of the irregular strings (Hanson, 1983). Similar results were obtained in an experiment investigating the recognition of fingerspelled words in which deaf adults were asked to report the letters of fingerspelled strings that were orthographically regular (e.g., *s-n-e-r-g-l-i-n*) or orthographically irregular (e.g., *f-t-e-r-n-a-p-s*). They more accurately reported the letters of the regular strings (Hanson, 1982b).

This superior performance on the regular strings suggests that skilled deaf readers, like skilled hearing readers, are sensitive to orthographic structure. As further support for this suggestion, nearly all of the incorrect letter reports in the experiment on fingerspelling were found to be orthographically permissible. Particularly striking was the finding that for the orthographically irregular strings, many of the reporting errors tended to result from the subjects' attempts to regularize the spelling of these strings.

Preparation of this article was supported by National Institute of Neurological and Communicative Disorders and Stroke Grant NS-18010.

For example, in recalling the string *f-t-e-r-n-a-p-s*, some subjects omitted the letter that made the sequence irregular and wrote *fernaps*. Others added a letter to make the sequence regular and wrote *afternaps*, while others rearranged the letters of the sequence and wrote *ferntaps*.

In addition to the ability to deal with the structure of individual words, reading requires holding words and their order of arrival in memory long enough to permit sentence comprehension. Short-term memory studies have been used to examine the nature of the internal representation (or code) used by deaf readers to mediate this comprehension process.

In studies of short-term memory with deaf college students, two primary findings have emerged. The first has been that these students, particularly the better readers, tend to use a speech-based code in the short-term retention of printed English words (Hanson, 1982a; Lichtenstein, in press, see pp. 111–114). These results are consistent with Conrad's (1979) finding that the better deaf readers among high-school-age students tended to use a speech-based code. These results extend Conrad's finding, however, in an important way: While the deaf students tested by Conrad attended schools that were strictly oral in their educational approach, the college students tested in more recent studies have had manual language experience (some have been native signers of American Sign Language). The second finding to emerge from the short-term memory studies with college students has been that deaf readers have difficulty in using a speech code. Even deaf readers who do use it, tend to use it less efficiently than hearing readers (Hanson, 1982a; Lichtenstein, in press, see pp. 111–114).

Given the difficulty in using a speech-based code, why might the better adult readers tend to prefer it over a manual code? A partial answer to this question is suggested by research on the retention of serial-order information. Since English is a language in which word order carries critical syntactic information, the retention of word order during sentence comprehension is essential. In an experiment comparing the memory of deaf and hearing college students for sequences of printed English words, deaf college students had poorer recall only when they were required to recall the words in their order of occurrence; the deaf students were comparable to the hearing students when recall of order was not required (Hanson, 1982a). Thus, the deaf students had specific difficulty in retaining information about the *order* in which words were presented. The extent of this difficulty appears to be correlated with deaf individuals' ability to use a speech code. In tests of short-term memory, those students with the larger memory spans have shown the greatest use of a speech code (Conrad, 1979; Hanson, 1982a; Lichtenstein, in press, see pp. 111–114). These results suggest that the retention of word order information depends on the ability to use a speech code.

In summary, this research suggests that deaf college students are quite proficient at using the morphophonemic structure of words in word recognition, but that even these readers experience persistent difficulties in the short-term memory processes that mediate comprehension. The difficulties appear to be related, at least in part, to inefficient use of a speech-based code.

The question of what the nature of the speech-based representation used by deaf readers is and how this representation is developed remains. Deaf readers could acquire information about a speech-based code from orthography or through speaking and lipreading. It may be that deaf readers' ability to use some form of speech-based code is not well reflected in the intelligibility rating of their speech. These intelligibility ratings are based on listeners' ability to understand the deaf speakers' utterances, and not on the deaf individuals' ability to utilize speech in reading. Further research therefore needs to be directed at determining how an effective speech-based code might be acquired by deaf individuals for the purpose of reading.

References

Brooks, L. (1977). Visual patterns in fluent word identification. In A. S. Scarborough (Ed.), *Toward a psychology of reading* (pp. 143–181). Hillsdale, NJ: Lawrence Erlbaum Associates.

Chomsky, N., & Halle, M. (1968). *The sound pattern of English.* New York: Harper & Row.

Conrad, R. (1979). *The deaf school child.* London: Harper & Row.

Gleitman, L. R., & Rozin, P. (1973). Phoenician go home? (A reply to Goodman). *Reading Research Quarterly, 8,* 494–501.

Hanson, V. L. (1982a). Short-term recall by deaf signers of American Sign Language: Implications for order recall. *Journal of Experimental Psychology: Learning, Memory, and Cognition, 8,* 572–583.

Hanson, V. L. (1982b). Use of orthographic structure by deaf adults: Recognition of fingerspelled words. *Applied Psycholinguistics, 3,* 343–356.

Hanson, V. L. (1983, August). *Access to orthographic regularities by deaf readers.* Paper presented at the meeting of the American Psychological Association, Anaheim, CA.

Hanson, V. L., Shankweiler, D., & Fischer, F. W. (1983). Determinants of spelling ability in deaf and hearing adults: Access to linguistic structure. *Cognition, 14,* 323–344.

Klima, E. S. (1972). How alphabets might reflect language. In J. F. Kavanagh & I. G. Mattingly (Eds.), *Language by ear and by eye: The relationship between speech and reading* (pp. 57–80). Cambridge: MIT Press.

Liberman, I. Y. (1983). A language-oriented view of reading and its disabilities. In H. Myklebust (Ed.), *Progress in learning disabilities* (Vol. 5, pp. 81–101). New York: Grune & Stratton.

Lichtenstein, E. H. (in press). The relationships between reading processes and English skills of deaf college students: Parts I & II. *Applied Psycholinguistics.*

Massaro, D. W., Taylor, G. A., Venezky, R. L., Jastrzembski, J. E., & Lucas, P. A. (1980). *Letter and word perception: Orthographic structure and visual processing in reading.* Amsterdam: North-Holland.

Mattingly, I. G. (1980). Reading, linguistic awareness and language acquisition. *Haskins Laboratories Status Report on Speech Research SR-61,* 135–150.

Venezky, R. L. (1970). *The structure of English orthography.* The Hague: Mouton.

Deaf Working Memory Processes and English Language Skills

Edward Lichtenstein

An important function of recoding strategies in working memory (WM, sometimes called short-term memory) during the reading process is to provide temporary storage of text surface structure (Baddeley, Eldridge, & Lewis, 1981; Kleiman, 1975). This short-term storage allows the reader to retain information about individual lexical items and the syntactic structures necessary to determine the correct underlying semantic relationships between the words in a sentence. Considerable research has shown that prelingually deaf students are likely to exhibit processes at the WM stage of reading that are different from those of hearing students in both quantitative and qualitative ways. This paper summarizes a series of studies (Lichtenstein, 1984, in press) that investigated the relationships between WM and recoding processes, background educational and linguistic variables, and a variety of English-language skills in a sample of 86 prelingually deaf college students.

When considering the problem of WM storage of linguistic information, there are two primary considerations. The first is simply capacity: Quantitatively, how much English linguistic information can the system hold? A large body of research has shown that deaf students generally have a limited WM capacity for linguistically encodable material. This is the case not only for English words; deaf students' capacity to retain a sequence of manually presented signs is also less than hearing students' capacity to retain a sequence of words (Bellugi, Klima, & Siple, 1975; Hanson, 1982; Kyle, 1980).

Recent studies involving both orally educated subjects (Conrad, 1979) and native signers (Hanson, 1982) have found that the ability to make effective use of a speech-coding mechanism is related to the ability to maintain a sequence of words in WM. The present research, which involved a heterogeneous group of students from a variety of educational and linguistic backgrounds, replicated the results of Conrad and Hanson. These studies may explain why deaf persons generally have shorter memory spans than hearing persons for linguistically codable materials. For most deaf students, neither the speech, sign, nor visual codes are as efficient as the speech code of hearing persons for the purpose of maintaining English linguistic information in WM, although the ability to effectively use a speech-based recoding process is positively correlated with WM capacity. As the Lichtenstein (in press) study indicated, when the effects of a speech-based recoding strategy are statistically controlled, the more central, cognitive components of deaf students' working memories seem to be as capable of maintaining sequential linguistic information as that of hearing persons. Inefficient peripheral rehearsal systems appear to account for the differences in WM capacity that are generally found between deaf and hearing students.

The research reported here was carried out under an agreement with the U.S. Department of Education.

The second issue concerns the internal representation of English linguistic information in WM. Subjects responded to two questionnaires concerning their use of recoding strategies in a variety of English information-processing tasks. These responses provided (a) information regarding the extent of use of speech- and sign-recoding strategies in reading and writing tasks and (b) descriptive data on the extent to which the codes provide a detailed internal representation of English grammatical information during sentence-memory and reading tasks. Interestingly, many students reported using both codes. Speech recoding was used by many students who rarely use speech for communication and by students with rather unintelligible speech. Sign recoding (generally reported in addition to speech) was used by many students who had learned to sign during their primary school years.

The strategies that students reported for using these codes showed considerable selectivity in recoding English grammatical information. For both speech and sign strategies, content morphemes were more likely to be recoded than were function words or morphological endings. The commonly reported strategy of not recoding to speech or to sign the function words in a sentence was found to be associated with limited working memory capacity. This finding suggests that the tendency not to recode English functors may be a strategy for dealing with English linguistic materials; this strategy is adapted to the individual's WM capacities. Given a limited capacity, the student recodes only the semantically more important information. Thus, the evidence suggests that neither the speech- nor sign-recoding systems provide the majority of students with a complete internal representation of English surface-structure information in WM during the reading process (Lichtenstein, 1984, in press).

Very few of the best readers made consistent use of a sign-recoding strategy (a finding in agreement with results reported by Treiman & Hirsh-Pasek, 1983). As found by Conrad (1979), overall reading and writing skills were positively correlated with the ability to depend upon a speech-based recoding strategy in WM. Conrad's population of students was orally educated. However, in this study, the advantage for those readers able to make efficient use of a speech-recoding strategy did not interact with type of educational background (oral versus TC education). Thus, there appear to be important consequences of the ability to depend upon speech to maintain English information in WM, consequences that are not related to the extent to which a student must depend upon oral communication for instructional purposes.

In order to explore the bases for these relationships, several analyses were made of the more specific relationships between the WM processing variables and skills in the various domains of English competence: syntax, morphology, and semantics. Semantic skills (vocabulary test scores and semantic errors in writing) showed little relationship to WM processes. This finding is consistent with research on the reading processes of hearing persons, which has found that recoding to speech is not a required process for accessing semantic information about individual words.

Syntactic skills (proper use of free functors) were positively related to WM capacity and to the ability to efficiently use a speech-based coding strategy. Logically, we might expect that as WM capacity increases, the ability to attend to sequential relationships among words and to internalize rules based on these relationships would be facilitated. In addition, the follow-up study found that, for both speech and sign recoding, students who tended not to recode the function words during reading had poorer syntactic skills than those who consistently recoded functors. Thus, while the tendency to be selective in the recoding of free functors may be an adaptive strategy for coping with a limited WM capacity, it may also effectively limit exposure to English grammatical information so as to cause serious gaps to develop in the students' knowledge of English syntax.

Skill in the use of English morphology was positively related to the ability to use a visual code to maintain information about word shape in WM. This finding suggests that the ability to retain information about the visual shape of words is useful in attaining skill with English morphology and knowledge about the internal grammatical structure of words. The follow-up study, which provided data on the recoding of morphological suffixes, found that the tendency not to recode morphological endings to speech was also associated with lower morphological skills.

In order to investigate the effects of background factors (e.g., age of learning sign language, oral vs. TC education) and preferred methods of communication (speech, ASL, manual English), the relationships of these variables to the English skills measures were examined, with the effects of the WM processing variables factored out. A similar analysis examined the hypothesis that use of ASL or of Pidgin Sign English (PSE) exerts specific influences on the writing of deaf students, especially on the use of articles, tense markers, pronouns, etc. In both cases there was no evidence of linguistic interference from either ASL or PSE. In addition, there was no evidence that the use of sign language in education interfered with the development of a speech-based recoding strategy (cf., Hanson, 1982).

The overall pattern of results suggests that the reading processes of deaf students, in particular WM processes and recoding strategies, may be influencing grammatical processing and the acquisition of English skills in distinctive ways. An important research question will be how to educate deaf students in a manner that takes into account the particular types of information-processing resources deaf students bring to the language-learning situation (see discussion in Lichtenstein, in press).

References

Baddeley, A., Eldridge, M., & Lewis, V. (1981). The role of subvocalization in reading. *Quarterly Journal of Experimental Psychology, 33*, 439–454.

Bellugi, U., Klima, E. S., & Siple, P. (1975). Remembering in signs. *Cognition, 3*, 93–125.

Conrad, R. (1979). *The deaf school child: Language and cognitive function*. London: Harper & Row.

Hanson, V. L. (1982). Short term recall by deaf signers of American Sign Language: Implications of encoding strategy for order recall. *Journal of Experimental Psychology: Learning, memory, and cognition, 8*, 572–583.

Kleiman, G. (1975). Speech recoding in reading. *Journal of Verbal Learning and Verbal Behavior, 14*, 323–339.

Kyle, J. G. (1980). Sign language and internal representation. In B. Bergman & I. Ahlgren (Eds.), *Proceedings of the First International Symposium on Sign Language Research* (pp. 207-221). Stockholm: Swedish National Association of the Deaf.

Lichtenstein, E. H. (1984). [Working memory representations and grammatical skills of deaf students]. Unpublished raw data.

Lichtenstein, E. H. (in press). The relationships between reading processes and English skills of deaf college students: Parts I and II. *Applied Psycholinguistics.*

Treiman, R., & Hirsh-Pasek, K. (1983). Silent reading: Insights from congenitally deaf readers. *Cognitive Psychology, 15*, 39–65.

Information Processing and Reading Achievement in the Deaf Population: Implications for Learning and Hemispheric Lateralization

Carol A. Kusché

At least two important factors have been found to be significantly related to good reading comprehension: (a) processing speed, which includes retrieval from semantic memory, scanning speed of working memory contents, linguistic understanding, and past language experience; and (b) short-term memory, which for hearing individuals seems to involve phonetic encoding (Golinkoff & Rosinski, 1976; Guttentag & Haith, 1978; Hess & Radtke, 1981). Automatic or unconscious processing of written material appears to be acquired with relative ease by most hearing children because they learn to transfer the patterns of spoken language, which have become habitual due to years of linguistic stimulation and practice, onto the secondary media of reading and writing (Fries, 1962; Wolff, 1973).

Reading, then, appears to be a language-based skill that ultimately depends upon automatic processing and unconscious linguistic awareness (Mattingly, 1972). The early language deprivation experienced by most deaf children, however, results in deficiencies in the primary linguistic knowledge available in long-term memory storage; because deaf children are generally weak in their automatic processing of the patterns, rules, and strategies for linguistic performance, they lack the repertoire necessary for easy transference to a new language-based skill.

Furthermore, research has indicated that deaf individuals also show deficits in short-term memory functioning. The following conclusions seem to emerge from the large body of available data.

1. Deaf children and adults tend to do poorly on memory-span tests or on tasks in which the order of information is important.

2. Encoding strategies differ between deaf and hearing subjects at all developmental levels studied.

3. Deaf subjects do not generally utilize phonetic encoding strategies.

4. There appears to be much variability among deaf subjects in types of encoding strategies that are utilized.

Cross-sectional pilot data collected by this author indicated that short-term memory development appears to show little improvement after the age of 9½ (strikingly reminiscent of the asymptote generally reported for reading comprehension scores). Twelve-year-old deaf children demonstrated memory abilities that were relatively retarded as compared to norms for hearing children of the same age. It was suggested that total communication comprehension skills may also be compromised by poor memory abilities, but this is an area in need of further research.

The complete version of this paper is available in microfiche or hard copy from ERIC Document Reproduction Service. Ask for Document No. ED 247 719.

Significant correlations between reading skills and short-term memory capacities have been reported for both deaf and hearing children (Blair, 1957; Carey & Blake, 1974; Hartung, 1970). It has been suggested that internal speech (i.e., phonetic encoding) is necessary for good reading achievement (Conrad, 1979). The data indicate, however, that it may be the kinesthetic or proprioceptive recoding associated with phonetic encoding that is actually the important factor (Hintzman, 1967). Hardyck and Petrinovich (1970) have suggested that an auditory-proprioceptive stimulus complex may be used as a stable mediator during the early process of learning to read. This stimulus complex allows for the development of neural analogues. Once developed, these neural analogues ultimately replace the auditory-proprioceptive process and render it unnecessary; automatic processing is then possible.

Deficiencies in linguistic knowledge (automaticity for language processing, memory capacities, reading achievement, etc.) suggest that another factor may be related that may ultimately prove to be of crucial importance, and that is left hemispheric specialization and lateralization for verbal memory and language-related functions. More specifically, research currently available suggests that early language deprivation may result in less than efficient myelinization and dendritic differentiation (i.e., an increase in the number of branches of neuronal dendrites and the synaptic interconnections between them) in the brain, which may be reflected in relatively weak hemispheric specialization and concomitant deficiencies in linguistic and memory-related functioning (see Rodda et al., pp. 94–99).

The human brain is asymmetrical and the left hemisphere appears to be specialized for language functions for most of the hearing population (Geschwind, 1979; Geschwind & Levitsky, 1968; Witelson & Paille, 1973). Asymmetrical differences between the two cerebral hemispheres are apparent even in human fetuses, which suggests that the left hemisphere's propensity toward developing superior language competence may have a solid anatomical base (Geschwind, 1979). More specifically, Broca's Area (in the frontal lobe above the Sylvian Fissure) appears to control expressive language and the muscles used in speaking, while Wernicke's Area (in the temporal lobe below the Sylvian Fissure) seems to be involved in receptive language and the connection of sights and sounds (Kesner & Baker, 1980). These two areas are connected by a bundle of nerve fibers.

Research with commissurotomized and aphasic hearing patients indicates that the right hemisphere of the brain is limited in its ability to remember sequential information and to mediate complex expressive speech (Gordon, 1983; Zaidel, 1976, 1977). Furthermore, discrepant hemispheric lateralization has been implicated for hearing children with dyslexia and other auditory-linguistic difficulties (Marcel, Katz, & Smith, 1974; Sommers & Taylor, 1972; Witelson, 1979; Witelson & Rabinovitch, 1972; see Rodda et al., pp. 94–99).

In a longitudinal study, Bakker (1979, 1983) found that hearing children who showed a left-ear advantage in kindergarten and shifted to a right-ear advantage one year later were ultimately the best fifth-grade readers; children who demonstrated the reverse shift were later the worst readers. Bakker hypothesized that proficient reading may be correlated with right-hemispheric control at an early age (when perceptual processing of script is still difficult) and with left-hemispheric speech control at later ages (when semantic and phonetic processing become more important). Given these findings, we might expect to find that reading problems in deaf children become more apparent as they progress through the elementary school years and beyond; this expectation is consistent with what educators have been observing for many years.

Frith (1983) distinguished between dyslexics, who show poor spelling and poor reading abilities, and dysgraphics, who demonstrate poor spelling but good reading skills. His research suggested that the former group was deficient in both lexical and phonetic processing, while the latter group did not show a deficit in the phonetic but only in the lexical route. Interestingly, he noted that "despite the theoretical possibility that there are [hearing] children whose reading problems are more severe than their spelling problems, such children are in practice difficult to find [although] they can be found readily in languages where orthography is regular, such as Spanish" (p. 460). Deaf children, as a group, tend to be better spellers than readers (Meadow, 1980). This finding suggests that phonemic processing is more problematic than orthographic processing, a hypothesis which is consistent with other data.

Research on deafness and hemispheric specialization for language is somewhat unclear because of methodological problems, but suggests that deaf children and adults do not typically show left-hemispheric specialization for linguistic functions (Kelly & Tomlinson-Keasey, 1977; Phippard, 1977). (See Rodda et al., pp. 94–99, for a more extensive review.) However, deaf adults who had deaf parents, have used sign language from birth, and have developed different types of sign aphasias as the result of strokes, do show left-hemispheric linguistic processing and right-hemispheric visual-spatial processing as is found with most hearing individuals (Bellugi, 1983). This finding is very important to note because it does not appear to be auditory deprivation or deafness per se that results in discrepant lateralization; it may well be, however, that problems result because of the lack of early language stimulation and training.

To the present author's knowledge, the effect of linguistic input on brain growth has not been studied. Research regarding the visual cortex has shown that for both people and animals, the key factor in rapid myelinization, which is important for efficient neural transmission, is not maturation but visual experience (Movshon & Van Sluyters, 1981). Animal research further indicates that an absence of different types of visual stimulation has serious permanent effects on neural development, including less myelinization of the optic nerve, the lack of development of important neural connections between eye and brain, the abnormal development of specific feature detectors, and the loss of binocular sensitivity of the nerve cells (Grobstein & Chow, 1975; Hirsch & Spinelli, 1970; Hubel & Wiesel, 1963). Studies of adults with uncorrected astigmatism (Freeman & Thebos, 1973) suggest that neural development in the visual cortex of humans also requires visual experience. It has been suggested that some neurons are environment-dependent and will not develop if the cortex is not stimulated by experience (Cummins, Livesey, Evans, & Walsh, 1979).

117

While the effects of linguistic input on brain growth have not been studied, it is known that hearing individuals are quite sensitive to auditory stimulation even at very young ages and that rapid changes take place in the speech areas of the brain during the first few years of life. Brain-wave recordings indicate that even infants show differences in the way the brain processes linguistic and nonlinguistic auditory stimulation (Molfese, Freeman, & Palermo, 1975) and that special mechanisms within the left hemisphere detect and analyze the sounds of human speech even among newborns (Molfese & Molfese, 1979). Milner (1976) traced the maturation of Broca's Area in hearing children and found that the emergence of speech accompanies cell maturation and the growth of neuronal connections. The two deepest of the six cortical layers begin to mature at the age of approximately one month, and the third layer of cortical tissue begins the myelinization process at about the time babies begin learning their first words. An especially rapid burst of growth occurs about the time children learn to put two words together, and the top three cortical layers (the supragranular layer) become myelinated during the time of greatest language acquisition (between the ages of 3 and 4). By the age of 4, the process of myelinization of Broca's Area is virtually complete. Furthermore, the number of dendritic interconnections increases dramatically during the first 2 years of life, with the greatest increase in dendritic arborization (branching) around Broca's Area during months 12 to 24—the period of time when language is first emerging (Kesner & Baker, 1980).

With regard to long-term memory development, the most important brain areas appear to be the hippocampus (for episodic long-term memory) and the cerebral cortex (for semantic long-term memory). Furthermore, dendritic growth and differentiation in these two areas seem to be closely related to memory performance and improvements in the organization of memory function. Research has shown, for example, that mentally retarded children have a lower than average number of dendritic spines, and the spines that they do have are very thin (Huttenlocher, 1974; Purpura, 1974). In addition, the degree of abnormality appears to be related to age and severity of retardation.

Good long-term memory performance is related to high levels of differentiation. Experiments with animals have demonstrated that malnutrition and dark, impoverished environments result in both deficient memory performance and decrements in dendritic differentiation; however, enriched environments, formal task training, and excessive sensory stimulation result in both improved memory development and increased dendritic differentiation (Kesner & Baker, 1980).

Although much of our available data are correlational in nature and therefore do not allow us to conclude causal relationships, a synthesis of the available information suggests the hypothesis that early language deprivation (not auditory deprivation) may result in deficient development of certain areas of the brain, especially with regard to myelinization and dendritic differentiation. This deficieny may be reflected in weaker hemispheric specialization and associated deficits in language and memory-related functions such as reading. While speculation is interesting, this line of reasoning suggests that research is badly needed. Future research utilizing the PET (positron emission tomography) Scan (see Corbett, p. 18) may provide us with some especially useful information. Related issues, such as sensitive periods, reversibility, and strategies for intervention, are clearly of crucial importance for the education of the deaf.

Given the findings that deaf individuals generally evidence deficiencies in linguistic processing, memory-encoding capacities, reading achievement, and possible hemispheric laterality, it is suggested that intervention and remediation are of crucial importance and should be instituted at as early an age as possible. The importance of the early detection of deafness is also clearly implied. Specific suggestions for educators are included in the complete version of this paper. However, it is strongly emphasized that reading programs designed for hearing children are inadequate for deaf children and that reading instruction should be developed specifically for the needs of the hearing-impaired population. Given the current deficiencies in reading achievement, it would seem that the development and assessment of such a curriculum should be a high priority in the education of deaf children.

References

Bakker, D. J. (1979). Hemispheric differences and reading strategies. *Bulletin of the Orion Society, 29,* 84–100.

Bakker, D. J. (1983). Hemispheric specialization and specific reading retardation. In M. Rutter (Ed.), *Developmental neuropsychiatry* (pp. 498–506). New York: Guilford Press.

Bellugi, U. (1983, August). *Brain organization: Clues from sign aphasia.* Paper presented at the Conference on the Development, Psycholinguistic, and Neurolinguistic Aspects of ASL. Seattle, WA.

Blair, F. X. (1957). A study of the visual memory of deaf and hearing children. *American Annals of the Deaf, 102,* 254–263.

Carey, P., & Blake, J. (1974). Visual short-term memory in the hearing and the deaf. *Canadian Journal of Psychology, 28,* 1–14.

Conrad, R. (1979). *The deaf schoolchild: Language and cognitive function.* London: Harper & Row.

Cummins, R. A., Livesey, P. J., Evans, J. G. M., & Walsh, R. N. (1979). Mechanism of brain growth by environmental stimulation. *Science, 205,* 522.

Freeman, R. D., & Thebos, L. N. (1973). Electrophysiological evidence that abnormal early visual experience can modify the human brain. *Science, 180,* 878.

Fries, C. C. (1962). *Linguistics and reading.* New York: Holt, Rinehart & Winston.

Frith, U. (1983). The similarities and differences between reading and spelling problems. In M. Rutter (Ed.), *Developmental neuropsychiatry* (pp. 453–472). New York: Guilford Press.

Geschwind, N. (1979). Specialization of the human brain. *Scientific American, 241,* 180–201.

Geschwind, N., & Levitsky, W. (1968). Human brain: Left-right asymmetries in temporal speech region. *Science, 161,* 186–187.

Golinkoff, R., & Rosinski, R. (1976). Decoding, semantic processing, and reading comprehension skill. *Child Development, 47,* 252–258.

Gordon, W. P. (1983). *Cerebral dominance: A guide for health care professionals.* Stanford, CA: Cortext Research & Development.

Grobstein, P., & Chow, K. L. (1975). Receptive field development and individual experience. *Science, 190,* 352–358.

Guttentag, R., & Haith, M. (1978). Automatic processing as a function of age and reading ability. *Child Development, 49,* 707–716.

Hardyck, C. K., & Petrinovich, L. F. (1970). Subvocal speech and material. *Journal of Verbal Learning and Verbal Behavior, 9,* 647–652.

Hartung, J. E. (1970). Visual perceptual skill, reading ability, and the young deaf child. *Exceptional Children, 37,* 603–608.

Hess, T. M., & Radtke, R. C. (1981). Processing and memory factors in children's reading comprehension skill. *Child Development, 52,* 479–488.

Hintzman, D. L. (1967). Articulatory coding in short-term memory. *Journal of Verbal Learning and Verbal Behavior, 6,* 312–316.

Hirsch, H. V. B., & Spinelli, D. N. (1970). Visual experience modifies distribution of horizontally and vertically oriented receptive fields in cats. *Science, 168,* 869–871.

Hubel, D. H., & Wiesel, T. N. (1963). Receptive fields of cells in striate cortex of very young, visually inexperienced kittens. *Journal of Neurophysiology, 26,* 994–1002.

Huttenlocher, P. R. (1974). Dendritic development in neocortex of children with mental defect and infantile spasms. *Neurology, 24,* 203–210.

Kelly, R. R., & Tomlinson-Keasey, C. (1977). Hemispheric laterality of deaf children for processing words and pictures visually presented to the hemifields. *American Annals of the Deaf, 122,* 525–533.

Kesner, R. P., & Baker, T. B. (1980). Neuroanatomical correlates of language and memory: A developmental perspective. In R. L. Ault (Ed.), *Developmental perspectives* (pp. 156–215). Santa Monica, CA: Goodyear Publishing.

Marcel, T., Katz, L., & Smith, M. (1974). Laterality and reading proficiency. *Neuropsychologia, 12,* 131–140.

Mattingly, I. G. (1972). Reading, the linguistic process, and linguistic awareness. In J. F. Kavanagh & I. G. Mattingly (Eds.), *Language by ear and by eye: The relationship between speech and reading* (pp. 133–147). Cambridge: MIT Press.

Meadow, K. P. (1980). *Deafness and child development.* Berkeley: University of California Press.

Milner, E. (1976). CNS maturation and language acquisition. In H. Whitaker & H. A. Whitaker (Eds.), *Studies in neurolinguistics* (Vol. 1, pp. 31–102). New York: Academic Press.

Molfese, D. L., Freeman, R. B., Jr., & Palermo, D. S. (1975). The ontogeny of brain lateralization for speech and nonspeech stimuli. *Brain and Language, 2,* 356–368.

Molfese, D. L., & Molfese, V. J. (1979). Hemisphere and stimulus differences as reflected in the cortical responses of newborn infants to speech stimuli. *Developmental Psychology, 15,* 505–511.

Movshon, J. A., & Van Sluyters, R. C. (1981). Visual neural development. *Annual Review of Psychology, 32,* 477–522.

Phippard, D. (1977). Hemifield differences in visual perception in deaf and hearing subjects. *Neuropsychologia, 15,* 555–561.

Purpura, R. P. (1974). Dendritic spine "dysgenesis" and mental retardation. *Science, 186,* 1126–1128.

Sommers, R. K., & Taylor, M. L. (1972). Cerebral speech dominance in language-disordered and normal children. *Cortex, 8,* 224–232.

Witelson, S. F. (1979). Developmental dyslexia: Research methods and interferences. *Science, 203,* 201–203.

Witelson, S. F., & Paille, W. (1973). Left hemisphere specialization for language in the newborn: Neuroanatomical evidence of asymmetry. *Brain, 96,* 641–646.

Witelson, S. F., & Rabinovitch, M. S. (1972). Hemispheric speech lateralization in children with auditory-linguistic deficits. *Cortex, 8,* 412–426.

Wolff, V. G. (1973). *Language, brain, and hearing: An introduction to the psychology of language with a section on deaf children's learning of language.* London: Methuen.

Zaidel, E. (1976). Auditory vocabulary of the right hemisphere after brain bisection or hemidecortification. *Cortex, 12,* 191–211.

Zaidel, E. (1977). Unilateral auditory language comprehension on the Token Test following cerebral commissurotomy and hemispherectomy. *Neuropsychologia, 15,* 1–13.

The Effectiveness of Cued Text in Teaching Pronoun Reference in Written English to Deaf Students

Harold W. Campbell

This study investigated the effectiveness of supplementing a written text with visual cues. The cues acted as prompts to help deaf students identify and comprehend pronoun reference.

The system of visual cues is called cued text. It was designed to make explicit the relationship between a pronoun and its referent. The cues were removed when the student demonstrated an ability to comprehend the relationship.

The study used three levels of cued text. At Level 1, the first letter of the noun referent was printed above the noun and circled. This same letter, *without* the circle, was printed above all pronouns referring to this noun referent, as seen in the following example.

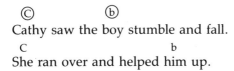

Ⓒ　　　　ⓑ
Cathy saw the boy stumble and fall.
　C　　　　　　　　b
She ran over and helped him up.

At Level 2, which represented multiple referents, the letters were combined.

Ⓜ　　　Ⓑ
Mary and Brian went out for pizza.
M, B
They didn't get home until after midnight.

At Level 3, the referent involved a phrase depicting an action or a concept. The cue was a circle with an arrow that was placed over the first word of the phrase. The arrow indicated that the referent extended to the end of the sentence.

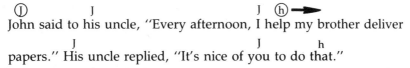

Ⓙ　　　　J　　　　　　　　　　J　ⓗ➤
John said to his uncle, "Every afternoon, I help my brother deliver
　　　　J　　　　　　　　　J　　h
papers." His uncle replied, "It's nice of you to do that."

Two research hypotheses were proposed for this study.

1. Hearing-impaired students will identify significantly more pronoun referents in sentences with cued text than they will in the same sentences with standard text.

2. Hearing-impaired students instructed with cued text will comprehend pronoun reference significantly better than a similar group of students instructed with a traditional approach.

The study sample consisted of 72 students, 11 to 15 years old, enrolled in the Intermediate Department of the Maryland School for the Deaf in Frederick. The students' average hearing threshold was 90 dB; their average performance IQ on the WISC-R was 108. It was not possible to randomly divide the students; therefore, a stratified division of the 16 intact reading groups was made, with the stratification variable being passage-comprehension ability. These two groups were then randomly assigned either to cued text instruction or traditional instruction.

The two dependent variables in this study were identification of pronoun referents and comprehension of pronoun reference. For the first dependent variable, a quasi-experimental group design was used in which the subjects were their own controls. Sixteen hearing-impaired students from the cued text reading groups participated. They were given two presentations of pronoun-reference problems. The first presentation was in standard text while the second presentation was in cued text. In both presentations, the target pronoun was underlined, so the student only had to circle its referent. The following examples illustrate the two presentations.

First: Eugene tried to take the leaves off Randolph's tail.

Second: *"They* won't come off," said Eugene.

The study results indicated that students did identify significantly more pronoun referents in sentences with cued text than in sentences with standard text ($p < .05$).

For the second dependent variable (comprehension of pronoun reference) a nonequivalent control group design was used. The control group of 33 students in eight reading groups received a traditional type of pronoun instruction in three 20-minute sessions each week for 8 weeks. Traditional instruction consisted of discussion of pronoun reference and practice with problem sentences. The target pronoun was underlined and the students were asked to circle the referent. In order to control for the variables of vocabulary and context, all reference problems were drawn from stories previously read in class.

The instructional method used with the 39 students in the eight experimental groups consisted of discussion of pronoun reference and practice with visual cues. The cues were applied to the students' reading texts. Houghton Mifflin Company supplied the 39 textbooks from their K–8 reading program. Weekly probe tests were given to all students in the sample to measure progress. For the traditional instruction groups, these probe tests determined the next level of instruction. For cued text instruction groups, the tests determined what cues should be removed from sentences.

The entire sample was pretested and posttested for comprehension of pronoun reference with an abbreviated form of two subtests from the Test of Syntactic Abilities (Quigley, Steinkamp, Power, & Jones, 1978). The test was abbreviated from 70 to 30 items by taking a stratified selection of items from each content area. Since the groups were statistically nonequivalent (with the control group being superior in most key variables), posttest scores were adjusted using pretest scores as a covariate. Results indicated that there were no statistically significant differences in comprehension between the traditional and cued text groups. Results from an item analysis of the instrumentation showed a negligible loss of internal reliability in the abbreviated subtests.

In addition, this study gathered data on types of pronoun reference. Pronouns are unique in that they have no inherent meaning; they can be understood only in relation to their referents. Wilbur, Montanelli, and Quigley (1976) determined the difficulty of different types of pronouns in highly restricted referent environments. No research has assessed how referent environments affect deaf students' comprehension of pronouns themselves.

A post-hoc analysis was conducted of the nearly 3,500 pronoun-referent problems used in this study. This analysis identified five characteristics of pronoun referents that appeared to influence students' ability to comprehend pronouns. These five characteristics, in descending order of influence, were (a) complexity of the referent (single, multiple, action, concept); (b) number of competing referents; (c) distance (in words) between the pronoun and its referent; (d) direct speech (as opposed to third person) contexts; and (e) type of noun referent (proper, common, inanimate). This classification system is in the process of being validated.

The study results have several implications for reading teachers. First, the study validated the theory of the effectiveness of using visual systems to cue syntactic relationships in written English. Cued text was shown to be an effective cue for helping deaf students to identify pronoun referents. Second, the study showed that cued text is as viable as a traditional instructional approach for teaching pronoun reference. Posttest scores for students in both instructional groups were essentially equivalent. Third, the study contributed to a more comprehensive definition of pronoun reference by tentatively identifying five referent characteristics that influence student comprehension of pronouns. This information could be used to sequence pronoun-reference instruction in the classroom.

It is recommended that future studies use a validated classification system of pronoun referents for an instructional period of 16 weeks. It is also recommended that visual cuing systems, like cued text, be assessed with populations (other than the hearing impaired) who have English-reading difficulties.

References

Quigley, S. P., Steinkamp, M. W., Power, D. J., & Jones, B. W. (1978). *The test of syntactic abilities*. Beaverton, OR: Dormac.

Wilbur, R. B., Montanelli, D. S., & Quigley, S. P. (1976). Pronominalization in the language of deaf students. *Journal of Speech and Hearing Research, 19*, 120–140.

A Child–Computer–Teacher Interactive Method for Teaching Reading to Young Deaf Children

Philip M. Prinz
Keith E. Nelson

Children who use computers in the classroom are often required to respond to statements and questions, and their responses have been required to fall within a small range of acceptable answers. This research project involved an investigation of the effectiveness of interactive microcomputer instruction for improving reading achievement in young deaf children.

Method

The research was conducted at the Pennsylvania School for the Deaf in Philadelphia. The software developed for the project included printed words, animated graphic representations of pictures, and manual signs to illustrate word meanings.

Subjects

The participants in this phase of the study were 12 deaf children between the ages of 2 and 5 years. They all exhibited average or better intelligence as indicated by a performance scale of an accepted intelligence test. Only subjects with a severe to profound hearing impairment were included. The children's modes of communication were not a criterion for selection. An initial assessment was conducted of each child's basic communication skills, including speech, speechreading, sign language, fingerspelling, and simultaneous communication (speech and sign). After the child's primary mode of communication was determined, communication measures were administered in that mode. These measures included a receptive and productive vocabulary test at the single-word/sign level, a sentence imitation test with items that increased in length and grammatical complexity, and a measure of comprehension of syntactic and semantic relationships. Baseline measures of the child's reading abilities were also completed. Based on this information, specially designed programs of instruction were developed for the children.

Equipment

The main equipment used in the project was the Apple II microcomputer system (+ 48K bytes), which was set up with a special, large interface keyboard (the EXPRESS-1 by Prentke Romich Co.), with interchangeable over-

This research was supported by Technology Effectiveness Research Grant No. 6008300361 from the U.S. Department of Education Office of Special Education and Rehabilitation Services.

The complete version of this paper is available in microfiche or hard copy from ERIC Document Reproduction Service. Ask for Document No. ED 247 720.

lays that allowed more flexibility than a regular computer keyboard. When the child selected a picture or sign, the corresponding word or phrase, as programmed, was printed on a printer and displayed on a large color monitor connected to the microcomputer.

Courseware

A software package—the ALPHA Interactive Language Series—was developed to assist hearing-impaired students who are just beginning to read. In the ALPHA programs, the computer displays items in the form of printed words, animated pictures, and optional animated graphic representations of manual signs.

Each child worked for one or two daily sessions of 10 to 15 minutes each for 32 weeks. The set of words, pictures, and graphics was gradually introduced. When the child pressed the appropriate word or sequence of words, the computer responded accordingly. For example, if the child pressed the keys for "dog chases horse," the video monitor would display both the printed words and redundant pictorial information. Then the same sentence could be repeated with animated signs on the TV screen. In addition, the teacher had the option of requesting more information or commenting on the child's message. This process could be carried out, for example, by asking the child if she or he wanted to see a big dog or a small dog or by telling the child something else about a dog and displaying appropriate print and graphics. This procedure served to create an atmosphere in which the child initiated and used printed information in an active, interactive, and pragmatic manner to exchange messages with another person.

The child's oral and manual skills (and any writing/printing skills) were also tapped by the teacher in the process of instruction, so that the child learned to communicate about the computer-assisted material and learned to flexibly extend the new reading knowledge and vocabulary beyond the computer.

Results

The children's progress in the use of the novel system was formally evaluated from the printers attached to the Apple II and the EXPRESS-1 keyboard. A preliminary analysis of child key presses, teacher key presses, and television displays after 10 weeks of reading instruction revealed that all of the children between the ages of 2 and 5 years demonstrated significant gains in word recognition and reading. The mean percentage of improvement for the 2- to 3-year-old children over 10 weeks was 31%. The percentage of improvement for the 4- and 5-year-old children for the same time period was 19%.

The subjects were given a sentence imitation test prior to and following microcomputer reading instruction. This test measured imitative responses in the children's best communicative mode (i.e., ASL or simultaneous communication). The results indicated that the overall mean percentage of improvement for the 2- to 3-year-old children was 42.3% and for the 4- to 5-year-olds was 50.3%. This finding is tentative but is at least encouraging to the notion that preschool reading instructional programs could enhance not only reading but also broader aspects of language skills.

Discussion

Initial results demonstrate that deaf children as young as 2 years of age can acquire reading comprehension and decoding skills. Also, preliminary results indicate that this computerized instructional approach has an impact on general language skills. Extensions of the present exploratory work will involve internal comparisons concerning optimal presentations of the signs, pictures, text, and teacher input for facilitating deaf children's processing of the material and their acquisition of new reading, writing, and general communication skills.

The present study involved redundant presentation of messages selected by the pupil. Assuming that one central goal of instruction is acquisition of new connections between text words or sentences and meanings to which the child already has access before instruction, then several interesting theoretical questions could be addressed through variations on the present interactive theme: Are some deaf children better processors and learners when only sign and text pairings occur in initial introduction of new textual information? and Are other children more efficient learners if text-picture associations are mastered before any emphasis is placed upon sign?

Moreover, the processes by which demonstrated advances in general language skills contribute to more rapid acquisition of text-related skills is a topic of keen interest. In sum, as this research is extended and refined, it will be possible to learn much about how different input combinations are used by deaf children in the acquisition of new reading and writing skills and new skills in using language in nontext modes.

This research should contribute to an understanding of the extent to which written English vocabulary and sign vocabulary are coded categorically in short-term and long-term memory by deaf children. Also, it should provide important information on the extent to which textual material is translated into a manual-based code for storage in memory. Future research should focus on variations in cognitive styles, information processing, and individual differences in relation to reading, writing, and general communication.

The overall significance of this research lies not only in testing a new cognitive approach to reading and writing in deaf children but also in the later educational options that would be opened by early success in reading instruction. In sum, this research attempts to minimize, through a new form of early cognitive training, many of the adverse social and educational consequences that are too often associated with congenital or acquired deafness.

Additional Reading

Geoffrion, L. D., & Geoffrion, O. P. (1983). *Computers and reading instruction.* Reading, MA: Addison-Wesley.

Mason, G. E., Blanchard, J. S., & Daniel, D. B. (1982). *Computer applications in reading* (2nd ed.). Newark, DE: International Reading Association.

Prinz, P. M., Nelson, K. E., & Stedt, J. D. (1982). Early reading in young deaf children using microcomputer technology. *American Annals of the Deaf, 127,* 529–535.

Analysis

John P. Madison

The authors of the five papers on reading and reading methodology share three basic, well-documented assumptions about deaf readers. The first is that learning to read is difficult for deaf children; each of the papers addresses this assumption in a different manner, but there is agreement that the process of learning to read for deaf children is not the same as for hearing children. Second, each accepts the overwhelming evidence that deaf readers demonstrate low achievement levels in reading (Furth, 1966; Trybus & Karchmer, 1977). The third assumption, although not specifically referred to in all of the papers but which can be inferred, is that intelligence and general ability among the deaf as a group is not measurably different from the general population. Using these assumptions as a central focus, the first three papers will be discussed as a group; then a discussion of the second group of papers will follow. The concluding discussion will summarize the main points and issues across all five papers.

Cognitive Processing and Reading

The relationships between cognitive processing and reading provide the central focus for the papers presented by Hanson, Lichtenstein, and Kusché. Each dealt specifically with memory as it relates to reading success. Hanson and Kusché used the term *short-term memory*, while Lichtenstein used *working memory*. On further analysis, it becomes clear that both terms when applied to reading are used to describe how linguistic information (surface structure) is stored in the brain until a semantic interpretation is possible. All three writers agreed that the differences between deaf and hearing readers in ability to store information in working memory accounted for lower scores among deaf readers. Their findings concur with a vast body of research that supports the importance of working memory in the comprehension of print. The nature and importance of this facet of reading research therefore offers an exciting challenge to those who develop reading programs for deaf children. One possibility is that reading programs can be developed that compensate for the apparent difference in the working memory capacity of deaf children.

It is assumed that working memory can be improved though training. The findings of these authors suggest that with this improvement would come a subsequent improvement in some of the skills associated with successful reading.

A second area of agreement among these three authors relates to the process of storing information in working memory. It is known that successful hearing readers recode text into a speech-based code for storage purposes. Deaf readers have three options for recoding information: They may use (a) a visual code (how the word looks), (b) a manual code (how the word is signed or fingerspelled), or (c) a speech-based code (how the word is pronounced). The relative efficiency of these code systems, their applicability to comprehension, and their interaction with each other during the learning-to-read stages were discussed by these authors. They agreed that various combinations of these codes are used by deaf readers, but all strongly concurred with the evidence that indicates that the most successful deaf readers use a speech-based code almost exclusively. This finding was not necessarily related to the individual reader's ability; nor to a preference for using speech as a vehicle for communication; nor to speech intelligibility, degree of hearing loss, or onset of deafness. In addition, for adult deaf readers no strong correlation was found between reading achievement and type of educational experience or instructional background (oral, sign, total communication).

The generalizations from this empirical evidence about working memory and recoding of linguistic information suggest that deaf children need reading programs that attend to the development of speech-based code systems. Specifically, the authors call for more attention to orthographic structure, instruction in the grammar of English, and speech training as methods to enhance phonetic encoding.

These recommendations presuppose that working memory can be developed; they also presuppose that if the codes used for storage of linguistic information do incorporate the phonemic, morphemic, and orthographic structures of English, then comprehension will be enhanced and the reading achievement of deaf readers will consequently improve. The implications of such recommendations for program development in the area of reading are indeed controversial. While evidence from the past 2 decades of research into the nature of reading has shifted emphasis away from the phoneme–grapheme–word level to the meaning level, these particular researchers have reemphasized the importance of these elements for success in reading. Requiring young deaf readers to become skilled in the phonemic and linguistic structures of English, as a co-requisite of learning to read, may place an overwhelming burden on deaf children and their teachers.

Reading for Meaning

The writers of the fourth and fifth papers in part 7 provide readers with a contrasting view of reading when compared to the first three authors. Campbell's paper described a new procedure for cueing text to provide deaf readers with visual prompts that assist the reader in understanding linguistic structures and concepts. Prinz and Nelson described and demonstrated an interactive computer program used to teach reading to preschool deaf children. Nolen and Wilbur (1984) have provided evidence to complement the work of Campbell and of Prinz and Nelson in regard to the teaching of complex syntactic structures of English in context instead of as isolated sentences. Nolan and Wilbur found that context had a strong positive effect on student comprehension of relative clauses.

Although these latter two papers deal with somewhat different aspects of reading, nonetheless they both focus on teaching reading in settings where meaning receives the highest priority. Nolen and Wilbur contend that meaningful context is helpful in learning to comprehend or obtain meaning from those linguistic structures which confuse and inhibit comprehension in deaf readers. This top-down or meaning-first view of teaching reading recommends that readers at all levels and of all ages should interact as much as possible with complete passages of text instead of isolated exercises that stress only individual sounds, words, or small units of language. Campbell agreed with this view of reading and, although his research is as yet in a formative stage, he proposed the technique of glossing text with visual cues to aid deaf readers in deriving meaning from complex structures.

The preschool children studied by Prinz and Nelson created sentences by pressing words on a large interface computer keyboard, which then transposed the words together with animated signs and pictures onto a screen (monitor). Children were then able to write and read stories (sentences) that they had created. The print form of these stories provided a record of performance for each child. The possibilities for doing research on reading development in deaf children appear to be unlimited, and at the same time this computer-based format provides an exciting active mode for learning to read and write.

Conclusion

The authors of all five papers, although representative of only a fraction of the research and investigation concerned with teaching reading to the deaf, do represent a range of points of view regarding both historical and current concerns. All of the papers assume a remedial view of teaching reading to deaf children. Existing reading programs for the deaf are almost all predicated on language-deficiency models. While some attention is given to those children who grow up in language-rich homes where sign (usually ASL) is the first or primary language, little reflection of this condition is evidenced at the program level in terms of available curricula in schools today. The reasons for this situation are clear and understandable: There are relatively small numbers of deaf children of deaf parents, and when these children enter school, they often encounter no programs that focus on their unique needs as compared to the needs of deaf children of hearing parents.

Those deaf children who do come from an environment where language and communication are present do not seem to fare noticeably better as readers when they reach adulthood, yet they should if given programs that challenge them and build on their strong existing language base. The need for more careful, controlled, longitudinal research into the various issues and topics raised in these papers is unmistakable. Practitioners responsible for the day-to-day teaching of reading to deaf learners need to be continually attentive to the findings of such researchers, especially those who provide specific recommendations and directions for teaching methodology.

If program developers and practitioners make the effort to look to researchers for guidance in making decisions about the teaching of reading to the deaf, they will find it; but they should not be surprised if they also come away with more questions than answers.

References

Furth, H. (1966). A comparison of reading test norms of deaf and hearing children. *American Annals of the Deaf, 111*, 461–462.

Nolen, S., & Wilbur, R. (1984). Context and comprehension: Another look. In D.S. Martin (Ed.), *International Symposium on Cognition, Education, and Deafness: Working Papers* (Vol. 2, pp. 389–403). Washington, DC: Gallaudet College.

Trybus, R., & Karchmer, M. (1977). School achievement scores of hearing-impaired children: National data on achievement test status and growth patterns. *American Annals of the Deaf, 122*, 62–69.

Related Educational and Research Issues

1. To what extent is the learning of reading by a hearing-impaired learner based on the interaction between meaning and decoding? Does the process move from meaning down to phonetic analysis, or does it move from phonetic analysis up to meaning?

2. What are the implications for instruction that derive from the answer(s) to the questions above?

3. To what extent can a hearing-impaired learner understand linguistic elements in isolation without understanding them in context? Or, understand them in context without understanding them in isolation?

4. How is cognitive style regarding field-independence vs. field-dependence related to the hearing-impaired learner's success in reading?

5. What role will Cued Speech have in improving reading comprehension?

6. What kinds of reading programs should be developed to meet the needs of deaf children of deaf parents? How will such programs differ from those provided for deaf children of hearing parents?

8 Measurement of Cognitive Potential in Hearing-Impaired Learners

Experimental Use of Signed Presentations of the Verbal Scale of the WISC-R with Profoundly Deaf Children: A Preliminary Report

Margery Silberman Miller

One traditional method of assessing the verbal thought processes of hearing children has been through administration of the verbal scale of standardized intelligence tests, such as the Wechsler Intelligence Scale for Children-Revised (WISC-R; Wechsler, 1974). It has been standard psychological testing practice, however, not to administer these verbal intelligence tests to deaf students. This practice is partly due to the field's present level of sophistication concerning the linguistic delays and/or differences of the deaf population (Bonvillian, Nelson, & Charrow, 1976; Quigley, & Power, 1972; Quigley, Wilbur, Power, Montanelli, & Steinkamp, 1976) and to the concern that these language delays will adversely affect student scores on verbal tests of intelligence.

Prior to the 1970s, oral education for deaf students predominated in the U.S. (Moores, 1978). Thus, tests of verbal intelligence were only administered orally. It was appropriate at that time to strongly discourage the use of verbal measures of intelligence because many deaf students did not comprehend what was being asked of them. However, with the educational climate presently favoring the incorporation of signs into deaf children's communication systems, it may no longer be necessary to rely solely upon nonverbal tasks to measure the intelligence of deaf individuals.

Because a majority of profoundly deaf students are consistently exposed to a system of signs (Jordan, Gustason, & Rosen, 1979), it appears appropriate to reexamine how these students perform on verbal intelligence tests. If these tests were administered in the students' preferred mode of communication, they could provide useful information regarding deaf students' ability to use symbols to comprehend and transmit verbal concepts.

It is not possible to provide only one accurate description of the sign system to which most young deaf children are exposed because of the varied communication systems used in preschool and early elementary programs and because of the varied communication patterns used in the homes of deaf children. Therefore, before undertaking a study to examine the verbal intelligence of deaf children, it was necessary to select the sign language varieties that would be used in translating verbal subtest items.

Three major sign language systems are presently being used in education programs in the U.S. These systems span the sign language continuum; however, there are no definite parameters to clearly define the movement from one variety of sign language to another on the continuum. The manual/visual codes for representing English are at one end of the continuum. These codes, which incorporate a "morpheme-to-morpheme representation of English" (Friedman, 1977, p. 3), are referred to as signed

The complete version of this paper is available in microfiche or hard copy from ERIC Document Reproduction Service. Ask for Document No. ED 247 727.

English. American Sign Language is at the other end of the continuum. ASL has its own syntactic construction and semantic devices; in recent years, it has been accorded full language status (Bellugi & Fischer, 1972; Bellugi & Klima, 1975; Bellugi, Klima, & Siple, 1974; Friedman, 1977; Hoemann, 1976; Wilbur, 1976).

At the center of the continuum is Pidgin Sign English (PSE), a system that uses many ASL signs but follows English word order (Woodward, 1973; Woodward & Markowicz, 1975). The term *Pidgin Sign English* does not represent one standardized system of signs; it, too, can be viewed according to its own continuum model. Although there is no clear demarcation between the variations of PSE, boundaries can be loosely defined according to which language structures (English or ASL) predominate the signed utterances. We shall use the term *Pidgin Sign English-English* (PSE-E) for the PSE variety that follows English word order but deletes most function words and signed English word-endings. The term *Pidgin Sign English-American Sign Language* (PSE-A) will be used to refer to the PSE variety that usually follows ASL word order and incorporates more of the nonmanual features of ASL than are found in the PSE-E variety.

Most deaf children function somewhere along the ASL–signed English continuum, using some form of Pidgin Sign English. Therefore, both of the PSE varieties and signed English are being included in a study being conducted by the author to examine the verbal intelligence of nonmultihandicapped, profoundly deaf children between the ages of 9 and 16. WISC-R Verbal subtest item translations have been developed in all three sign language varieties.

Study Procedures

The 30 profoundly deaf subjects included in the study met the following selection criteria: age of onset of deafness at or before 24 months; hearing thresholds of 90 dB (pure tone average) or greater in the better ear; consistent use of sign language in an academic setting by the time the child was 6 years old; absence of additional handicapping conditions, such as cerebral palsy, epilepsy, severe emotional disturbance, mental retardation, Usher's Syndrome, or visual-perceptual disorders; and a WISC-R Performance IQ score of 80 or better.

Each subject in the study was randomly assigned to one of three experimental groups. One of the three selected sign systems (signed English, PSE-E, or PSE-A) was selected as the first presentation mode. The remaining two modes were used as back-up modes if the answer to a test item was initially incorrect. If a subject still responded incorrectly after the three sign presentations, the printed version of the test item was presented. The printed stimulus was included because recent studies indicate that printed presentations may be more effective for transmitting complex material than signed presentations (Trybus, 1978).

Preliminary Findings

The testing phase of this study was recently completed and preliminary findings are encouraging. The mean Verbal IQ score obtained by this sample, when calculated with four subtest scores (Information, Similarities, Arithmetic, and Comprehension), was 97.8. The mean Verbal IQ score obtained by the sample, calculated with five subtest scores (Information, Similarities, Arithmetic, Comprehension, and Digit Span), was 96.3.

These data are currently under analysis to provide further information about deaf children's performance on the Verbal scale of the WISC-R. Once this phase has been completed, the author will begin work on a full standardization of the testing procedure for signed administrations of the Verbal subtests of the WISC-R for deaf children.

References

Bellugi, U., & Fischer, S. D. (1972). A comparison of sign language and spoken language. *Cognition, 1,* 173–200.

Bellugi, U., & Klima, E. (1975). Aspects of sign language and its structure. In J. Kavanagh & J. Cutting (Eds.), *The role of speech in language* (pp. 171–203). Cambridge: MIT Press.

Bellugi, U., Klima, E., & Siple, P. (1974) Remembering in signs. *Cognition, 3,* 93–125.

Bonvillian, J. D., Nelson, K. E., & Charrow, U. E. (1976). Language and language-related skills in deaf and hearing children. *Sign Language Studies, 12,* 211–250.

Friedman, L. (1977). *On the other hand.* New York: Academic Press.

Hoemann, H. (1976). The transparency of meaning of sign language gestures. *Sign Language Studies, 7,* 151–161.

Jordan, I. K., Gustason, G., & Rosen, R. (1979). An update on communication trends at programs for the deaf. *American Annals of the Deaf, 124,* 350–357.

Moores, D. F. (1978). *Educating the deaf: Psychology, principles, and practices.* Boston: Houghton Mifflin.

Quigley, S., & Power, D. (1972). *The development of syntactic structures in the language of deaf children.* Urbana, IL: Institute for Research on Exceptional Children.

Quigley, S., Wilbur, R., Power, D., Montanelli, D., & Steinkamp, M. (1976). *Syntactic structures in the language of deaf children* (Report No. DEG-0-9-232175-4370). Urbana: University of Illinois.

Trybus, R. J. (1978, May). What the Stanford Achievement Test has to say about the reading abilities of deaf children. In *Proceedings of the Gallaudet Conference on Reading in Relation to Deafness* (pp. 213–221). Washington, DC: Gallaudet College, Division of Research.

Wechsler, D. (1974). *Manual for the Wechsler Intelligence Scale for Children-Revised.* New York: Psychological Corporation.

Wilbur, R. (1976). The linguistics of manual language and manual systems. In L. Lloyd (Ed.), *Communication assessment and intervention strategies* (pp. 425–500). Baltimore: University Park Press.

Woodward, J. (1973). Some characteristics of Pidgin Sign English. *Sign Language Studies, 3,* 39–46.

Woodward, J., & Markowicz, H. (1975). *Pidgin sign languages.* Paper presented at the International Conference on Pidgins and Creoles, Honolulu, HI.

Determining First Language Composition Using Cognitively Demanding/Context-Reduced Tasks

Barbara Luetke-Stahlman

The focus on an assessment of cognitively demanding/context-reduced language activities rather than cognitively *un*demanding/context-embedded language tasks is a relatively new procedure when making decisions regarding bilingual and/or bimodal hearing-impaired students. Traditionally, for example, a hearing-impaired student's ability to articulate known words (a cognitively undemanding task) in a highly supportive contextual situation (i.e., context embedded) may have caused educators and parents to believe that he or she could comprehend teacher instruction presented only orally. But Cummins (1981) suggested that assessment tasks should consider two planes: (a) context-embedded/context-reduced and (b) cognitively undemanding/cognitively demanding.

In applying the Cummins theory to situations that arise in the field of hearing impairment, it seems logical that educators and parents should allow hearing-impaired students the opportunity to systematically demonstrate the composition of their first language rather than attempt to predict it. Thus, the present study began with a specific question: Given several possible languages and/or systems (L/S), do any of these L/S function more efficiently as a first language for a hearing-impaired child who is learning cognitive/academic tasks?

Method

Subjects

In the first study (designed by the author under the direction of Dr. Fred Weiner, Pennsylvania State University; Luetke-Stahlman & Weiner, 1982), three Spanish deaf females enrolled in the St. Christopher's Hospital Nursery program for hearing-impaired preschoolers in Philadelphia, Pennsylvania, served as subjects. The children attended school approximately 5 hours a day and engaged in structured activities aimed primarily at language development.

Subject 1 was age 4 years, 4 months and had been attending the program for approximately 4 months. Her teacher judged her to benefit minimally from the use of her hearing aid; yet she wore it consistently. Subject 1 had a bilateral profound (unaided) sensorineural hearing loss. She communicated primarily through mixed sign and voice and also gesture. She lived with her parents (who had emigrated from Puerto Rico) and a 5-year-old sister, all of whom had normal hearing. Her mother used sign and oral English to communicate with her. The family did not want the daughter to use Spanish in school.

The complete version of this paper is available in microfiche or hard copy from ERIC Document Reproduction Service. Ask for Document No. ED 247 715.

Subject 2 was 3 years, 5 months. The child and mother had attended one year of a parent-infant program and the child had been enrolled in the 3-year-old classroom for approximately 6 months. Subject 2 had a hearing aid but refused to wear it. The teacher reported that the child had good unaided hearing although she had a bilateral moderate-to-severe (unaided) sensorineural hearing loss. She communicated primarily through mixed sign and voice but also used gesture and voice alone. She lived with both hearing parents (who had also emigrated from Puerto Rico) and six siblings, two of whom were also hearing impaired. Her mother used sign, gestures, oral Spanish, and oral English to communicate with her. The teacher reported that Subject 2's parents primarily spoke Spanish, while her older hearing siblings primarily spoke English.

Subject 3 was 4 years, 11 months and had been enrolled in school for approximately 6 months. She consistently wore a hearing aid and was judged by her teacher as having good aided hearing. Her unaided hearing was judged as poor and she had a moderate-to-severe (unaided) sensorineural hearing loss. She communicated primarily through sign and voice mixed with fingerspelling and sign language. She used both oral English and/or Spanish, but use of speech decreased when she was communicating with peers. Subject 3's family came from Puerto Rico. The family's communication was primarily English alone, but Spanish alone, sign, and English mixed with sign were also used.

Languages and/or Systems

The language and/or systems (L/S) that were selected for study in this investigation were those potentially available in school programs educating hearing-impaired children from Spanish-speaking homes. The investigation inputs were oral English alone, English-sign mixed, oral Spanish alone, Spanish-sign mixed, and sign alone.

The English utilized was of a Madison, Wisconsin dialect, the author's first native language. The English-sign mixed system included both oral English and American Sign Language (ASL) signs. The oral Spanish used was spoken by the first author. The sign component of the Spanish-sign mix also included oral Spanish and ASL signs. (No Spanish sign language was used in the study.) All signs were reviewed by two trained interpreters at the St. Christopher's Hospital program so that all stimulus questions were in the St. Christopher's Hospital sign dialect. The sign-alone phrases were presented without voice.

Tasks

The three tasks (noun, verb, adjective learning) chosen for use in the study were at a "cognitively demanding" (Cummins, 1980) level for each subject. The choices of pictures (instead of real objects) reduced the contextual support in the learning process. Thus, the child's performance on the cognitively demanding/context-reduced tasks (which required problem-solving ability without presenting contextual support) were good predictors of her future English-learning ability according to Cummins' model (1979, 1981).

Results and Discussion

From the results of a first investigation, it appeared that the three subjects demonstrated three different L/S preferences for learning noun, verb, and adjective vocabulary items. Subject 1 used sign as the most efficient L/S. She performed poorly on the vocabulary tasks taught through oral English and oral Spanish. Her best performance came when sign alone was used or when it was combined with English or Spanish. This finding was consistent with the fact that Subject 1 had a profound bilateral sensorineural hearing loss and was reported to benefit minimally from the use of a hearing aid. For Subject 1, then, neither her Spanish heritage nor any exposure to a second language (i.e., English) facilitated vocabulary learning. Instead, the handicap was the significant factor.

Subject 2 completed the noun vocabulary task, failed to meet criterion for verb vocabulary, and did not have time to participate in the adjective vocabulary task. On the basis of results obtained for noun vocabulary, it would appear that Subject 2 could learn through oral Spanish or sign. Most likely, vocabulary acquisition using an English-sign mix was due to the sign component because performance was so poor for the English-alone condition. These results again were predictable from the case history. Subject 2's moderate-to-severe hearing loss enabled her to learn through an oral-only language (Spanish). Her inability to learn through English alone was predicted from the fact that her parents primarily spoke Spanish at home. For Subject 2, heritage and handicap seemed significant in determining which L/S facilitated vocabulary learning.

Subject 3's behavior on the assessment tasks presented the most mixed results. For the noun and verb vocabulary tasks she seemed to present a similar learning pattern to Subject 1 where sign or sign-mix produced the greatest learning. In the adjective vocabulary task, however, oral English alone seemed to produce as much learning as sign or sign-mix. This inconsistent pattern, however, could be predicted from the case history. That is, her hearing loss was only moderate-to-severe and improved significantly when she wore her hearing aid. Furthermore, the mother was English-dominant while the father and caretaker spoke Spanish. Given her improved aided hearing, she was exposed to a great deal of English at both home and school. For Subject 3, then, her heritage played no role in predicting which L/S would facilitate learning. Instead, her handicap and her exposure to an English-speaking society were educationally significant.

In a second study, this author (1984) replicated the L/S assessment procedure using elementary-aged, hearing-impaired subjects. Single-subject methodology requires extensive planning, implementation, and analysis; therefore, the usefulness of an ASL Ability Rating Scale (Luetke-Stahlman, 1984) that could be substituted for this procedure was analyzed, as was a Language Base Rating Scale (Luetke-Stahlman) that could be used to identify the strength of a student's language base. The findings substantiated the results found by Luetke-Stahlman and Weiner (1982). The L/S of greatest cognitive/academic benefit to a student cannot be predetermined but must be systematically assessed.

These studies illustrated that neither heritage nor etiological classi-fication dictate a specific language use by hearing-impaired students. All hearing-impaired children should be afforded the opportunity to demon-strate which of the potential languages and/or systems are beneficial to them in learning academically related skills. The instructional language and/or system used as the primary method of instruction should, then, be deter-mined by evaluating four variables: (a) the language and/or system of the caretaker, (b) the onset date of exposure to sign language and/or systems, (c) the degree of usable aided hearing ability, and (d) the language and/or system demonstrated to be the most effective for learning cognitively demanding/context-reduced tasks.

While the necessity to acquire English literacy skills is obviously a major goal of education in the United States, it is not the case that an (oral and/or manual) English-immersion instructional model is the only one by which to achieve that goal with hearing-impaired children.

References

Cummins, J. (1979). Cognitive/academic language proficiency, linguistic inter-dependence, the optimum age question and some other matters. *Working Papers in Bilingualism, 19,* 197–205.

Cummins, J. (1981). The role of primary language development in promoting edu-cational success for language minority students. In *Schooling and language mi-nority students: A theoretical framework.* Los Angeles: National Dissemination and Assessment Center.

Luetke-Stahlman, B. (1984). Replicating single-subject assessment in deaf elemen-tary age children. *American Annals of the Deaf, 129,* 40–44.

Luetke-Stahlman, B., & Weiner, F. (1982). Assessing language and/or system prefer-ences of Spanish-deaf preschoolers. *American Annals of the Deaf, 127,* 789–796.

Application of Feuerstein's Mediated Learning Construct to Deaf Persons

Kevin J. Keane

Cognitive competence refers to the structural ability to adequately adjust and adapt to life situations (Scarr, 1981). In this context, structure refers to the cognitive/intellective and affective schemas that promote adaptations to novel situations. Beyond the biological/physiological level, the construction of these schemas, according to Feuerstein (1979), is affected by two modalities of learning: direct learning experience and mediated learning experience. Through direct exposure, an individual is constantly bombarded by stimuli; the individual's reactions to these stimuli produce lasting effects in his or her behavioral repertoire. In mediated exposure, direct experience with environmental stimuli is transformed through the actions of an "experienced, intentioned, and active human being" (Feuerstein, 1979, p. 110). Through a repertoire of actions—such as selecting stimuli for exposure, framing environmental events, focusing the individual in terms of salient aspects, and feeding back environmental events—the mediating agent orients and organizes the phenomenological world for the child. In so doing, this caring person transmits appropriate learning sets and habits "which in turn become important ingredients of his [the child's] capacity to become modified [structurally changed] through direct exposure to stimuli" (Feuerstein, 1980, 16).

According to Feuerstein's (1979, 1980) mediated learning theory, then, both modalities of learning (i.e., direct learning and mediated learning) are perceived as essential to development. However, the contention is that through mediated learning, the ability of the individual to benefit from direct experience is not only enhanced but is essential for continued direct exposure learning. The importance of mediated learning experience (MLE) is underscored by Feuerstein as a "prerequisite to effective, independent, and autonomous use of environmental stimuli by the child . . . and to the development of an attitude toward thinking and problem-solving that is actively and efficiently involved in organizing the world of stimuli impinging on the individual from both internal and external sources" (1979, pp. 71–72).

Insufficient mediated learning exposure results in cultural deprivation (i.e., an alienation from one's own culture) marked by a significant reduction in the ability of an individual to adapt to and become modified by his or her own culture. This alienation may be produced by a number of determinants, including sociological, geopolitical, psychophysical, and economic conditions (Feuerstein, 1979). Feuerstein stressed that the concept of cultural deprivation in this framework "refers to an intrinsic criterion of the specific culture, namely the lack of the process inherent to the concept of culture itself: *intergenerational transmission*" (p. 39). Thus, emphasis is placed

The complete version of this paper is available in microfiche or hard copy from ERIC Document Reproduction Service. Ask for Document No. ED 249 743.

upon the intergenerational communication or transmission of culture as opposed to popular notions of culture involving group organizations and the by-products or artifacts of that culture. Furthermore, in formulating this definition, Feuerstein rejected the more commonly accepted referent of an "extrinsic criterion by which the culture of certain ethnic subgroups is considered as depriving their members, thereby negatively affecting their cognitive capacities" (p. 39). Hence, culture itself in the philosophy of mediational learning *cannot* be viewed as a depriving factor.

Mediated Learning Theory and the Deaf

Feuerstein (1979, 1980) has delineated a number of cognitive deficiencies that are manifest in a culturally deprived (MLE-deprived) individual. Similar cognitive/behavioral deficiencies have been noted in studies with deaf populations (Altshuler, 1964; Altshuler, Deming, Vollenweider, Rainer, & Tender, 1976; Binder, 1970; Chess & Fernandez, 1980; Hess, 1960; Levine, 1956, 1981; Myklebust, 1960; Rainer, Altshuler, Kallmann, Deming, 1969), along with parallels in academic retardation (Bonvillian, Charrow, & Nelson, 1973; Cooper & Rosenstein, 1966; Furth, 1966; Levine, 1981; Tomlinson-Keasey & Kelly, 1978). Levine (1976), for example, has indicated that as a group the deaf population mirrors the performance of traditionally defined culturally disadvantaged individuals along certain cognitive/behavioral parameters of performance. Likewise, Schlesinger and Meadow (1972) and Sarlin and Altshuler (1978) have observed similarities between these two populations in certain aspects of psychological adaptation and attainment.

The suggested similarity between deaf and culturally disadvantaged individuals may be a reasonable hypothesis, given (a) Feuerstein's (1979, 1980) notion of cultural deprivation (which is proximally linked to a breakdown in the intergenerational transmission of culture) and (b) the environmental milieu in which most hearing-impaired children are raised. For example, more than 90% of deaf children are born to hearing parents; for the majority of these parents, their own child is their first encounter with the handicap of deafness (Schlesinger & Meadow, 1972). As a result of this unexpected encounter, many of these parents may go through various stages of guilt, anger, grief, and depression in coping with the reality of having a hearing-impaired child (Mindel & Vernon, 1971), and the normal channels of parent-child communication may be significantly altered. The nature of these coping mechanisms and communication problems may, in turn, significantly affect the parents' nurturing role in the environment of the deaf child (Quigley & Kretschmer, 1982), thereby disrupting the mediational learning process. The organization of environmental stimuli and events may not be adequately interpreted for the child.

Conceptually, mediated learning theory may also provide a framework for understanding the differential cognitive development within the deaf population. For example, studies involving deaf children of deaf parents as compared to deaf children of hearing parents indicate that the former perform significantly better on measures of educational achievement (Vernon &

Koh, 1970), intellectual achievement (Brill, 1969; Conrad, 1979; Ray, 1979), and social/behavioral adaptations (Meadow, 1980; Schlesinger & Meadow, 1972). In general, it is agreed that deaf parents are more accepting of their child's hearing impairment and have a more facilitative communication system for parent-child interaction (Corson, 1973; Meadow, 1980; Vernon, 1967; Vernon & Koh, 1970). These two factors would indicate a greater opportunity for mediated learning to occur for deaf children of deaf parents. However, an additional third factor is posited: Deaf parents are often singularly visually oriented and, therefore, may be more adept at visually orienting the mediational aspects of learning for their deaf children.

The comparative performance between deaf children of hearing parents and deaf children of deaf parents may serve to reinforce the importance of mediated learning in the development of cognitive competence. Also, since more than 90% of deaf children are born to hearing parents, the degree and nature of mediated learning available may serve to clarify the differential cognitive development within this group.

With regard to the educational milieu of the deaf, Meadow (1980) postulated that as the deaf child moves into the educational environment, his or her low achievement may cause teachers to feel frustrated, discouraged, and depressed. This result may cause a circular effect, with the low achievement leading to lowered expectations, thus continuing an environment where the cognitive potential of the deaf child is not tapped. In essence, then, the problems for some deaf and traditionally defined culturally disadvantaged individuals may result from the inability to maximally profit from mediated learning experiences resulting, to varying degrees, in a "state of reduced cognitive modifiability . . . to direct sources of stimulation" (Feuerstein, 1980, p. 15).

Mechanisms for Change

The ability to adapt oneself to external reality (i.e., autoplastic adaptation) requires "the presence of adequate cognitive processes and autonomous exercise of control over those functions that render the cognitive system flexible and constantly modifiable" (Feuerstein, 1980, p. 3). When, through the syndrome of cultural deprivation, these cognitive processes are deficient, reduced, or underdeveloped, an intervention procedure is necessary. The intent of the intervention procedure delineated by Feuerstein (1979, 1980) is to promote structural cognitive change within the culturally deprived individual. For this purpose Feuerstein developed two procedures: the Learning Potential Assessment Device (LPAD) and the Instrumental Enrichment (IE) program.

The Learning Potential Assessment Device (LPAD) is a clinical performance assessment that departs theoretically and procedurally from traditional psychometric procedures. Traditional psychometric procedures assess previous environmentally learned abilities; the LPAD, on the other hand, consists of a battery of instruments that assesses the ability of an individual to learn. Learning, in this context, refers to an individual's ability to modify existing cognitive structure through exposure to mediated intervention. The LPAD permits the investigation of deficiencies that may impede performance, classifies them according to a continuum of information processing, and seeks to mediate them in the testing situation itself so that the cognitive potential of an individual may be measured more directly. As such, the LPAD attempts to rectify the mismatch between the nature of the cognitive deficits in culturally deprived individuals and the nature of the instruments used in assessing these deficits.

Feuerstein (1979), in his work primarily with retarded-functioning adolescents, has demonstrated high degrees of modifiability or potential among large numbers of individuals across the populations he has studied. In a recent study with a preadolescent profoundly deaf population (ages 9–13) of hearing parents, Keane (1983) and Keane and Kretschmer (1983) found that an experimental group exposed to mediated intervention on an LPAD battery performed significantly better ($p < .01$) than a comparison group that received the instruments according to traditional psychometric procedures. The experimental group also performed better than another comparison group that received the battery under a testing-the-limits procedure. Further, this research also involved a pretest–posttest design to investigate the pervasiveness of mediated intervention (i.e., the transfer of learning). The experimental group receiving mediated treatment demonstrated significant transfer of learning along defined cognitive and behavioral parameters.

Instrumental Enrichment (IE), on the other hand, is a long-term cognitive intervention program specifically developed for adolescents. The intent of IE is to promote structural cognitive change in the individual. As such, IE develops the cognitive prerequisites for learning. Instrumental Enrichment consists of academic content-free activities related to 14 different cognitive functions. However, based upon knowledge of the functioning of culturally deprived individuals, IE does not assume spontaneous generalization to other areas. Rather, a critical element in this curriculum is a technique called *bridging*, whereby the teacher overtly promotes transfer of skills to both real-life and academic situations through discussion for insight. At this time, a few schools and programs for the deaf are involved in implementing this curriculum with certain deaf populations, and preliminary results are becoming available (Martin, 1984; Rohr-Redding & Innes, 1984; see Jonas & Martin, pp. 172–175).

Conclusion

Feuerstein's (1979, 1980) theoretical construct (mediated learning theory) concerning the etiological nature of cultural deprivation may apply also to certain deaf populations. Initial studies on the cognitive modifiability of a deaf population indicate this population responds with high degrees of modifiability when exposed to mediated treatment (Keane, 1983; Keane & Kretschmer, 1983; see Rohr-Redding, pp. 168–171). In terms of educational practice, these findings indicate a level of potential that is not usually apparent from the academic performance of this population.

Diagnostically, initial studies indicate that cognitive deficiencies similar to those delineated by Feuerstein (1979) with other populations are also evident within the deaf population studied. It would seem that the pervasiveness of these deficiencies affects the learning ability of these deaf children. In approaching the complex phenomenon of learning, it appears logical that these deficiencies affecting the mental act need to be addressed in order to promote independent learning. To facilitate this task, more research is needed. Further investigation of Feuerstein's theoretical construct of mediated learning as it applies to deaf populations could impact upon educational curricula, preservice and inservice teacher education, cognitive/intellectual assessment, and, finally, parent-infant education programs that serve deaf children.

References

Altshuler, K. (1964). Personality traits and depressive symptoms in the deaf. In J. Wortes (Ed.), *Recent advances in biological psychiatry.* New York: Plenum Press.

Altshuler, K., Deming, W., Vollenweider, J., Rainer, J., & Tender, R. (1976). Impulsivity and profound early deafness: A cross-cultural inquiry. *American Annals of the Deaf, 121,* 331–339.

Binder, O. (1970). *The relation between verbal language and impulsivity in the deaf.* Unpublished doctoral dissertation, Wayne State University, Detroit.

Bonvillian, J., Charrow, V., & Nelson, K. (1973). Psycholinguistic and educational implications of deafness. *Human Development, 16,* 321–345.

Brill, R. (1969). The superior I.Q.'s of deaf children of deaf parents. *The California Palms,* 1–4.

Chess, S., & Fernandez, P. (1980). Impulsivity in rubella deaf children: A longitudinal study. *American Annals of the Deaf, 125,* 505–509.

Conrad, R. (1979). *The deaf school child.* London: Harper & Row.

Cooper, R., & Rosenstein, J. (1966). Language acquisition of deaf children. *Volta Review, 68,* 58–67.

Corson, H. (1973). *Comparing deaf children of oral parents and deaf parents using manual communication with deaf children of hearing parents on academic, social, and communication functioning.* Unpublished doctoral dissertation, University of Cincinnati, Cincinnati.

Feuerstein, R. (1979). *The dynamic assessment of retarded performers: The learning potential assessment device, theory, instruments, and techniques.* Baltimore: University Park Press.

Feuerstein, R. (1980). *Instrumental enrichment.* Baltimore: University Park Press.

Furth, H. (1966). A comparison of reading test norms of deaf and hearing children. *American Annals of the Deaf, 111,* 461–462.

Hess, W. (1960). *Personality adjustment in deaf children.* Unpublished doctoral dissertation, University of Rochester, Rochester, NY.

Keane, K. (1983). *Application of mediated learning theory to a deaf population: A study in cognitive modifiability.* Unpublished doctoral dissertation, Columbia University, New York.

Keane, K., & Kretschmer, R. (1983). *The effect of mediated learning intervention on task performance with a deaf population.* Manuscript submitted for publication.

Levine, E. (1956). *Youth in a soundless world, a search for personality.* New York: New York University Press.

Levine, E. (1976). Psycho-cultural determinants in personality development. *Volta Review, 78,* 258–267.

Levine, E. (1981). *The ecology of early deafness.* New York: Columbia University Press.

Martin, D. (1984). Enhancing cognitive performance in the hearing-impaired college student: A pilot study. In D. S. Martin (Ed.), *International Symposium on Cognition, Education, and Deafness: Working Papers* (Vol. 2, pp. 561–577). Washington, DC: Gallaudet College.

Meadow, K. (1980). *Deafness and child development.* Berkeley: University of California Press.

Mindel, E., & Vernon, M. (1971). *They grow in silence.* Silver Spring, MD: National Association of the Deaf.

Myklebust, H. (1960). *The psychology of deafness.* New York: Grune & Stratton.

Quigley, S., & Kretschmer, R. (1982). *The education of deaf children: Issues, theory, and practice.* Baltimore: University Park Press.

Rainer, J., Altshuler, K., Kallman, F., & Deming, W. (Eds.). (1969). *Family and mental health problems in a deaf population.* Springfield, IL: Charles C. Thomas.

Ray, S. (1979). *An adaptation of the "Wechsler Intelligence Scales (Performance) for Children-Revised" for the deaf.* Unpublished doctoral dissertation, University of Tennessee.

Rohr-Redding, C., & Innes, J. (1984). Can thinking skills be incorporated into a curriculum? In D. S. Martin (Ed.), *International Symposium on Cognition, Education, and Deafness: Working Papers* (Vol. 2, pp. 578–587). Washington, DC: Gallaudet College.

Sarlin, M., & Altshuler, K. (1978). On the inter-relationship of cognition and affect: Fantasies of deaf children. *Child Psychiatry and Human Development, 9*(2), 95–103.

Scarr, S. (1981). Testing for children: Assessment and the many determinants of intellectual competence. *American Psychologist, 36,* 1159–1166.

Schlesinger, H., & Meadow, K. (1972). *Sound and sign: Childhood deafness and mental health.* Berkeley: University of California Press.

Tomlinson-Keasey, C., & Kelly, R. (1978). The deaf child's symbolic world. *American Annals of the Deaf, 123,* 452–459.

Vernon, M. (1967). Relationship of language to the thinking process. *Archives of Genetic Psychology, 16,* 325–333.

Vernon, M., & Koh, S. (1970). The effect of manual communication on deaf children's educational achievement, linguistic competence, oral skills, and psychological development. *American Annals of the Deaf, 115,* 527–536.

Additional Reading

Carlson, J., & Dillon, R. (1978). Measuring intellectual capabilities of hearing-impaired children: Effects of testing the limits procedures. *Volta Review, 80,* 216–224.

Chess, S. (1975). Behavior problems of children with congenital rubella. In D. Naiman (Ed.), *Needs of emotionally disturbed hearing-impaired children.* New York: New York University School of Education, Health, Nursing, and Art Professions.

Craig, W., & Collins, J. (1970). Analysis of communicative interaction in classes for deaf children. *American Annals of the Deaf, 115,* 79–85.

Dillon, R. (1979). Improving validity by testing for competence: Refinement of a paradigm and its application to the hearing-impaired. *Educational and Psychological Measurement, 39,* 363–371.

Dillon, R. (1980). Cognitive style and elaboration of logical abilities in hearing-impaired children. *Journal of Experimental Psychology, 38,* 389–400.

Feuerstein, R., & Rand, Y. (1977). *Studies in cognitive modifiability: Redevelopment of cognitive functions of retarded early adolescents.* Jerusalem: Hadassah-Wizo-Canada Research Institute.

Gerweck, S., & Ysseldyke, J. (1975). Limitations of current psychological practices for the intellectual assessment of the hearing-impaired: A response to the Levine study. *Volta Review, 77,* 243–248.

Goetzinger, C., & Rousey, C. (1959). Educational achievement of deaf children. *American Annals of the Deaf, 104,* 221–231.

Harris, R. (1978). The relationship of impulse control to parent hearing status, manual communication, and academic achievement in deaf children. *American Annals of the Deaf, 123,* 52–67.

Leitman, A. (1968, February). *The workshop classroom.* Paper presented at the Symposium on Research and Utilization of Educational Media in Teaching the Deaf, Lincoln, NE.

Liben, L. (Ed.). (1978). *Deaf children: Developmental perspectives.* New York: Academic Press.

McCrone, W. (1979). Learned helplessness and level of underachievement among deaf adolescents. *Psychology in the Schools, 16,* 430–434.

Putnam, G. (1896). How to study. *American Annals of the Deaf, 41,* 265–274.

Quigley, S., & Frisina, D. (1961). *Institutionalization and psycho-educational development of deaf children.* Washington, DC: Council for Exceptional Children.

Stuckless, E., & Birch, J. (1966). The influence of early manual communication on the linguistic development of deaf children. *American Annals of the Deaf, 111,* 452–469, 499–504.

Wolff, S. (1977). Cognition and communication patterns in classrooms of deaf students. *American Annals of the Deaf, 122,* 319–327.

LPAD Applications to Deaf Populations

Jeffery P. Braden

The Learning Potential Assessment Device (LPAD) (Feuerstein, 1979) advocates a test-teach-test model for assessing intellectual potential. The LPAD differs from traditional psychometric models both in its procedures (which require questioning the subject about responses and providing feedback to the subject about performances) and in the underlying psychological theory used to interpret cognitive behavior. A brief overview of the LPAD's theoretical underpinnings is provided in Keane's paper (see pp. 141–147). The focus here is upon clinical and theoretical issues raised by applying the LPAD to deaf populations.

Clinical Issues

LPAD techniques are recommended for the assessment of deaf children with multiple disabilities and deaf people from unusual experiential backgrounds (e.g., those from other cultures who have never attended a school program). The benefits of the LPAD are threefold: (a) the LPAD provides a systematic model for assessing a wide variety of cognitive functions; (b) the examiner tests, then teaches tasks to the subject, then tests again to determine the accessibility of the deficient functions to remediation attempts; and (c) the model and related test results provide a descriptive/prescriptive profile of the subject's capabilities, rather than a normative/labeling outcome. LPAD methods are uniquely superior to psychometric methods for assessing deaf children from nonstandard backgrounds because psychometric methods cannot be assumed to be valid for these deaf subjects; psychometric tests also produce classifications of dubious value.

There are some problems in applying the LPAD to deaf children. The first major difficulty is communication. Because LPAD techniques assess the molecular (underlying) structure of cognitive performance, the examiner must question the subject about molar (overt) behaviors. This procedure is extremely difficult for deaf children from nonstandard backgrounds or those with multiple disabilities because they typically do not differentiate question forms (e.g., Why? vs. How?). The development of remediation attempts then presents the second major difficulty with LPAD use. Currently, few teachers are trained in the instructional program that parallels the LPAD (Instrumental Enrichment [IE], Feuerstein, 1980). Those teachers who are trained in IE are not usually taught how to tailor IE to LPAD results. It remains to be seen how LPAD and IE techniques will compare to current approaches used to assess and then instruct low-functioning deaf children.

The complete version of this paper is available in microfiche or hard copy from ERIC Document Reproduction Service. Ask for Document No. ED 247 716.

Theoretical Concerns

The theoretical assumptions underlying the LPAD have been invoked to explain group differences on standard intelligence (IQ) tests. LPAD theory assumes that cognitive skills are learned in the process of cultural transmission. Feuerstein (1979) suggested that minority children have more cognitive deficiencies because minority parents do not transmit their culture to their children. Similar reasoning (see Keane, pp. 141–147) has been cited to explain cognitive deficiencies in deaf children.

The problem with this line of argument may be simply stated: Deaf children perform much better than minority children on nonverbal IQ tests. Because some deaf children theoretically experience less cultural transmission than ethnic minority groups (i.e., some deaf children of hearing parents are not exposed to certain forms of language until they enter school; some experience punitive parental interactions more often than their hearing peers; and all are members of a subculture different from their hearing parents), they would be expected to perform more poorly than minority peers. We have found that deaf children's nonverbal IQ performance is quantitatively similar to majority children's nonverbal performance, which contradicts the cultural transmission model of group differences (Braden, 1984).

The implications of the preceding discussion are twofold. First, environmental explanations of minority children's lower mean nonverbal IQ's (e.g., dialect differences, parenting styles, etc.) are inadequate because they cannot simultaneously account for poor minority group performance and average deaf nonverbal IQ scores. Second, the contemporary tendency to characterize deaf children as a minority group in order to explain deaf/hearing differences on cognitive measures should be subjected to careful scrutiny.

Conclusions

The LPAD promises to provide a valuable adjunct to current assessment techniques used with deaf children. This point is particularly applicable to those deaf children with unusual backgrounds and/or multiple disabilities. Although some difficulties exist in LPAD administration and in the educational application of LPAD results, LPAD techniques nonetheless are superior to traditional psychometric methods in some situations. It is therefore suggested that the time needed for LPAD training of professionals (a minimum of 2 weeks) would be worthwhile for professionals who are heavily involved in the assessment of deaf children.

Although the LPAD appears welcome for clinical reasons, its theoretical foundations as applied to deaf populations may be fallacious—not in the cognitive model employed for collecting and interpreting LPAD results, but rather in using LPAD theory to explain cognitive differences between majority and minority groups. The essential point is that while LPAD techniques can be recommended for clinical purposes, the extension of LPAD theory (or other hypotheses characterizing deaf children as a minority group) to account for the cognitive performances of deaf children should be avoided.

References

Braden, J. P. (1984). The factorial similarity of the WISC-R performance scale in deaf and hearing samples. *Journal of Personality and Individual Differences, 5,* 403–409.

Feuerstein, R. (1979). *The dynamic assessment of retarded performers: The learning potential assessment device, theory, instruments, and techniques.* Baltimore: University Park Press.

Feuerstein, R. (1980). *Instrumental enrichment.* Baltimore: University Park Press.

A Factor-Analytic Study of Intellectual Development in Deaf and Hearing Children

Abraham Zwiebel
Donna M. Mertens

Two major schools of thought have attempted to explain cognitive functioning in the deaf: Myklebust's (1964) organismic shift hypothesis and Furth's (1971) view that no difference exists between deaf and hearing subjects in conceptual performance, at least up to concrete-operational thinking. The results of factor-analytic studies of the differential ability structure for deaf and hearing children (Bolton, 1978; Farrant, 1964; Holmberg, 1966; Juurmaa, 1963) have generally agreed with Myklebust's organismic shift hypothesis. Myklebust hypothesized that the deaf were quantitatively equal, but qualitatively inferior, to the hearing in that the deaf develop a more concrete, and, therefore, less abstract intelligence. Myklebust and Brutton (1953) stated that deafness "restricts the child functionally to a world of concrete objects and things" (p. 93).

Bolton (1978) found little support in the factor-analytic studies for Furth's (1971) position that the deaf reach a plateau in their thinking. Furth (1964) labeled the deaf as "linguistically deficient" because they do not use "the living language as heard and spoken in our society" (p. 47). This linguistic deficiency supposedly restricts the cognitive development of deaf individuals to concrete-operational thinking. Furth emphasized that the use of verbal tests to assess deaf children's intelligence was not fair.

The position in the present study was that neither the factor-analytic work that supports the Myklebust hypothesis nor Furth's conclusion concerning the plateau reached by the deaf are accurate representations of the nature of intelligence in a deaf population. The major problem with the factor-analytic work is that it has aggregated data across age groups and thus obscured differences in developmental progression. Even the most recent study by Bolton (1978) did not find any rationale for different factors in deaf and hearing populations using limited IQ stimuli such as performance scales. Many studies report that deaf children lag behind hearing children at early ages, but that the lags are often not observed in older children (Canabal, 1970; Hoemann & Briga, 1980).

Available evidence suggests that the condition of deafness imposes no limitation on the cognitive capabilities of individuals (Moores, 1982; Ottem, 1980; Rittenhouse & Spiro, 1970). No evidence suggests that a deaf person thinks in more concrete ways than a hearing person. Previous findings of a plateau in the development of deaf intelligence seem to have been the result of using tests and instructions that were inappropriate to the deaf population. A fair test of the intelligence of deaf children must (a) ensure the ability of the experimenter to communicate the instructions to the deaf, (b) avoid the heavily verbal nature of many intelligence tests, and (c) cover the

We offer a special note of thanks to Steve Wolk, Chair, Department of Educational Foundations and Research, Gallaudet College, for his guidance and support during the data analysis and reporting.

entire intellectual span, including evaluation of abstract thinking. The Snijders-Oomen Nonverbal Intelligence Test (SON) fits all of these criteria (Harris, 1982; Kearney, 1969; Kyle, 1980).

The present study used factor-analytic techniques to examine the nature of cognitive development in deaf children. The factor analyses were done separately for younger and older groups in order to determine developmental differences; the SON was used as a measure of intelligence. This test is appropriate for assessing the intelligence of deaf children in that the items are restricted to the performance type that can be visually demonstrated and imitated. In addition, the subscales cover all the subareas of intelligence.

Methodology

Subjects

The subjects included 251 deaf children ages 6 to 15 (approximately 25 children from each age level) who were randomly selected (stratified by age and sex) from the population of all Israeli deaf children in special education settings in 1975 and 1976. The deaf children were divided evenly by sex, 125 boys and 126 girls, with the same proportion (50%) at each age level. This sample represents 62% of the total population. Twelve percent of the sample were deaf children of deaf parents, most also had deaf siblings. Thirty percent of the deaf children of hearing parents also had at least one deaf sibling.

The demographic data indicate a slightly greater representation from the lower socioeconomic level of the Israeli population. More than 85% of the subjects were profoundly deaf from birth. All the children attended oral-oriented educational settings (the only system in Israel). Sixty percent of the deaf subjects were in segregated schools and 40% were in different degrees of mainstreamed settings. Most of them wore hearing aids and had a moderate level of oral communication skill that enabled them to communicate with their parents and others. Manual communication was found only among deaf children with deaf parents.

The hearing sample consisted of 101 children aged 10 to 12 who were chosen from three schools representing three socioeconomic levels. They were matched to the deaf group on all of the demographic variables.

Procedure

The SON was administered individually to all the children by a trained psychologist following the test manual directions (Snijders & Snijder-Oomen, 1959), using pantomime and general clues. The administration was the same for both deaf and hearing subjects.

Instrumentation

Israeli norms were created for the SON (Zwiebel & Rand, 1975). Reliabilities were found to range from .76 on the memory subscales to .88 on the arrangement subscale, with an overall Kronbach α of .84. The SON was found to correlate at .61 with the Draw-a-Person Test and at .55 with the teacher's rating of the children's intelligence.

The SON includes 4 subtests and 11 subscales. Because four of the subscales are designed only for small children, no variance was associated with them in the present sample. Consequently, these four subscales were eliminated from the data analysis. The following subscales were used:

1. *Mosaic B:* The child uses flat squares to build a pattern shown on a card (motor-perceptual skills).

2. *Block Design:* The child constructs a pattern with cubes (motor-perceptual-thinking skills).

3. *Picture Memory:* A small card with one or more pictures is shown for a few seconds, after which the subject must pick them out on a large card (memory skill).

4./5. *Picture Series:* There are two picture series subscales that are based on difficulty level. The child must arrange pictures in a logical order to make a story (information and general comprehension).

6. *Picture Analogies:* The child is shown an example of an analogy in a concrete pictorial relation (e.g., broken-unbroken; empty-full). The child then has to apply the abstract principle to other materials (concrete thinking).

7. *Figure Analogies:* This test is the same as the picture analogies except that abstract figures are used instead of concrete pictures (abstract thinking).

Data Analysis

Factor analysis was used to identify the constructs that underlie the scales of the SON. The specific technique used was principal factoring with iteration, followed by varimax rotation (Nie, Hull, Jenkins, Steinbrenner, & Bent, 1975). This strategy simplified and stabilized the factor structure.

Results

The heavy loading on the figure analogy test for the hearing group of 10- to 12-year-olds indicates an abstract thinking component (see Table 1). This component is not evidenced in the deaf group of the same age as the hearing group. However, for deaf subjects who are slightly older than the hearing group, the abstract thinking factor does appear.

Prior research based on these data (Zwiebel & Milgram, 1982) has found that the deaf were not inferior to the hearing in terms of intellectual abilities. Using an appropriate measure such as the SON, the deaf appeared to be capable of abstract thinking; there is only a slight delay in its appearance in the deaf. One interpretation of the results is that the SON's visual stimuli may be processed more verbally by the hearing and more visually by the

Table 1
Factor-Analytic Results of the SON for Deaf and Hearing Children by Age Level

Subscales	All Deaf	Deaf (Age 6–9)			Deaf (Age 10–12)		Deaf (Age 13–15)		Hearing (Age 10–12)	
					Factors					
	1	1	2	3	1	2	1	2	1	2
Mosaic B	.56	.03	.90	.02	.04	.82	.65	.22	-.18	-.13
Block Design	.61	.56	.29	.05	.35	.40	.15	.66	.64	.40
Picture Memory	.57	.20	.06	.71	.61	.17	.39	.40	.69	-.09
Picture Series A	.58	.33	.38	.05	.57	.17	.57	.12	.04	.13
Picture Series B	.73	.95	.03	.06	.51	.32	.53	.56	.60	.27
Picture Analogy	.62	.33	.47	-.28	.56	.25	.67	.35	.00	.17
Figure Analogy	.44	.18	.08	-.21	.33	-.13	.25	.68	.37	.80

deaf. Therefore, in coping with such visual stimuli, the deaf may tend to use a more visual thinking technique (as is seen in the single factor in the deaf population as a whole). Overall, the hearing subjects tend to use a verbal technique in coping with the same stimuli, but this technique does not affect the results. The older deaf children, ages 13 to 15, appeared to adopt the technique used by the hearing. Perhaps the oral training experiences of the older deaf students contributed to their adoption of the verbal style of processing the information and to their demonstration of abstract thinking a few years later than their hearing peers.

Consequently, neither Myklebust's nor Furth's explanations appear to accurately reflect the intellectual development of the deaf. The present study supports previous findings that no difference exists in the pattern of cognitive development in deaf and hearing children. However, differences do seem to exist in the rate of development and in the processes or techniques used by the two groups. It is possible that these techniques are influenced by environmental conditions such as communication mode. Continued research is necessary using appropriate measurement techniques and analyzing the data such that a developmental progression can be determined. In addition, a deaf group that uses manual communication could contribute to the explanation of this research. Perhaps these results pave the way for a new understanding of the cognitive development in deaf children and the techniques they use to process information.

References

Bolton, B. (1978). Differential ability structure in deaf and hearing children. *Applied Psychological Measurement, 2*(1), 147–149.

Canabal, J. V. (1970). *Comparison of deaf and normally hearing children on analogy items under different methods of instructions at different age levels.* Unpublished doctoral dissertation, St. John's University, New York.

Farrant, R. (1964). The intellective abilities of deaf and hearing children compared by factor analysis. *American Annals of the Deaf, 109,* 306–325.

Furth, H. G. (1964). Research with the deaf: Implications for language and cognition. *Psychological Bulletin, 62*, 145–162.

Furth, H. G. (1971). Linguistic deficiency and thinking: Research with deaf subjects, 1964–1969. *Psychological Bulletin, 76*, 58–72.

Harris, S. H. (1982). An evaluation of the Snijders-Oomen nonverbal intelligence test for young children. *Journal of Pediatric Psychology, 7*, 239–251.

Hoemann, H., & Briga, J. (1980). Hearing impairment. In J. Kauffman & D. Hallahan (Eds.), *Handbook of Special Education* (pp. 222–248). Englewood Cliffs, NJ: Prentice-Hall.

Holmberg, G. R. (1966). *A factor analytic study of the intellective abilities of deaf children as measured by the "structure of intellect" model.* Unpublished doctoral dissertation, University of Nebraska.

Juurmaa, J. (1963). On the ability structure of the deaf. *Jyvaskyla Studies in Education, Psychology, and Social Research,* No. 4.

Kearney, J. E. (1969). A new performance scale of cognitive capacity for use with deaf subjects. *American Annals of the Deaf, 114*, 2–14.

Kyle, J. G. (1980). Measuring the intelligence of deaf children. *Bulletin of British Psychological Society, 33*, 54–57.

Moores, D. F. (1982). *Educating the deaf: Psychology, principles, and practices* (rev. ed.). Boston: Houghton Mifflin.

Myklebust, H. (1964). *The psychology of deafness.* New York: Grune & Stratton.

Myklebust, H., & Brutton, M. (1953). A study of visual perception in deaf children. *Acta Oto-Laryngologica,* Supplementum, 105.

Nie, N. H., Hull, C. H., Jenkins, J. G., Steinbrenner, K., & Bent, D. H. (1975). *SPSS.* New York: McGraw-Hill.

Ottem, E. (1980). An analysis of cognitive studies with deaf subjects. *American Annals of the Deaf, 125*, 564–575.

Rittenhouse, R., & Spiro, R. (1970). Conservation-interrogation of deaf and normal hearing children. *Journal of Childhood Communication Disorders, 3*(2), 120–127.

Snijders, J., & Snijders-Oomen, N. (1959). *Non-verbal intelligence tests for deaf and hearing subjects* (A manual). Groningen, Holland: J. B. Wolters.

Zwiebel, A., & Milgram, N. (1982). Cognitive and communicative development in deaf children. *Israel Journal of Behavioral Sciences, 27*, 382–396.

Zwiebel, A., & Rand, Y. (1975). SON test for Israeli deaf children: New norms and applications. Ramat Gan, Israel: Bar-Ilan University.

Analysis

Kenneth I. Epstein

This analysis of the papers in part 8 considers the fundamental question, What techniques of cognitive assessment are the most useful in assessing the hearing-impaired learner and why? This analysis begins with a brief overview of some important historical events that helped to shape the measurement of cognitive potential. It then considers some of the recent thinking outside the field of deafness about what measurement experts should be doing. Finally, it relates the results reported in this volume to the history and the hopes for the future in the area of cognition and deafness.

Historical Review

Mental measurement has a relatively short but fascinating history. One can trace that history to attempts to create a biological rationale for white supremacy or to studies designed to find the relationships between intellectual functioning and such physical characteristics as brain weight or cranial capacity. However, the history that is most relevant to the measurement of intelligence as a psychological construct does not begin until the turn of this century. Boring (1950, pp. 570–571) listed nine laboratories in the United States and Europe that were beginning to experiment with psychological tests of intellectual functioning during the 1890s. In 1904, Alfred Binet began a study for the French Minister of Public Education to identify children who were not successful in normal classrooms, so that special educational programs could be established to help them.

Binet's work is especially interesting because of its empirical nature and its practical objective. In 1909, he developed batteries of short, everyday types of tasks that he believed to involve basic processes of reasoning such as "direction (ordering), comprehension, invention, and censure (correction)" (cited in Gould, 1981, p. 149). That approach is decidedly atheoretical; and, there is no search for a basic human characteristic. We also see no attempt to build a theory of intelligence. "One might almost say, 'It matters very little what the tests are so long as they are numerous'" (Binet, 1911, cited in Gould, 1981, p. 149).

Gould (1981, p. 155) summarized Binet's approach by identifying three principles for the use of his tests.

1. The scores are a practical device; they do not buttress any theory of intellect. They do not define anything innate or permanent. We may not designate what they measure as intelligence or any other reified entity.

2. The scale is a rough empirical guide for identifying mildly retarded

and learning-disabled children who need special help. It is not a device for ranking normal children.

3. Whatever the cause of difficulty in children identified for help, emphasis shall be placed upon improvement through special training. Low scores shall not be used to mark children as innately incapable.

Binet's principles seem remarkably modern to us today. They could have been written by an advocate of the proper use of mental tests in response to the kind of criticism of testing that has been heard recently, and they fit very well with the philosophies expressed in this volume.

An historical perspective is important as we analyze the measurement of cognitive potential of hearing-impaired individuals because of the mistakes that occurred between Binet's time and today. We should review the mistakes and abuses of the past and try to avoid repeating them.

This history is fully described in Steven Jay Gould's book, *The Mismeasure of Man* (1981). The important point for this analysis is that most of the work on mental testing has been based on two assumptions. The first is that intelligence is something real and tangible, similar to some material object. The second is that one's share of intelligence is governed primarily by heredity. In other words, we may differ with respect to how well we use the intelligence we have, but we each have a set amount.

It is only a small leap from the belief that intelligence is a stable entity to the extremist conclusion that the genetic pool can be improved by preventing individuals with only minimal amounts of it from reproducing. Given these assumptions, one can also see the logic of restricting educational opportunities to those individuals with enough intelligence to benefit from it. Otherwise, time and resources would be wasted.

As Charles Spearman said in 1927 as part of the rationale for the English 11+ tests, "If once, then, a child of 11 years or so has had his relative amount of g measured in a really accurate manner, the hope of teachers and parents that he will ever rise to a much higher standing as a late-bloomer would seem to be illusionary" (cited in Gould, 1981, p. 295). In addition, this approach to testing tends to lead to self-fulfilling prophecies.

> Any inference made about the developmental course of an individual will of necessity end up shaping its environmental conditions, thus helping to fulfill the prediction. This may have the effect of drastically limiting the prospects in life for the individual who presumably should have been served by the diagnosis and the prediction. (Feuerstein, 1979, p. 24)

Test development techniques and the interpretation of the results of data analysis are guided, implicitly or explicitly, by one's theoretical position. For example, many human anatomical variables are found to be distributed according to the normal (Gaussian) curve. One would expect that if intelligence were a stable substance, it would also be normally distributed in the population. Any person who has taken a basic psychological or educational measurement course knows that test results are more or less normally distributed and that there are techniques available to permit us to achieve closer approximations to a normal curve if needed. However, there are many possible explanations for a normal distribution of a variable, and the fact that data are normally distributed does not necessarily mean that a physical quantity is being measured.

Gould's (1981) description of the development of factor analysis is an excellent example of the interactions among one's point of view, theory, and analysis. As Gould reported, Spearman was interested in determining whether or not it was possible to identify a single dominant factor that would explain why tests designed to measure different aspects of intelligence tended to be highly correlated with one another. His investigations led to the development of the principal-components technique of factor analysis and the identification of a dominant factor. Spearman called that factor g. However, by using the technique now known as varimax rotation, one can cause g to disappear and be replaced by several more or less equally important factors. Thurstone developed the varimax technique in 1938, partly as a way to refute Spearman's theoretical position. By expanding Spearman's principal-components technique with his varimax rotation, Thurstone was able to replace g with his seven primary mental abilities: verbal comprehension, word fluency, numerical and computational skills, spatial visualization, associative memory, perceptual speed, and reasoning. Either theory can be supported by the same data, depending on which equally mathematically valid technique one chooses to use. The problem is not with the technique, which can be very helpful in simplifying complex data; the problem is with attaching too much meaning to the results and with believing that the factors are more than a mathematical abstraction.

Recent Developments

There are several recent areas of research and development that propose alternatives to this traditional view of measurement of cognitive potential. Three will be addressed in this analysis: the Learning Potential Assessment Device (LPAD), mastery learning, and aptitude-treatment interaction (ATI).

Learning Potential Assessment Device (LPAD)

The LPAD is an alternative assessment procedure developed by Reuven Feuerstein (1979). Originally intended to diagnose the reasons for retarded performance in individuals and their learning potential, the procedure has been used with some success to assess the potential of hearing-impaired children (see Jonas & Martin, pp. 172–175; Keane, pp. 141–147; Braden, pp. 148–150). The LPAD is based on a model of the learner that is considerably different from that which assumes a stable intelligence. Feuerstein's book, *The Dynamic Assessment of Retarded Performers* (1979), describes his view of intellectual development and the development of the LPAD as a natural consequence of that model. Intelligence is viewed as a dynamic changing variable, so that individuals can learn cognitive skills. The appropriate form of assessment is one that measures the potential for learning as directly as possible.

> We define intelligence as the capacity of an individual to use *previously acquired experiences* to adjust to new situations. The two factors stressed in this definition are the capacity of the individual to be modified by learning and the ability of the individual to use whatever modification has occurred for future adjustments. (Feuerstein, 1979, p. 76)

The LPAD is a device that must be used by a trained clinician. It does not have norms, and the administration of the device varies with each individual tested. The intent of the device is to permit the clinician to make valid judgments about why individuals have difficulties with cognitive tasks and to assess their potential for learning how to approach and solve problems.

Mastery Learning

Bloom's mastery-learning model is based on the premise that new skills and knowledge are built on a well-defined foundation of prerequisities, and that if individuals have this foundation, they can master the new skills and knowledge. Individuals vary with respect to the time needed to acquire new skills or with respect to the type of learning environment best suited to them. It may also be necessary to delay instruction for the new skills in order to strengthen the prerequisite foundation. Bloom (1980) provided some suggestions for how measurement practice needs to change to match more closely the mastery philosophy. He stated, "Perhaps the most important methodological change is the movement from what I have termed stable or static variables to variables that are alterable either before the teaching-learning process or as a part of these processes" (1980, p. 18). Two of Bloom's alterable variables—cognitive-entry characteristics and formative testing—are especially relevant for measurement.

Cognitive-entry characteristics are those skills and knowledge that individuals bring with them to the learning situation. These characteristics can be defined as the set of prerequisite skills and knowledge necessary to learn new material. Correlations between such variables and achievement in the content to be learned are typically in the + .70 range and above. One should contrast this strong relationship with the typical + .50 to + .70 correlations found in studies comparing measures of general intelligence to achievement. In addition, these variables are alterable in the sense that if a student is found to be deficient in some prerequisite skill, then that skill can be taught.

Formative testing is the use of tests to monitor the progress of learning. This type of testing is contrasted to summative testing, which is designed to measure performance after instruction is completed. Formative testing views the teaching and learning processes as dynamic. One needs to know what students are doing on a frequent and regular basis in order to modify and improve instruction on an individual basis. The test results provide the feedback that the teacher needs for making changes in the learning environment.

Aptitude-Treatment Interaction

Aptitude-treatment interaction (ATI) research focuses on the relationships among aptitude, instructional treatments, and achievement. "'Aptitude' as a construct refers to psychological characteristics of individuals that predispose and thus predict differences in later learning under specified instructional conditions" (Snow, 1980, p. 41). All teachers know that individual students vary widely in the kind of instruction that seems to work best for them. ATI research systematically explores this phenomenon.

Despite the appeal of the ATI idea and the anecdotal evidence that abounds for the phenomenon, it has remained a very difficult research area. The reasons for this phenomeon include the complexity of the instructional process, the difficulty in determining which set of variables is most important for predicting achievement, and the measurement techniques themselves. "[The apparent complexity of ATI phenomena] makes the task of optimizing instruction for individuals in real school settings very much a continuous, local diagnosis, description, and evaluation activity" (Snow, 1980, pp. 40–41).

Snow summarized recent ATI research and tied it to research in cognitive psychology. He concluded,

> Educational measurement has not yet differentiated the complex constructs of aptitude and achievement sufficiently, or inquired directly into their psychological content and process structure, or connected these to possible instructional conditions. But research toward a process theory of aptitude and achievement in instruction is moving ahead today on a broad front. (1980, p. 56)

These three modern measurement ideas—dynamic assessment with the LPAD, measurement of alterable variables, and measuring aptitude with the ATI purpose of facilitating learning—are philosophically remarkably similar. All reject the notion of an unchanging intelligence; all focus on instruction. All are extremely positive in their views of the potential of individuals to successfully learn. Snow summed it up very well by stating, "And the main purpose of aptitude and achievement measurement in education, in my view, is diagnosis of instructional effects for the individual learner, usually with the aim of improving instruction for each individual learner . . . that is, they should explain instructionally relevant individual differences" (1980, p. 48).

160

Implications of Recent Research

The symposium papers in part 8 and the discussion that they stimulated suggest that measurement of cognitive potential in hearing-impaired individuals is at the point of breaking away from traditional approaches and is ready to take advantage of more recent thinking. The paper by Zwiebel and Mertens and part of that by Braden belong to the factor-analytic tradition. Miller's paper focused on more valid uses of a traditional intelligence test. Luetke-Stahlman proposed the measurement of variables that are not traditionally assessed, but which could have strong instructional implications. Keane and Braden discussed applications of the LPAD to hearing-impaired individuals. Discussion of these papers at the symposium tended to center on interpreting results and applying results to instructional situations.

Zwiebel and Mertens and Braden presented us with factor-analytic results that support the idea that hearing-impaired individuals are not very different from the hearing population. The Zwiebel and Mertens data suggest that there may be differences between the two populations for young children, but that by the early teens the factor structures of the two populations are very similar. Braden's paper made the point that the factor structure of the hearing-impaired population is far more similar to the white hearing population than to the black hearing population and that hearing whites and hearing blacks are considerably more different from each other than are hearing-impaired persons from hearing whites. Braden cautioned researchers to be careful about comparing the hearing-impaired population to culturally disadvantaged groups. At least from a factor-analytic point of view, hearing-impaired persons are apparently not similar to culturally disadvantaged hearing persons.

These factor-analytic results add to the body of literature which indicates, "that no evidence suggests less than the normal range of intellectual potential among the hearing-impaired group" (Levine, 1976). These studies are important in the sense that they tend to dispel misconceptions about the potential of hearing-impaired individuals, but they are limited. One of Sigel and Brinker's criticisms (see pp. 209–221) regarding the research represented by these papers was that they did not see a psychology of deafness emerging. Rather, there appears to be too much comparison of the hearing impaired with other populations. Too many researchers appear to be asking whether hearing-impaired people are like hearing people or behave like hearing people. There are not enough asking the direct question, What are hearing-impaired people like?

It is now time to move beyond comparison studies. If factor-analytic studies are planned for the future, they must focus on describing the characteristics of hearing-impaired individuals directly. They should also be directed toward using the results to improve the cognitive functioning of hearing-impaired individuals. For example, the Zwiebel and Mertens results suggest that hearing-impaired individuals may undergo an important change in their cognitive functioning as they become older. What are the behavioral manifestations of this change? Would it be desirable to provide instruction at an early age to hasten the change? How can these results help to explain the way that hearing-impaired individuals develop cognitively?

The WISC-R is one of the most widely used intelligence tests available. Its nonverbal subscales have been normed for hearing-impaired individuals, but there has been a reluctance to use its verbal subscales because of the fear that the need for specific English-language skills would invalidate any results. Miller's work attempts to assess verbal intelligence without the confounding effects of English.

There seems to be no doubt that Miller's technique can significantly increase the likelihood that responses to WISC-R verbal items will be based on knowledge of the content rather than on understanding the wording of the item. This development is certainly an improvement. However, Miller's technique does not address the question of content validity. Much of the argument about bias in mental testing has revolved around the cultural awareness apparently assumed by the test items. Whether or not the WISC-R is culturally biased against hearing-impaired individuals is an unanswered question.

Cultural bias may not be a *red herring*, if we can recall Binet's advice of 70 years ago. He observed that results based on many items of varied content seemed to be of practical value, but he was extremely reluctant to generalize beyond those practical results. Miller's technique may provide a much-needed tool to support cognitive research with verbal components. The key is to be certain that results are carefully interpreted and used.

English is often assumed to be the second language of prelingually deaf individuals. For prelingually deaf persons with deaf families, the first language may be a dialect of American Sign Language (ASL). For prelingually deaf persons with hearing families, it is difficult to identify precisely what their first language is. It appears to be a mix of English and sign, often referred to as Pidgin Sign English (PSE). PSE's relative similarity to English differs according to the individual and may depend on such factors as schooling, home environment, extent of the hearing loss, and contact with the deaf community.

Luetke-Stahlman's research is concerned with identifying an individual's first language and assessing his or her linguistic skills using tasks that are highly predictive of success in an instructional setting. Her approach views education of the deaf as presenting problems similar to bilingual education. She points out that children's comprehension of instructional material may be inhibited by as much as 50 to 90% if there is a language mismatch between teacher and student. She is clearly interested in improving communication in the classroom.

Linguistic competence, as Luetke-Stahlman used the concept, could easily be included in Bloom's category of cognitive-entry characteristics. Linguistic competence is highly correlated with academic success, and linguistic skills can be improved. In addition, Luetke-Stahlman's results, which showed differences in achievement as a function of language competency and the language match between teacher and student, could form part of the basis for future ATI research. The relatively narrow definition of linguistic competence implied by this assessment technique is of some concern. There is also a question of the validity of the bilingual approach with a hearing-impaired population. To the extent that Luetke-Stahlman's work is viewed as primarily research in linguistics, this validity may be a problem. However, as a practical technique to support improvement in classroom instruction, it shows great promise.

The Keane and Braden papers suggested that the LPAD can be used successfully with hearing-impaired students. Braden introduced Feuerstein's model and raised some interesting questions about the theoretical appropriateness of the model for deaf individuals. Keane's interest in test administration methodology and the transfer of learning that appears to occur as a result of strictly following Feuerstein's administration procedures has important practical implications.

If it is reasonable to view deaf children in much the same way as one views culturally deprived groups, then the Feuerstein model would fit nicely. However, Braden's data do not support the cultural deprivation model. Nor is it reasonable to view deaf individuals in the same way as Feuerstein viewed his original subject pool of retarded performers. Yet, the LPAD seems to work as a diagnostic device. There is now a need to extend Feuerstein's theoretical base to develop a theoretical rationale for the use of the LPAD with deaf individuals.

Keane's results raise several interpretation questions. He showed that LPAD results vary systematically as a function of test administration procedures. He also showed that the learning which occurs during the LPAD administration can transfer positively to other tests. The question left unanswered is how to use the results in the classroom. This question is particularly important when using the LPAD because the results are not interpretable in traditional psychometric intelligence-testing terms. The value of LPAD results also becomes questionable if students are not in an instructional environment that is based on Feuerstein's model.

As one reads these papers and others presented at the symposium, one is struck by the amount of evidence suggesting that hearing-impaired individuals are much more like their hearing peers than different from them. We then may ask ourselves, "If deaf learners are cognitively similar to hearing learners, why do instructors have so much trouble in helping them to learn?" The typical answer has been some statement such as, "They can't hear." While this answer may seem overly simplistic, there is much that can be learned from it. We began by asking what the most appropriate assessment techniques are; the answer may be, "Those techniques that are most sensitive to the fact that the examinees can't hear."

Thus, Miller's adaptation of the WISC-R permits more valid assessment of verbal intelligence. Luetke-Stahlman's techniques point the way toward proper identification of an individual's first language and the assessment of it. The LPAD, heavily dependent on a qualified administrator, can present a more complete picture of an individual's potential than can traditional techniques. All of these procedures are specifically designed or can be tailored for a hearing-impaired population.

Assessment procedures designed for deaf examinees must now be combined with instruction designed for deaf students. The Bloom mastery-learning model can be useful. Its focus on frequent feedback to the instructor, its empirical approach to finding effective instructional methods, and its emphasis on the learner as an individual make it very attractive. Aptitude-treatment interaction research can also assist us now. Hearing-impaired individuals have one very important instructionally relevant aptitude: They cannot hear. Instructional treatments must recognize and be sensitive to that fact. If we can bring assessment and instruction closer together, and if we remember that our students cannot hear, then we can do something about helping them to learn effectively.

References

Bloom, B. S. (1980). The new direction in educational research: Alterable variable. *New Directions for Testing and Measurement, 5,* 17–30.

Boring, E. G. (1950). *A history of experimental psychology* (2nd ed.). New York: Appleton-Century-Crofts.

Feuerstein, R. (1979). *The dynamic assessment of retarded performers: The learning potential assessment device, theory, instruments, and techniques.* Baltimore: University Park Press.

Gould, S. J. (1981). *The mismeasure of man.* New York: W. W. Norton.

Levine, E. S. (1976). Psychological contributions. In R. Frisina (Ed.), *A bicentennial monograph on hearing impairment: Trends in the USA* (pp. 23–33). Washington, DC: A. G. Bell Association.

Snow, R. E. (1980). Aptitude and achievement. *New Directions for Testing and Measurement, 5,* 39–59.

Related Educational and Research Issues

1. In testing a hearing-impaired learner, to what extent is the use of multiple languages helpful (ASL, English, Pidgin Sign English)?

2. What variables affect a hearing-impaired learner's response to tests of cognitive potential?

3. To what extent can psychologically based evaluations predict classroom success?

4. What types of retraining techniques are necessary to help teachers use data from psychologically based instruments of measurement?

5. What special retraining is now needed for psychologists who have responsibility for testing hearing-impaired learners?

9 The Effects of Cognitive Intervention Programs

Can Thinking Skills Be Incorporated into a Curriculum?

Cindy Rohr-Redding

Teachers who work with hearing-impaired adolescents frequently express deep concern and frustration about some of their students' serious deficiencies in problem solving. Student performance in both classroom discussions and written work indicates that students (a) are unable to organize and synthesize information for taking tests, (b) do not spontaneously compare and apply information across subject areas, (c) cannot follow written and oral directions without demonstration, (d) do not read between and beyond the lines, (e) have difficulty in seeing relationships between assignments, and (f) are not able to generalize the information learned in the classroom to life experiences. Previous studies have established these concerns as valid. Hearing-impaired children have demonstrated specific cognitive deficiencies in such areas as memory (Karchmer & Belmont, 1976), concept application (Meadow, 1980), opposition (Furth, 1964; Meadow, 1980), analogic reasoning (Meadow, 1980), superordinate reasoning (Johnson, 1981), and classification (Best & Roberts, 1975). However, both Furth and Meadow have found that hearing-impaired learners perform as well as hearing children on cognitive tasks such as understanding parts versus wholes. Thus, we see normal performance by hearing-impaired children on some cognitive tasks and not others.

If we accept the evidence that some cognitive deficiencies do exist for hearing-impaired individuals but that no evidence suggests less than the normal range of intellectual potential among the hearing impaired, it is apparent that a cognitive intervention program used in an educational setting might promise improvement of these skills.

Instrumental Enrichment (IE) was developed by Reuven Feuerstein (1978, 1980) in response to the need for mediated learning experiences to facilitate the development of thinking skills among culturally disadvantaged groups emigrating to Israel. A mediated learning experience is a process by which an experienced person selects and interprets the stimuli impinging on a learner. While mediating, IE teachers often use such phrases as, "You should continue to look for the best answer," or "Your strategy is not working; think of another way to solve the problem."

Instrumental Enrichment consists of content-free paper-and-pencil activities relating to 14 specific cognitive functions. This program provides an excellent tool for instruction (especially in relation to the results of those studies cited earlier) for the following reasons:

1. It gives the students repeated opportunities to reflect on their own thinking processes. Students in the program have begun comparing

The complete version of this paper is available in microfiche or hard copy from ERIC Document Reproduction Service. Ask for Document No. ED 247 729.

different strategies they have used to arrive at the same answer or are contemplating the need to change strategies midstream when trying to reach a solution.

2. It develops the prerequisites for learning and does not assume that those prerequisites already exist.

3. It does not assume that the student will automatically generalize the skill to other areas. Instead, the teacher overtly and actively promotes transfer by the student of skills to both real life and curricular situations through classroom *bridging* exercises. (Classroom activities integrating IE with subject matter occur at least twice per week.) For example, two areas of emphasis in the first year of the program are the reduction of impulsivity and the need to be precise. In discussing the application of these strategies in relation to the subject area, the teacher would ask the students to explain one way that their impulsiveness in completing a homework assignment resulted in having incorrect answers; or the teacher would ask students to identify another strategy that the main character in the story might have used to more efficiently and accurately resolve the conflict in the story.

A strong validation of the importance of training students in intellectual skills is made by Sternberg (1983); he has listed several criteria that any worthwhile training program should meet. Among them is the importance of training students in strategies, and he specifically mentions Feuerstein's Instrumental Enrichment as a successful example of such a program.

A special 2-year pilot project at the Model Secondary School for the Deaf (Washington, D.C.) studied a control group of 17 students and an experimental group of 10 students using measures of cognitive functioning to assess the success of this systematic intervention program. (The paper in this volume by Jonas & Martin, pp. 172–175, describes in more detail the results of a later and more extensive study using the same program.) The experimental and control groups were matched on the basis of age, sex, degree of hearing loss, and reading ability. Three questions needed to be answered in an evaluation of this effort. First, could the students learn the training task itself? Second, could the students generalize the training to a specific curricular situation? Third, could the training generalize to other situations? To answer these questions, three separate data collections were planned.

The Raven's Standard Progressive Matrices (1958), an untimed multiple-choice test of general intellectual capacity, was administered to both the experimental and control subjects. The Stanford Achievement Test—

Hearing-Impaired Version (SAT-HI) Reading Comprehension subtest, which requires multiple-choice responses, was also selected to assess the individuals' ability to construct a coherent interpretation of an extended prose passage as well as to measure specific decoding skills. *All* MSSD students were given the entire test battery. In addition, each experimental and control subject was interviewed individually using a prescribed problem-solving format to examine the use of problem-solving strategies. The students were videotaped while they responded to three questions asked by qualified hearing-impaired users of American Sign Language.

The results supported the fact that IE is an intervention program that promotes logical and abstract thinking, as demonstrated in the individual growth in scores on the Raven's Progressive Standard Matrices. The IE group gained an average of 6.3 while the control group gained 2.9 points in a one-way variance on the number of correct items.

The experimental group showed a higher mean scaled score (154.1) than the control group (150.6) on the SAT-HI Reading Comprehension subtest. A test for significance of difference between the pre- and posttests revealed an increase for the experimental group ($p < .05$), while no such difference was found within the control group (Kluwin, 1982). This trend in favor of the experimental group when comparing pre- and post-SAT-HI Reading Comprehension subtest scores within the experimental and control groups, indicates that the program was contributing some positive impact on the development of prerequisite skills for reading comprehension.

At the end of the second pilot year, some important and consistent effects were reported for the students receiving IE instruction.

1. Hearing-impaired students now approached problem-solving situations in the curriculum more systematically by analyzing component parts of a problem and with less impulsivity. While bridging, students have been able to develop a variety of plans to assist them with problems in management, memorization, and research.

2. Students improved in their understanding of the reasons behind required assignments, which increased their motivation when solving problems in English and mathematics. They spontaneously used categorization techniques such as semantic mapping, webbing, matrices and outlines, because they recognized a need for such strategies in assisting them to learn.

3. Significant growth in sign language vocabulary was observed. After 2 years in the program, students incorporated such vocabulary as "elaborate, imagine, point of view, precise, impulsive, irrelevant, mediate, explicit, implicit, overlap, and organize" into their daily problem-solving discussions.

4. Students now cooperated with peers in problem-solving tasks with less simplistic criticism of peers' work and with an increase in positive attitude. Students were able to suggest alternative strategies to each other for solving problems, while providing insight into the

quality and depth of answers. They had developed a peer evaluation system for feedback on assignments.

5. The experimental students more frequently were able to describe several strategies to solve a problem and could defend their opinions on the basis of logical evidence. Students were always prepared to challenge the strategies and solutions of a peer. They stated, "An answer is not acceptable without proof."

6. Students had become less obsessed with the end results or terminal behavior of an objective and more interested in the means (process) by which the objective was reached. Instead of comparing answers, they compared systems of planning and possible approaches.

Systematic cognitive intervention for adolescent hearing-impaired learners is thus demonstrated to be effective in a classroom setting, provided the appropriate materials and adequate teacher training are available. Hearing-impaired adolescents can indeed improve their cognitive skills, and adolescence (while late in the developmental cycle) is clearly not too late for effective intervention in their cognitive performance.

References

Best, B., & Roberts, G. C. (1975). *Cognitive development in young deaf children.* (Grant No. OEG 093321894533[032]). Minneapolis: University of Minnesota Research, Development, and Demonstration Center.

Feuerstein, R. (1978). *Instrumental enrichment.* Baltimore: University Park Press.

Feuerstein, R. (1980). *Instrumental enrichment: An intervention program for cognitive modifiability.* Baltimore: University Park Press.

Furth, H. (1964). *Thinking without language.* New York: Free Press.

Johnson, J. (1981, April). *Hearing-impaired learner with special needs.* Paper presented at the Symposium on Media and the Hearing-Impaired, Lincoln, NE.

Karchmer, M. A., & Belmont, J. M. (1976, November). *On assessing and improving deaf performance in the cognitive laboratory.* Paper presented at a meeting of the American Speech and Hearing Association, Houston, TX.

Kluwin, T. N. (1982). *Evaluation of the instrumental enrichment training project for the Model Secondary School for the Deaf, 1981–82.* Unpublished manuscript.

Meadow, K. (1980). *Deafness and child development.* Berkeley: University of California Press.

Raven, J. C. (1958). *Standard progressive matrices.* London: H. K. Lewis.

Sternberg, R. J. (1983). Criteria for intellectual skills training. *Educational Researcher, 12*(2), 6–13.

Cognitive Improvement of Hearing-Impaired High School Students Through Instruction in Instrumental Enrichment

Bruce S. Jonas
David S. Martin

If one accepts the fact that certain specific cognitive deficiencies exist for hearing-impaired individuals but that no evidence suggests less than the normal range of intellectual potential among hearing-impaired individuals as a group (Drever & Collins, 1928; Levine, 1976; Vernon, 1968), then it is apparent that a specific program of activity in an educational setting may promise improvement in the deficient areas of cognition.

Reuven Feuerstein (1978, 1980) developed the instructional program Instrumental Enrichment (IE) based on a set of theoretical assumptions relating to the cognitive modifiability of low-functioning adolescents. The IE goals include (a) improving performance in spatial relations, (b) improving performance in abstract analogies, (c) improving the ability to use more than one rule to solve a problem, (d) fostering more systematic approaches to problem solving, (e) fostering more accurate reading and following of directions, and (f) increasing use of appropriate language for planning and sequencing events. The IE methodology involves student manipulation of content-free paper-and-pencil activities in such skills as comparison, analysis, orientation in space, and organization, followed by discussion for insight into the mental processes used and how they also apply to the study of various subject matter. For the school using IE, some secondary or spillover effects include improvement in reading, math, and writing skills, as well as in work habits, classroom behavior, and social behavior.

An evaluation aimed at assessing how IE promoted this set of goals for hearing-impaired students was implemented during the 1982–84 academic years at the Model Secondary School for the Deaf (MSSD) at Gallaudet College. (This study expanded the pilot study reported by Rohr-Redding; see pp. 168–171.) The research design was a pre- and posttest model on experimental (IE) and control (non-IE) groups, each comprised of 39 students. Experimental and control groups were matched on the basis of sex, age, and level of class placement (remedial, regular, or advanced).

In order to measure and compare relative gains for all the goals listed, eight measurement instruments were administered as pretests prior to October 1982 and as posttests in the spring of 1984. These instruments were (a) Raven's Progressive Matrices (1958), (b) Kit of Factor-Referenced Cognitive Test (KFRCT)—Diagramming Relationships (Ekstrom, French, Harman, & Derman, 1976), (c) KFRCT—Letter Sets, (d) Written Problem Solutions, (e) Teacher Observation Checklist, (f) Stanford Achievement Test—Hearing-Impaired Version (SAT-HI) Reading Comprehension, (g) SAT-HI Math Concepts, and (h) SAT-HI Math Computation. The three psychometric tests listed here (a,b, and c) all measured aspects of ability to reason abstractly

The complete version of this paper is available in microfiche or hard copy from ERIC Document Reproduction Service. Ask for Document No. ED 247 725.

and to group concepts into logical and analogical forms. The written problems (d) posed life-adjustment situations to students in order to measure logical problem-formulation and language sequencing. The teacher observation checklist (e) profiles the efficacy of this approach toward providing general study skills and improving classroom and social behavior. The three SAT-HI subtests (f, g, h) relate to the long-term goals of improvement in reading and mathematics.

Results

After 2 years in the program, the Instrumental Enrichment group demonstrated important and consistent trends. The IE group's performance gain on the Raven's Progressive Matrices was more than four times higher than that of a suitably matched group of control students (8.1 gain for the IE group vs. 1.8 for the control group), representing a statistically significant difference ($p < .02$). The other two psychometric tests, Diagramming Relationships and Letter Sets, showed no significant findings, but the trends for the Instrumental Enrichment group were in the direction hypothesized. Both of these factor-referenced tests were linguistically too difficult for most of the students tested.

For the Problem-Solving Solutions as a whole, the Instrumental Enrichment group performed better than the control group. The significant difference was in Problem #3: "Suppose you and a friend from MSSD are having dinner at a restaurant in Washington, D.C., away from the MSSD campus. Your friend gets *very sick*, but no one else in the restaurant knows ASL; What would you do?" IE students' written responses to this problem showed highly significant improvement ($p < .01$, according to independent raters). The IE students tended to (a) use more steps, (b) systematize those steps in the solution more often, and (c) increase their usage of both contingencies and if/then sentence constructions on the posttest.

After only one year, the Instrumental Enrichment group also showed significant gains on two items on the Teacher Observation Checklist. Teachers reported significant improvements in the following work habits ($p < .02$) and classroom/social behaviors ($p < .03$):

1. Correcting mistakes spontaneously

2. Settling down to work rapidly at beginning of class

3. Taking responsibility for making up work missed

4. Giving relevant and complete answers to questions

5. Taking responsibility for personal materials

6. Making a minimum number of errors and erasures

7. Reading and following directions spontaneously

8. Expecting oneself to be precise.

Students also showed significant improvements in the following class-room and social behaviors:

1. Being willing to help others in class

2. Working well with others in a group

3. Being considerate of others' feelings and listening to others

4. Acting without impulsivity

5. Avoiding involvement in fights and arguments

6. Approaching new tasks positively and working with confidence

7. Volunteering to do extra work

8. Being enthusiastic about learning.

The three SAT-HI achievement subtests (Reading Comprehension, Math Concepts, and Math Computation) all showed significant increases ($p < .05$) for the IE group. Over a period of 2 years, the Reading Comprehension scores for the IE group increased by 15.6 scaled-score points, while those for the controls gained 8.8 points. Math Concepts scores for the IE group gained 24.1 points while control scores rose by only 14.3 points. Math Computation scores for IE students gained 19.1 points while controls showed a gain of 12.2 points. One of the English teachers explained these changes in her students by noting that the teaching of comparisons, organization, and strategies are crucial prerequisites to the reading and writing process. It also appears that these skills, when applied to math, contributed to the SAT-HI performance gains.

Discussion

Many hearing-impaired students tend to have a *touch-finish* attitude about homework and class time (i.e., they attempt a task only once and then drop it), instead of developing an academic response or taking a project to its full completion. Often students do not feel an intrinsic need to compare, extrap-olate, and analyze. In order to relate these cognitive skills to school subject areas, students need mediated learning experiences to move from thinking to reading, writing, and mathematics. Instrumental Enrichment apparently develops skill in metacognition (i.e., students' ability to think about their own thinking processes). IE also apparently enables students to stay more often with a project until its completion; develop an intrinsic need to com-pare, extrapolate, and analyze; and apply these skills to academic subjects.

Conclusions

From this study of a systematic cognitive intervention, we may therefore draw the following conclusions:

1. Adolescence is apparently not too late to begin a systematic program of cognitive improvement for the hearing-impaired learner.

2. Teacher training is an essential prerequisite for curricular intervention involving content-free cognitive materials that are integrated into regular subject matter.

3. Dissemination of these results to other programs for the hearing impaired is now appropriate.

4. A larger student sample and the resulting more complex evaluation design are now appropriate for investigation and replication of these apparent effects with the hearing-impaired population.

References

Drever, J., & Collins, M. (1928). *Performance tests of intelligence.* Edinburgh: Oliver & Boyd.

Ekstrom, R. B., French, J. W., Harman, H. H., & Derman, D. (1976). *Kit of factor-referenced cognitive tests.* Princeton: Educational Testing Service.

Feuerstein, R. (1978). *Instrumental enrichment.* Baltimore: University Park Press.

Feuerstein, R. (1980). *Instrumental enrichment: An intervention program for cognitive modifiability.* Baltimore: University Park Press.

Levine, E. S. (1976). Psychological contributions. In R. Frisina (Ed.), *A bicentennial monograph on hearing impairment: Trends in the USA* (pp. 23–33). Washington, DC: A. G. Bell Association.

Raven, J. C. (1958). *Standard progressive matrices.* London: H. K. Lewis.

Vernon, M. (1968). Five years of research on the intelligence of deaf and hard-of-hearing children: A review of literature and discussion of implications. *Journal of Research on Deafness, 1*(4), 1–12.

Enhancing Cognitive Performance in the Hearing-Impaired College Student: A Pilot Study

David S. Martin

Instructors who work with hearing-impaired college students frequently express deep concern and frustration about some of their students' serious deficiencies in problem-solving skills in both classroom and written work. The concern often relates to the students' difficulty with manipulating more than one variable, conceptualizing what a textbook or journal author is saying, forming conclusions, dealing with hypothetical data, and spatial reasoning. Yet, research with hearing-impaired persons has documented that (a) no basic malfunctions are present in the cognitive abilities of that general population and (b) any inferiorities in cognitive performance may be attributed to experiential and linguistic deficits and communication handicaps (Levine, 1976, p. 28).

The relationship between language and cognition is both essential and complex. A major body of research during the past 50 years indicates that language in social interaction is critical to effective cognitive development (Vygotsky, 1962, 1978; Wertsch, 1978). The work of Halliday (1973) and Tough (1977) has reinforced Vygotsky's work and given new insights into the degree of linguistic use by children in attacking cognitive problems. In addition, Klein (1981) has found that using language enables the learner to restructure mental schemata, perceive reality in new ways, and redesign the strategies employed to solve problems (p. 447). Thus, it is highly appropriate that an intervention program for hearing-impaired learners in the area of cognitive development should recognize and use language in a systematic manner since, as previously noted, the linguistic deficits of hearing-impaired learners are considered to be partly responsible for some of their difficulties in cognition.

The literature on the improvement of cognitive skills in the college-age learner strongly supports the efficacy of separate training in those skills. Brabeck (1983) found that the greatest cognitive change occurs during a student's first 2 years of college. Mentkowski and Strait's (1983) research on cognitive instruction of college-age students in analogic reasoning has shown dramatic improvement as the result of instruction, although similar effects have not been found in regard to syllogistic reasoning. Even minimal training in cognitive strategies has resulted in long-term effects (Dansereau et al., 1975). Weinstein (1977) found that the more successful learners use meaningful elaboration strategies, albeit often covertly. Hence, the merits of specific training in these skills is supported (Weinstein et al., 1980). In addition, training was found to be superior to merely giving simple instructions (Weinstein et al., 1981).

The author acknowledges the valuable cooperation and assistance of Anna Hauptman, PhD, in the design, implementation, and analysis of this pilot study.

The complete version of this paper is available in microfiche or hard copy form ERIC Document Reproduction Service. Ask for Document No. ED 247 726.

Thus, the literature establishes a clear need for interventions to improve the cognitive performance of hearing-impaired learners of college age. The optimum time for this intervention may be during the freshman and sophomore years, yet there is relatively little evidence of prior efforts to carry out such interventions systematically.

Pilot Program

In an effort to develop a program for enhancing the cognitive skills of hearing-impaired college-age students, the author conducted a pilot study in the spring of 1983. All of the subjects in the study were education majors at Gallaudet College. The experimental group contained 24 students who were enrolled in a curriculum foundations course or an educational psychology course. The control group contained 10 students who were enrolled in a parallel educational psychology course.

The experimental group was given activities based on Feuerstein's (1980) Instrumental Enrichment program. The paper-and-pencil cognitive activities were included in alternate 45-minute class sessions for a period of 15 weeks. The activities were drawn from five instruments related to improving the specific skills of (a) projection of virtual relationships, (b) orientation in space, (c) comparison, (d) analytic perception, and (e) following precise instructions. Each activity was followed by a discussion-for-insight into how that particular skill could be applied to (a) teaching children that same skill, (b) the other subject matter of the course itself, (c) professional teaching behaviors such as lesson planning and materials selection, and (d) life (outside world) functioning such as finding a job and selecting a mate.

Results

The experimental and control groups were given several pre- and posttests to measure their cognitive skills. The groups showed no significant differences on the Uncritical Inference Test (Haney, 1967). Results on a special comparisons test requiring written analysis of similarities and differences between two complex cartoons were content-analyzed by independent judges for precision, detail, and relevancy of the similarities and differences described. Scores were assigned on that basis to each subject's test. The posttest data showed improvement in the experimental subjects' abilities to state similarities, state differences, be precise in description, and explain the meaning behind pictorial stimuli.

On a self-rating scale of 10 generic cognitive behaviors relating to problem-solving habits, trends indicated that the experimental subjects also increased in their self-reported tendency to follow directions, carry out coursework carefully, correct their own mistakes, and take the time to think through an answer before writing it on paper.

Responses to a picture completion test requiring perception of wholes in response to given parts were summed across items for each experimental subject and submitted to the Wilcoxon Test for differences between pre- and posttests. No statistically significant difference was found between test administrations.

Results on a learning style test showed a clear trend in the experimental group toward preference for a visual versus a verbal modality and toward preference for reflectivity versus impulsivity.

The self-perceived improvement within the experimental group in taking the time to think through a problem on the self-rating scale and the clear trend toward reflectivity on the learning style indicator validate each other well; these data constitute evidence that the intervention succeeded in reducing impulsivity. The clear trends favoring greater precision and improved abilities to accurately describe similarities and differences would attest to the success of even a brief 15-week intervention in promoting those generic cognitive skills.

The following conclusions can be drawn from this pilot study:

1. The college-age hearing-impaired population is indeed amenable to observable and measurable gain in cognitive functioning level.

2. The integration of supplemental cognitive interaction activities of a content-free nature is feasible in the context of the subject matter in at least preprofessional studies at the college level.

3. Specific faculty development is necessary to train instructors in the methodology of such an intervention.

4. Additional research is now required with more varied and larger samples of hearing-impaired students of college age in additional subject matter contexts to validate, replicate, and enlarge upon the findings of this pilot study.

The potential for improvement in cognitive performance of the hearing-impaired learner as late as the college level is clearly suggested by this study. The involvement of such populations at campuses other than Gallaudet will now be welcomed by the investigator for the next phases of the study.

References

Brabeck, M. M., (1983, April). *Intellectual development in the college years: How strong is the longitudinal evidence?* Paper presented at the conference of the American Educational Research Association, Montreal, Canada.

Dansereau, D. F., et al. (1975, June). Effective learning strategy program: Development and assessment (Report No. AFHRL-TR-75-H). *Resources in Education.* (ERIC Document Reproduction Service No. ED 111 740)

Feuerstein, R. (1980). *Instrumental enrichment: An intervention program for cognitive modifiability.* Baltimore: University Park Press.

Halliday, M. A. K. (1973). *Explorations in the function of language.* London: Edward Arnold.

Haney, W. V. (1967). *Uncritical inference test.* Evanston, IL: Northwestern University.

Klein, M. L. (1981). Key generalization about language and children. *Educational Leadership, 38,* 446–448.

Levine, E. S. (1976). Psychological contributions. In R. Frisina (Ed.), *A bicentennial monograph on hearing impairment: Trends in the USA* (pp. 23–33). Washington, DC: A. G. Bell Association.

Mentkowski, M., & Strait, M. J. (1983, April). *A longitudinal study of student change in cognitive development and generic abilities in an outcome-centered liberal arts curriculum: Boston College.* Paper presented at the conference of the American Educational Research Association, Montreal, Canada.

Tough, J. (1977). *The development of meaning.* New York: John Wiley & Sons.

Vygotsky, L. S. (1962). *Thought and language.* Cambridge: MIT Press.

Vygotsky, L. S. (1978). *Mind in society.* Cambridge: Harvard University Press.

Weinstein, C. E. (1977, April). Cognitive elaboration strategies. *Resources in Education.* (ERIC Document Reproduction Service No. ED 144 953)

Weinstein, C. E., et al. (1980, August). Training versus instruction in the acquisition of cognitive learning strategies. *Resources in Education.* (ERIC Document Reproduction Service No. ED 208 018)

Weinstein, C. E., et al. (1981). Training versus instruction in the acquisition of cognitive learning strategies. *Contemporary Educational Psychology, 6*(2), 159–166.

Wertsch, J. V. (Ed.). (1978). *Recent trends in Soviet psycholinguistics.* White Plains, NY: M. E. Sharpe.

Improving Cognitive Skills in Deaf Adolescents Using LOGO and Instrumental Enrichment

Charles H. Dietz

Young deaf children generally live in environments where they neither hear nor speak a language common to their parents. To these children, written symbols may have little meaning; in addition, they have few opportunities to discuss and share their experiences with adults. Without easy communication with the adults around them, many deaf children are denied what Israeli psychologist Reuven Feuerstein calls *mediated learning experiences;* this deprivation impacts on their cognitive development (Feuerstein, 1980). These children may not experience adult thought patterns and skills upon which to model their own and may not have the cognitive skills necessary to perceive and process information. They need a way to learn these cognitive skills so that they can form appropriate concepts and abstractions (Dietz & Williams, 1981).

A Proposed Solution

As a means of providing mediated learning experiences in which students can learn cognitive skills, a course was conceived that combined two approaches, each of which purported to improve thinking skills. The two approaches selected were the use of the computer language LOGO, developed by Seymour Papert as a means of providing an environment rich in ideas for students, and the Instrumental Enrichment developed by Feuerstein for "retarded performers" (Feuerstein, 1980).

LOGO was developed for use by children to aid them in learning to interact with and control a computer. Papert suggested that "learning to communicate with a computer may change the way other learning takes place" by allowing children to build their own cognitive structures (1980, 6–7). LOGO provides a natural process of communication and a vehicle for the building of microworlds of ideas in which to explore and develop cognitive structures.

Feuerstein, on the other hand, suggested that it is possible to modify the cognitive structures of adolescents through a program of intervention. His Instrumental Enrichment (IE) program has been used extensively in Israel and in the U.S. with various classifications of retarded performers. During the past 3 years, this program has been in use with groups of students at MSSD with apparent success (see Jonas & Martin, pp. 172–175; Rohr-Redding, pp. 168–171).

Course Description and Method

The 12 students in this pilot course were divided into two classes of 6 students each at the Model Secondary School for the Deaf (Washington,

D.C.). These 17- to 20-year-old students had all failed their previous mathematics course and had not had success with mathematics beyond the fourth grade level. Some of these students had personal and behavioral adjustment problems, and several had additional physical handicaps. In previous classes, they had shown dependence on teacher guidance and continuous feedback, lack of persistence in solving problems, and little systematic planning behavior.

During the first 2 weeks of the course, these students were introduced to LOGO through lessons designed to progress from a high degree of guidance and structure to a final open-ended investigation. The emphasis at this stage was the development of exploration and independence. After 2 weeks, the written lessons were discontinued since most students showed interest in pursuing design ideas of their own. From this point, all LOGO activity was student directed. Teacher intervention occurred only to encourage or teach a new LOGO command or technique as the need arose. Extensive sharing of ideas and peer teaching occurred. By the end of the course, all students had mastered most LOGO graphics commands and were able to write and edit original programs involving several levels of complexity. Three students had begun to use the more abstract, nongraphics, list-processing commands. The course became less structured, and the classroom atmosphere was quite close to that suggested by Papert in *Mindstorms* (1980).

Instrumental Enrichment (IE) paper-and-pencil cognitive activities were first introduced during the third week of the course. One day each week for the next 6 weeks was devoted to IE. These classes were teacher centered and involved extensive discussion. The students resisted the IE activities and continuously expressed an interest in getting back to their LOGO projects. After the 6 weeks, IE was dropped with the hope of reintroducing it later in the course. In January, IE was again introduced into the classes for a 6-week period, again with similar student reaction. Since a very positive learning environment had been developed with LOGO and since the IE activities seemed to be threatening that environment, the decision was made to drop IE from the course completely.

In February, three hearing-impaired low-achieving students from the Kendall Demonstration Elementary School were brought into one of the classes and were tutored in LOGO by students in the class (see Luft, p. 184). This tutoring occurred once a week until May.

In September and again in late May, four tests were administered to the students by a clinician. The measures selected were the Raven's Progressive Matrices (Raven, 1958), the Hiskey-Nebraska Test of Learning Aptitude (Block Design and Spatial Reasoning subtests) (Hiskey, 1966), and the Woodcock Reading Mastery Test (Word Comprehension subtest) (Woodcock, 1973). Complete pre- and posttest data were gathered on 10 of the original 12 students. (Two students could not continue the second half of the course due to scheduling conflicts.) The purpose of these tests was to see if any change in abstract reasoning, spatial abilities, or reading skills could be detected.

Conclusions

Based upon informal observations by the teacher and by the administrator of the pre- and posttests, the students in this course did benefit in the following ways:

1. They were able to learn LOGO. Two students actually began to use some of the more abstract, nongraphic list-processing abilities of the language.

2. Students' attitudes and habits toward their work in this class improved; they became more independent, persistent in dealing with difficult problems, and willing to explore on their own without continuous feedback from the teacher. There was also evidence of improved and extended planning behaviors and more positive attitudes toward school.

3. Improved self-confidence was indicated on the part of half of the students by expressing an interest in learning more about computers and wanting to enter computer-related jobs in the future. Since the conclusion of the course, all except one student has graduated, and at least two of them have entered vocational or college programs related to computer professions.

4. There was evidence of improvement in understanding of geometric concepts, but no test of geometry was a part of this project.

Three of the four tests administered showed little evidence of change between pre- and posttest scores. On the Hiskey-Nebraska Block Design test, however, 8 out of 10 students showed improvement, and 6 of these showed improvement of more than 3 years as computed by the norms associated with the test. This test seems to measure spatial ability on a rather concrete level. Since these data are based on only 10 students in an informal study, additional investigation is suggested with this measure and other spatial measures of a similar type

Do any of these benefits transfer to other areas of academic work or to life? Have the cognitive abilities of these students improved as a result of their experience with LOGO? Neither of these questions can be answered definitely as yet. The data from some of the pre- and posttest measures are inconclusive, and no follow-up of these students into other academic work was possible.

The experiences of this project do suggest that the use of LOGO with academically unsuccessful deaf students is promising, and formal investigations of its value should now be made. The combination of LOGO with the Instrumental Enrichment program was not successful in this particular instance. IE does appear to be an effective program in its own right; however, the classroom atmosphere encouraged by independent LOGO explorations may not be compatible with the more teacher-centered approach of the IE program and its discussions for cognitive insight. In addition, the once-a-week IE intervention may not have been sufficient to produce an accumulative effect. Finally, the apparent success of this LOGO program should encourage the search for other alternative learning approaches for students who are not successful in traditional settings.

References

Dietz, C., & Williams, C. (1981). Teaching mathematics to the hearing-impaired. In V. Glennon (Ed.), *Teaching mathematics to exceptional children and youth* (pp. 321–358). Reston, VA: National Council of Teachers of Mathematics.

Feuerstein, R. (1980). *Instrumental enrichment: An intervention program for cognitive modifiability.* Baltimore: University Park Press.

Hiskey, M. (1966). *Hiskey-Nebraska test of learning aptitude.* Lincoln, NE: Union College Press.

Papert, S. (1980). *Mindstorms: Children, computers, and powerful ideas.* New York: Basic Books.

Raven, J. C. (1958). *Standard progessive matrices.* London: H. K. Lewis.

Woodcock, K. W. (1973). *Woodcock reading mastery tests.* Circle Pines, MN: American Guidance Services.

LOGO Instruction for Low-Achieving Elementary-Age Hearing-Impaired Children

Pamela Luft

In a preliminary project involving the LOGO computer language in a tutorial setting, three students from the Kendall Demonstration Elementary School (Washington, D.C.) joined a class of secondary-level students. The purpose was to provide all students with a positive math experience and to uncover possible abilities that had been unused in standard academic classes.

All participants were low-achieving hearing-impaired students. The Kendall students had mild to moderate additional handicaps in the academic, social-emotional, and/or physical areas. The secondary students had failed two previous math courses.

The students worked in pairs. Each pair met on five to seven occasions. The Kendall teacher introduced her students to ZOOM (a simplitied form of LOGO). The secondary students who were familiar with LOGO tutored the elementary students in further applications and also introduced ZOOM.

Several activities were employed during the project.

1. Students or the teacher gave LOGO commands to another student to proceed through, step by step.

2. Transparencies of objects (houses, cars) and of maps provided formats to trace onto transparencies stuck to the screen.

3. A secondary student hid his or her eyes while a Kendall student drew the object on the screen; the group had to guess the object.

Observations of Kendall students provided useful information regarding overall school performance. The results of this experience can be reported as follows:

1. Low-achieving elementary students were poor at goal setting and had few previous experiences in self-directed activities.

2. Individual learning styles were illuminated by the LOGO experience. New insights into risk taking, achievement motivation, frustration-tolerance, and perfectionism were useful in other academic classes.

3. Higher expectations of student maturity and the social skills of Kendall students were coupled with higher motivation and the prestige of visiting the high school.

This instructional experience was beneficial for all participants, including the teachers. Future projects are now planned that will focus on measuring change, on determining how learning-adaptation relates to academic progress, and on standardizing the tutorial content of these experiences.

Philosophical Inquiry Among Hearing-Impaired Students

Ron B. Rembert

In November 1981, the Regional Day School for the Deaf in Fort Worth, Texas, provided the setting for the first of several philosophical discussions among hearing-impaired students. These discussions, which stretched over a 2-year period, arose initially from the reading and interpretation of a philosophical novel for children, *Harry Stottlemeier's Discovery* (Lipman, 1974), a book that challenges students to develop and use certain thinking skills. The development and use of various thinking skills was the primary objective of the efforts to launch a Philosophy for Children program at the Regional Day School for the Deaf. This report highlights the problems and prospects of (a) implementing the program, (b) practicing the program, (c) extending the program, and (d) evaluating the program.

The Philosophy for Children program created by Matthew Lipman of the Institute for the Advancement of Philosophy for Children (IAPC) at Montclair State College in New Jersey set the stage for the project. Lipman established the IAPC in 1972 to promote the development of thinking skills through philosophical discussion among students in grades 3–10. The classroom discussions emerge from reading and studying philosophical novels for children in which the characters discover the power of logic and the benefits of thinking analytically. The benefits become most apparent when the students accept the challenge to *think about thinking*—the metacognitive goal underlying the entire program.

In implementing the program with hearing-impaired children, this author's greatest difficulty was in preparing for discussion sessions rather than mere question-and-answer activities. The distinction between these two types of activities rests upon the different set of expectations defining each activity. For example, the teacher of the experimental group established the expectation that the emphasis during discussions would be placed on the exploration of complex concepts such as thinking, dreaming, hoping, and imagining, rather than on the regurgitation of simple definitions of these terms. In addition, the teacher established the expectation that each student act as a participant who follows the line of questioning required in exploring complex concepts, not as a competitor who strives only for personal success or achievement.

The six hearing-impaired students in the experimental group embraced these expectations but faced some problems in satisfying them. Strategies for helping the students overcome such problems included (a) using a spe-

Special thanks to Mr. William Moffatt, principal at the Regional Day School for the Deaf (Fort Worth, Texas), and Mrs. Rose Marie Schweitzer and Mrs. Jane Braswell, two teachers at that school, for their help and their encouragement in launching the Philosophy for Children program.

The complete version of this paper is available in microfiche or hard copy from ERIC Document Reproduction Service. Ask for Document No. ED 247 724.

cial set of exercises on ambiguity to help students anticipate the range of meanings of complex concepts, (b) devoting entire discussions to a single philosophical question whose final answer never emerges, and (c) building ideas upon the ideas of previous students in an effort to draw all students into the inquiry.

In practicing the program, the students met for two 45-minute sessions each week throughout one school year. Thinking-skill exercises focusing upon issues of ambiguity, immediate inferences, cause-and-effect reasoning, the drawing of distinctions, inductive reasoning, or conceptual analysis established the agenda for the discussions. However, many philosophical issues for which no exercises had been planned surfaced spontaneously during the sessions. Whether prepared before the class or generated during it, the exercises stemmed from those contained in Lipman, Sharp, and Oscanyan's *Philosophical Inquiry: An Instructional Manual to Accompany Harry Stottlemeier's Discovery* (1979).

An attempt was made to extend the Philosophy for Children program to the general curriculum. The goal was to make conceptual analysis and inductive reasoning into integral parts of the school program. Thinking-skill exercises were adapted to be used with a social studies text, *The United States and Its Neighbors* (Helmus, Arnsdorf, Toppin, & Pounds, 1982). The exercises focused attention upon certain logical confusions embedded in the discussions about world exploration in general and the discoveries of the Vikings in particular. This phase of the program proved successful.

In evaluating the program, students were asked to complete an Analytic Thinking Questionnaire created by Dr. Ron Reed (1979), director of the Analytic Thinking Program at Texas Wesleyan College. The majority of students in the experimental group at the Regional Day School for the Deaf reported the following changes as a result of the program:

1. They learned to express themselves more clearly.

2. They found their reading in traditional subject areas to be more meaningful.

3. They understood their teacher better than they did before participating in the program.

4. They were better able to accept the feelings of others.

The teachers noted that the development and use of thinking skills through the Philosophy for Children program had strengthened the analytic skills of the students in other subject areas. In addition, the teachers recognized greater patience and endurance on the part of the students in sustaining philosophical inquiry over the 2-year period.

Several implications for students, teachers, and the curriculum arise from these experiences in implementing the Philosophy for Children program at the Regional Day School for the Deaf. For the students, the Philosophy for Children program raises questions that lie at the heart of their education: What is a discussion? What roles must be adopted by the participants in a discussion? What attitudes must they exhibit? What skills must they demonstrate? Another implication for instruction is the advantage of this special set of language experiences, especially those involving ambiguity. But the most important implication for students rests in the challenge provoked by the Philosophy for Children program to think about thinking. The Philosophy for Children program encourages students to think about thinking in all subject areas.

For teachers, the Philosophy for Children program promotes the acquisition of those thinking skills required to be an inquiring teacher, one who initiates inquiry. These skills include the effort to raise questions about logical matters, to uncover assumptions in the text and in discussions, and to analyze the meaning of important concepts. Finally, the Philosophy for Children program has the potential to bridge subject areas in the typical school curriculum by identifying and labeling the basic set of skills required for study in each subject area. To the extent that such bridging occurs, hearing-impaired students and teachers will appreciate an integrated educational experience that is grounded in the effort to think about thinking.

References

Helmus, T., Arnsdorf, V., Toppin, E., & Pounds, N. (1982). *The United States and its neighbors* (The World and Its People Series). Morristown, NJ: Silver Burdett.

Lipman, M. (1974). *Harry Stottlemeier's discovery.* (Target grades: 5–6). Upper Montclair, NJ: Institute for the Advancement of Philosophy for Children.

Lipman, M., Sharp, A., & Oscanyan, F. (1979). *Philosophical inquiry: An instructional manual to accompany Harry Stottlemeier's discovery.* Upper Montclair, NJ: Institute for the Advancement of Philosophy for Children.

Reed, R. (1979). *Analytic thinking questionnaire.* Unpublished manuscript.

Additional Reading

Lipman, M. (1976). *Lisa.* (Target grades: 7–9). Upper Montclair, NJ: Institute for the Advancement of Philosophy for Children.

Lipman, M. (1978). *Suki.* (Target grades: 8–10). Upper Montclair, NJ: Institute for the Advancement of Philosophy for Children.

Lipman, M. (1980a). *Mark.* (Target grades 8–10). Upper Montclair, NJ: Institute for the Advancement of Philosophy for Children.

Lipman, M. (1980b). *Social inquiry: An instructional manual to accompany Mark.* Upper Montclair, NJ: Institute for the Advancement of Philosophy for Children.

Lipman, M. (1980c). *Writing, how and why: An instructional manual to accompany Suki.* Upper Montclair, NJ: Institute for the Advancement of Philosophy for Children.

Lipman, M. (1981). *Pixie.* (Target grade: 4). Upper Montclair, NJ: Institute for the Advancement of Philosophy for Children.

Lipman, M. (1983). *Kio and Gus.* (Target grade: 4). Upper Montclair, NJ: Institute for the Advancement of Philosophy for Children.

Lipman, M., & Sharp, A. (1977). *Ethical inquiry: An instructional manual to accompany Lisa.* Upper Montclair, NJ: Institute for the Advancement of Philosophy for Children.

Lipman, M., & Sharp, A. (1982). *Looking for meaning: An instructional manual to accompany Pixie.* Upper Montclair, NJ: Institute for the Advancement of Philosophy for Children.

Lipman, M., Sharp, A., & Oscanyan, F. (1980). *Philosophy in the classroom.* Philadelphia: Temple University Press.

Sternberg, R. J. (1979, March). The nature of mental abilities. *American Psychologist,* 214–230.

Pegasus Project for the Hearing Impaired

Jane M. Krahe

During the past 10 years, the trend in schools and programs for the hearing impaired has been toward increased use of manual communication in general and manual English codes in particular. This trend, coupled with the increase in preschool and parent-education programs, has resulted in an increasing number of hearing-impaired students with English skills that are equal to those of hearing children. Many of these students are in day schools, day classes, or mainstreamed programs; consequently, they have had limited contact with other hearing-impaired students with similar English skills. In addition, there are not many programs for gifted hearing-impaired children.

In an attempt to address this problem, exploratory discussions were begun with Lorraine Bostick and Laura Katz, directors of Pegasus programs for gifted hearing students, located in Orange County, California, at the University of California, Irvine (UCI), campus. This program sponsors a variety of classes to provide stimulating and challenging opportunities to high-ability students who are eager to explore subjects on an in-depth or fast-paced level. The program also provides a supportive environment for academic and social interaction for students from preschool through high school.

The Pegasus staff was quite interested in expanding their programs to include hearing-impaired students. An experimental program was set up during the summer of 1983 to include hearing-impaired students in Pegasus's Project Explore! UCI, which serves students entering the sixth, seventh, and eighth grades. Project Explore! was selected because it is an academic and cultural enrichment program with courses designed to stimulate complex thinking and problem-solving behaviors in high-achieving, gifted, motivated, or capable under-achieving students. This program seemed to meet the identified needs of an unserved segment of the hearing-impaired population.

Program Implementation

Pegasus Project for the Hearing Impaired (PPHI) began in the fall of 1983. The program was offered to all incoming sixth through ninth grade hearing-impaired students who could demonstrate evidence of reading at grade level as measured by a standardized achievement test. Interested students also had to submit a letter of recommendation from authorized school personnel familiar with their school functioning ability.

The complete version of this paper is available in microfiche or hard copy from ERIC Document Reproduction Service. Ask for Document No. ED 247 728.

Nine students met the criteria and were enrolled in Pegasus Project for the Hearing Impaired. Seven of the students used total communication and two students used an oral/aural-only approach to communication. The students ranged in age from 11 to 15 years. Sixty-three hearing students entering grades 6 to 8 participated in Project Explore!

The staff serving PPHI included a Pegasus program director, a site administrator/teacher for PPHI, a sign language teacher, 11 of the regular Pegasus teachers who had students mainstreamed in their courses, and 5 full-/part-time sign language interpreters.

Program Description

Each of the 63 hearing students selected six courses of about 1½ hours in length. Courses offered included computer programming, literature, fine arts, physical and biological sciences, math enrichment, and sign language. The hearing-impaired students selected four courses from the same offerings and all enrolled in a special class—Issues for the Hearing Impaired—that met daily. This course gave hearing-impaired students an opportunity to explore deaf history, consider traits of productive deaf adults, and consider other relevant issues in the field of hearing impairment. All students were free to select those courses they desired, and interpreters were provided as needed. The sign language class and the issues class met at the same time and joined together for the last 15 minutes of each period to provide one-to-one interaction between hearing-impaired and hearing students.

The day began with a 25-minute group session for all Project Explore! students and staff. A variety of involvement activities focused on bringing the group together and preparing them for the demands of their courses. These activities included exercise, stress and relaxation techniques, mind bogglers/teasers, and student sharing of various courses and activities. Two sessions were used to explain deafness to the hearing students, to have hearing-impaired student volunteers share their backgrounds and feelings about being hearing impaired, and to answer questions from hearing students. The sign language class also did an end-of-course presentation demonstrating their manual communication skills.

Following morning exercises, students attended their first classes, had a short nutrition break, attended their second and third classes, and then had lunch. During lunchtime, students were free to use the UCI snack bars and food machines at a variety of locations on campus as long as they followed the rule of staying in pairs at all times. This time was used voluntarily for the sign language class, the issues class, and any other interested students to increase their interactive communication. Students could also use the library facilities, and those students in computer programming could use the time on computers in the lab. Following lunch, students attended their afternoon classes and then met at a designated location for transportation home.

A final end-of-session party for the issues class and the sign language class proved to be a truly integrated social experience.

Discussion

The consensus of directors, staff, students, and parents was that PPHI was a highly successful project. This assessment was noted in questionnaires, observations, and comments by persons working with and observing the program. Interaction and acceptance among the students was very good, with both hearing-impaired and hearing students reaching out to each other. Hearing-impaired students easily followed the interpreters in classes and morning activities, and they participated equally with the hearing students.

Only one of the Pegasus staff had had previous experience with hearing-impaired students in a mainstreaming situation; however, the other teachers were openly involved in a preparatory staff inservice training. In addition, a PPHI site administrator gave a staff, parent, and student inservice workshop on deafness. Other information was provided on a one-to-one basis as needed throughout the 3½-week session.

The PPHI students rated almost all classes good, with the high-level involvement courses like computer programming, chemistry, mime, architectural drawing, and the deaf issues class receiving the highest ratings. Students felt challenged by the level of questioning utilized in courses and by the problem-solving activities and projects presented.

The greatest weakness demonstrated by the PPHI students was in the area of written language. Although their English-language abilities enabled them to adequately follow and participate in fast-paced instruction and verbal discussions, reports and papers showed a continued need to emphasize written language skills. It is anticipated that this area will become a core part of the deaf issues class in the future.

Summary

Pegasus Project for the Hearing Impaired, as a component of the Pegasus Project Explore! UCI, demonstrated that high-ability hearing-impaired students can successfully function with and benefit from the type of curriculum and teaching strategies used with high-ability hearing students. The intelligence of these students, their high level of cognitive engagement with material, and their creativity, in combination with developed language skills, represent a unique capability in a small segment of the hearing-impaired population. This ability can best be challenged by people trained to work with gifted individuals together with those knowledgeable about hearing impairment.

The Use of Visual Aids by Interpreters: A Cognitive Model for Mainstreamed Education

Manjula B. Waldron
Thomas J. Diebold

Public Law 94-142 has effected change in the public schools by placing more hearing-impaired students than in the past into mainstreamed settings with interpreter services. This increased number of mainstreamed students includes many with limited English-language skills. These students may experience difficulties with new concepts and subject matter because of a language barrier. To overcome the language barrier, new strategies must be developed that may change the roles and responsibilities of both the classroom teacher and the classroom interpreter to meet the needs of their students.

The traditional classroom interpreter has been trained to assume that the information signed to the deaf student can be assimilated as efficiently as hearing students assimilate auditory information. This assumption is not always valid because the novelty or complexity of the information to be acquired affects that assimilation. This assumption has often led to the conclusion that if the student fails to assimilate the information, then he or she is not ready for mainstreaming. In this paper an alternative strategy for overcoming the language barrier in a mainstreamed environment is explored: the supplemental use of visual aids by the classroom interpreter.

The Need for a Permanent Record and Spatial Presentations

Wilson (1981) found that reexposure was one critical factor for learning new concepts among deaf students. With new or difficult concepts the student often needs a permanent record of the presentation; a signed interpretation cannot provide that record. Currently, notetakers in the classroom do provide a permanent record to the deaf student; however, the information is not available until the end of the day, it does not contain planned graphics, and it is limited to the notetaker's own understanding of the information.

The spatial properties of graphic visual aids are a second critical factor for efficient presentation of information to deaf students. Reynolds and Booher (1980) and Waldron and Rose (1983) found that deaf students use a visual/spatial symbolic presentation utilized by hearing students. Materials that are largely pictorial with some verbal labeling were found to be useful.

The Use of Visual Graphics

The premise for the of visual graphics is that if the deaf student has demonstrated a conceptual understanding of the content area, then it is possible to deliver the information in a form that the student will understand and remember.

The proposed use of graphics expands the interpreter's available modes of communication to include the use of visual/pictorial representations as a supplement to simultaneous speech and sign language (see Figure 1).

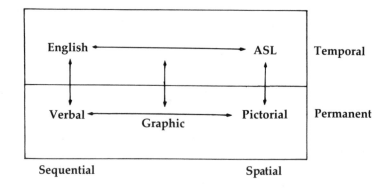

Figure 1. Interpreters' use of visual graphics together with temporal interpretation.

Permanent information supplements temporal or passing information while capitalizing on the spatially oriented processing strengths of hearing-impaired students. Currently the interpreter in the classroom moves back and forth along the sign language continuum (English↔ASL), depending on the situation and complexity of the information. In the proposed model, the interpreter additionally moves along the visual-aids continuum, using a pemanent graphic product to supplement the sign language interpretation. The visual aids range from completely verbal/sequential materials (printed text) to completely spatial/pictorial materials (word-free diagrams) (Wileman, 1980).

New Tasks for the Educational Interpreter

Insofar as possible, the interpreter and the teacher should review the material to be taught in advance, assess the deaf student's prior understanding of the topic, and then develop an appropriate visual aid to supplement the signed interpretation. A prior knowledge and understanding of the material to be presented is therefore required for the interpreter. Cain (1981) has noted the importance of this condition for mainstreamed college students. The persons adapting the material into a graphic form must be skilled in conveying conceptual meanings through signs, graphics, words, or any other medium available to the student, because frequently an impromptu explanation may be necessary. An example of a visual aid used by a teacher-interpreter team follows.

Sample Presentation Using Visual Aids

Situation.   Seventh-grade students were directed to answer the questions printed at the end of a 12-page short story in their literature book. The deaf student had difficulty with one section of the questions labeled *Point of View:* How did each of these characters react when the raccoon returned to the woods? (Characters in the story were listed.) Unlike his hearing classmates, the deaf student did not understand the idiom, *point of view*. The student told his interpreter that he understood the story but did not know how to respond to this particular section of the questions.

Traditional model.   The interpreter directed the student to ask the teacher for help. The interpreter accompanied the student to the teacher's desk and interpreted the teacher's response to the student. The teacher asked the students what their point of view was, how they felt about the situation, or what their opinion was of what happened. The deaf student was still unsure of what the question was asking.

Proposed model.   The interpreter drew and labeled a diagram to illustrate the concept *point of view* (see Figure 2). The diagram pictured two people looking at a scoreboard; one man wore an OSU sweatshirt and was smiling, while the other man wore an MSU sweatshirt and was frowning. The scoreboard was labeled *situation*. A dotted line extended from each man's eye to the scoreboard, and both lines were labeled *point of view*. The interpreter asked the student how each person felt about the score. After the student responded "happy" and "sad," the interpreter then printed the phrase "felt = point of view." The interpreter then asked why each person had a sad or happy point of view about the situation.

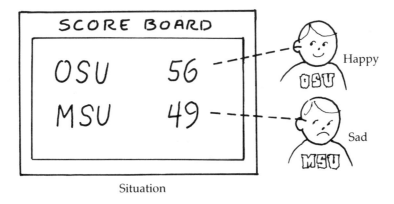

Situation

Figure 2. A visual presentation of the concept *point of view.*

After the deaf student correctly answered the question, the interpreter drew a picture of the raccoon walking towards the woods and labeled it *situation* (see Figure 3). The interpreter drew faces looking at the situation, with the dotted lines labeled *point of view* extending from each face. The interpreter labeled each one of the faces as characters from the story. At that point the student made the visual association with the concept and correctly answered the question. The student then had a pictorial copy to reaccess the phrase *point of view* until he learned it.

Situation

Figure 3. A visual aid to help students answer story-related questions.

Implications of Using Visual Aids

The supplemental use of visual aids by the educational interpreter raises several issues that must now be addressed. These issues include coordination, training, reimbursement, workload, staffing, budgeting, and monitoring. Further research on and application of visual thinking and graphic communication for the deaf must also be explored to integrate the disciplines of psychology, graphic design, art, and education.

The ideas presented here derive from actual classroom situations with a sound theoretical basis. No claim is yet made for validation of these techniques through research; rather, the supportive evidence is anecdotal and should be viewed as such. However, the potential of this model to help hearing-impaired students improve comprehension and succeed in the mainstreamed setting warrants serious further study. This concept also has possible applications to some nonhandicapped students as well as to special students with limited language skills.

References

Cain, B. E. (1981, May). Teaching chemistry to the hearing-impaired. *Journal of College Science Teaching, 10,* 364–366.

Reynolds, H. N., & Booher, H. R. (1980). The effects of pictorial and verbal instructional materials on the operational performance of deaf subjects. *Journal of Special Education, 14*, 175–187.

Waldron, M. B., & Rose, S. (1983, May). Visual thinking for severe language handicapped children through the use of computer graphics. *Journal of Computer Based Instruction, 9*, 206–210.

Wileman, R. E. (1980). *Exercises in visual thinking.* New York: Hastings House.

Wilson, J. J. (1981, September). Notetaking: A necessary support for the hearing-impaired student. *Teaching Exceptional Children, 14*, 38–40.

Analysis

Philip S. Saif

Overview

The research studies and program descriptions represented in part 9 may be categorized according to the age group of their target audience, the instructional approaches used, and the nature of the data analyses.

The study using the Philosophy for Children program (Rembert) targeted the age group of 7- to 12-year-olds, used a philosophical or Socratic approach to teaching, and carried out descriptive analyses of results. The Instrumental Enrichment program used in the Jonas and Martin study at the Model Secondary School for the Deaf targeted the age group of 15 and older, used an activity-based and discussion-based approach, and carried out statistical analyses of data. The Instrumental Enrichment intervention used in the Martin study with the Gallaudet College group targeted the age group of above-20 years old, also used an activity-based and discussion-based approach, and used both descriptive and statistical analyses of data.

Rohr-Redding's Instrumental Enrichment description used a comparative approach, as did Dietz's study using the LOGO computer intervention. In both cases, students using the intervention were compared to students with whom these teachers had previously worked and who did *not* have that intervention. The Krahe outline of the Pegasus project used descriptive approaches and a summary of test data, while the Waldron and Diebold description of the mainstreaming project used mainly observation as an approach. All of these latter four papers centered on the secondary school population.

Specific Analyses

In the Rembert study, the author wished to replicate an approach that had previously been carried out with hearing students using Lipman's Philosophy for Children program; Lipman's analysis of his own program represents an expansion of John Dewey's original five steps of "how we think." Rembert reported no significant differences at the implementation level; however, no detail is given as to how he came to that conclusion other than the statement of pre- and posttest results. Apparently, a test developed by Shipman and Lipman was the criterion. The study could have profited from examining how deaf students have difficulty with linguistic idioms—a possible critical prerequisite in a Socratic context.

The Jonas and Martin study was basically sound; it should be continued in view of the results obtained and to study these subjects for 2 additional years to determine which tests truly differentiate experimental from control subjects. Their design was also appropriate, although the nature of a residential school and the resulting ease of communication between experimental students may have contaminated some of the results. In regard to the observation data from experimental group teachers, we see some lack of agreement between their observations and the achievement test results with students. It is possible that the teachers' enthusiasm may have caused them to partially overlook some student errors or that the measures used were not entirely appropriate to the task. Again, as in the Rembert study, the teaching of linguistic idioms proved to be a necessary prerequisite to student achievement and should be examined further.

The Martin study focused on the college-age population but, unfortunately, used a larger number for the experimental group than the control group. The attempt to transfer the Instrumental Enrichment program used in the study with high school students to a college-age population may be questioned in that this college population results from a more selective school admissions policy than does the high school group. Perhaps a comparison between the two groups and their results using the Instrumental Enrichment program is best left unmentioned since their comparability may be questioned.

The related program description of Instrumental Enrichment by Rohr-Redding makes very clear that teacher enthusiasm about the Instrumental Enrichment program and its implementation is a critical variable. By reading this description together with the studies by Jonas and Martin, and Martin, one finds some differences in the description of the actual intervention and in the methodology of assessing student results. However, the Rohr-Redding paper is basically supportive of the two other studies related to it.

The Dietz study of the effects of the computer program LOGO is exciting, and if it could now add supportive data through empirical procedures, it would be indeed excellent. Some clarification would be helpful in regard to whether this intervention was done through the acquisition of new skills or also through some behavior modification techniques.

The Krahe description of Project Pegasus provides a brief view of an excellent program for challenging the gifted hearing-impaired student. The description itself is concise and provides an attractive programming alternative for such students at the secondary level.

The Waldron and Diebold description on the mainstreaming program is based on an excellent concept. Clarification of this model would be obtainable through observation of the program in action.

Generalizations

These papers and the lively discussions of them that occurred at the symposium prove that high interest in these topics exists in our field at this time.

All seven papers could perhaps be relabeled under the category of "Pilot Studies in Cognitive Education of the Deaf," in that they are all rather small-scale investigations that could profit from extension and replication.

Recommendations

Several recommendations are implied by these descriptions and studies, and these may be useful to future investigators in the area of active intervention in the cognitive processing of hearing-impaired students. These recommendations consist of the following:

1. Longitudinal studies of the effects of cognitive intervention programs are now a necessity. The nature of intervention programs in the instructional context is that short-term effects may be seen quickly, but we must know if those effects are only an artifact of the setting or are truly the result of changing the cognitive processing of these subjects. By the same token, sometimes effects are not immediately seen; yet, it would be erroneous to conclude that no effect has resulted since long-term intervention is sometimes necessary for changing lifelong cognitive habits. Longitudinal studies could also confirm whether delayed effects of a positive or negative nature are outcomes of such intervention attempts.

2. It is important to articulate the ideology and the theoretical rationale with which any intervention is identified. Most of these programs stress skills per se, but more detail is needed as to what purposes these skills serve in the respective interventions. Future investigations should provide sufficient detail on this aspect of rationale for classroom interventions.

3. The relationship between these skills and academic knowledge must also be strengthened in any description or analysis of intervention attempts. For example, the analyses of the Instrumental Enrichment program refer to the bridging act by which the teacher actively promotes application of cognitive skills to academic subject matter. All such interventions should follow that procedure explicitly.

4. Further attention is also needed to the entire area of application of these programs, specifically in respect to:

   a. identification of the students' styles of thinking as a help to the classroom teacher in planning instruction.

   b. stimulation of students to think at one (or more) levels beyond their present levels of thinking.

   c. the importance of disagreement in student answers to teacher questions; such disagreement can give important insight into students' cognitive functioning.

d. the power of such intervention programs to stimulate meta-cognitive awareness in students.

In sum, these efforts at classroom-level interventions in cognitive performance of hearing-impaired learners are laudable; they are examples of active work by professionals who have taken the responsibility to try to change and improve the generic cognitive functioning of students. The degree to which other active professionals fully understand cognitive processes and the concepts of these papers will now directly affect our future successes in helping hearing-impaired learners of all ages to reach their full potential.

Related Educational and Research Issues

1. In attempts to improve the level of cognitive performance of hearing-impaired learners in the classroom, what provisions should be made for individual differences?

2. To what extent is the improvement of cognitive performance dependent on the increase of linguistic ability?

3. To what extent should school programs to improve cognitive performance be embedded in subject-matter context, and to what extent should they be taught in a content-free manner?

4. How should teachers be retrained so as to enable them to induce cognitive improvement in hearing-impaired learners?

5. What types of diagnostic information would be most useful to teachers in planning programs of cognitive improvement?

6. What classroom instructional strategies are most appropriate for young as opposed to older hearing-impaired children in cognitive improvement programs?

7. To what extent can regular writing activities result in an enhancement of the cognitive performance of hearing-impaired learners?

8. What cognitive factors affect writing competence in hearing-impaired learners?

9. How, if at all, would or should intervention strategies by the teacher be adapted according to the language preference of the students (ASL, PSE, English)?

10 A Synthesis: Cognition, Education, and Deafness

A Macroanalysis of the Research on Deafness and Cognition

Steve Wolk

In analyzing the research on deafness and cognition, certain terms must first be defined. For the purposes of this paper, the most important term to define is cognition. Neisser succinctly defined cognition as "the activity of knowing: the acquisition, organization, and use of knowledge" (1976, p. 1). According to Anderson, "Cognitive psychology is dominated by the *information processing approach*, which analyzes cognitive processes into a sequence of ordered stages. Each stage reflects an important step in the processing of information" (1980, p. 31). Anderson (1975) also made a useful and meaningful distinction between the *representational* and *executive* levels of the cognitive system. There is little doubt that the current cognitive perspective represents the most prominent approach to the study of learning and thinking among psychologists and educators. Professionals who are involved in the education of deaf students and the study of deafness can ill afford to neglect this perspective.

The contents of this volume and a representative review of the published literature (Austin, 1975; Belmont, Karchmer, & Pilkonis, 1976; Liben, Nowell, & Posnansky, 1978; McCabe & Pehrsson, 1980; Ottem, 1980; Quigley & Kretschmer, 1982; Somers, 1977) reveal that researchers today are pursuing a variety of questions related to the cognitive processes of deaf children and adults. However, this overall research effort and the related accumulation of knowledge appear to suffer from two major weaknesses common to most academic research in the social sciences: (a) the absence of a guiding and consistent theoretical or conceptual orientation underlying the research question or questions across research studies and (b) the inconsistent and often confusing use of divergent research methodologies and related operational definitions. The purpose of this paper is to review these weaknesses and to suggest an overall approach to the study of cognition and deafness that is more efficient and effective.

The Conceptual Distinction Between Representational and Executive Processing

A common and useful distinction drawn by cognitive theorists is the one between *representational* and *executive* levels of processing (Anderson, B. F., 1975; Gagné, 1977). This conceptual distinction is significant because it highlights two major capabilities of the cognitive system: the ability to *re-present* information extracted from the environment and the ability to *execute* often complex manipulations of this abstracted knowledge. B. F. Anderson and Gagné both have argued that this latter ability also implies that the executive system maintains an awareness of and an intentionality for action.

The distinction between representational and executive processes is highly useful to the study of cognition since it often helps to differentiate processes that are responsible for the acquisition of knowledge (e.g., perception or memory storage) from processes that are responsible for the manipulation and use of knowledge (e.g., memory retrieval, language comprehension, or problem solving). If this distinction is valid, then it should reinforce among researchers the need to identify what type of process (representational or executive) is being analyzed within the cognitive system. Clearly, different external and internal influences may be critical to each level of processing, and both experimental and naturalistic research designs must identify the level of analysis and explanation being applied to the study of cognition.

These comments should not be taken to imply that the representational and executive systems are discrete and noninteractive. B. F. Anderson (1975), J. R. Anderson (1980), and other theorists assume that most actions, behaviors, and important academic responses (e.g., recall of past knowledge for a test situation, reading comprehension, or mathematics computation) involve complex interactions between the representational and executive systems or levels of processing.

It is clear from a review of the papers in this volume, as well as from a review of a representative selection of published research studies, that researchers in deafness have not recognized this basic distinction to a significant degree in their research questions. They also have not initiated their design of research studies with this conceptualization of the cognitive system in mind. Although Quigley and Kretschmer (1982) acknowledge that some research in deafness has been guided by an information-processing model of learning, nonetheless this conceptualization, as well as the important distinctions noted previously, do not characterize the majority of research studies in the field. Parenthetically, it is not always clear that researchers have distinguished the study of what is being acquired or represented (cognitive structure) from the activity responsible for the acquisition of this structure (cognitive process). For example, the study of human memory can focus upon what is stored (e.g., propositional networks or iconic traces), or it can focus upon how such structures are established and subsequently utilized (e.g., elaboration or cued retrieval).

Most important, however, is the fact that a useful and basic distinction between representational and executive cognitive processing is not reflected in the current body of research literature on deafness and cognition. Equally important, that research which does exist tends to focus heavily upon representational processes.

A major exception to the emphasis on representational processes is the collection of studies that have examined deaf subjects' performance on

Piagetian tasks (Dolman, 1983; Furth, 1964; Murphy-Berman, Witters, & Harding, 1984; Rittenhouse, Morreau, & Iran-Nejad, 1981; Rittenhouse & Spiro, 1979; Witters-Churchill, Kelly, & Witters, 1983). The predominant types of analysis reflected in these studies are either a comparison of deaf/hearing performance-level differences or an examination of task/procedural factors (e.g., mode or type of instructions given to subjects) that appear to critically influence deaf subjects' performance. More will be said later about this latter type of Piagetian study and its significance for the study of cognition and deafness.

The general collection of research literature, which has largely employed conservation tasks that are assumed to require strong logical reasoning skills for successful performance, has not systematically analyzed the thinking (executive) and reasoning processes of deaf subjects to any significant degree. Ironically, the classic clinical methodology of Piagetian research (Ginsburg & Opper, 1969), which is most suitable for characterizing an individual's thinking processes, has been forsaken in these studies for the statistical analysis of group central tendencies in performance on a restricted range of Piagetian-type tasks. Thus, the researchers who have selected Piagetian tasks for study in order to characterize the cognitive skills of deaf subjects have failed to take full advantage of the complexities of such tasks in order to analyze the levels of processing underlying successful or unsuccessful task performance.

To some extent, this convergence of study on basic representational activity seems reasonable, given that (a) many deaf subjects are distinguishable for their perceptual handicap and (b) perception and short-term memory for perceptually extracted information are critical representational processes. Thus, if we exclude the plethora of research concerning language acquisition and the applied areas of reading and writing achievement, much of the cognitively oriented research has focused upon the representational processes of perception and memory.

Studies of discrimination learning, simple associative learning, and coding of information during short-term memory processing have been well represented in the research literature (Ottem, 1980). These studies have certainly contributed to a clarification of the manner in which deaf individuals represent information early in the cognitive processing of information. The findings often are consistent with professional intuition: The limited language experiences of the deaf child influence the manner in which information is encoded through perception and short-term memory. Verbal information is often processed more effectively along visual and spatial dimensions (O'Connor & Hermelin, 1976; Wallace & Corballis, 1973); however, some studies have suggested that deafness does not always preclude processing along auditory and temporal dimensions (Beck, Beck, & Gironella, 1977; Belmont, Karchmer, & Pilkonis, 1976).

Disparate Research Methods

This brief examination of the findings on short-term memory processing of verbal information by deaf subjects introduces a second major weakness of much of the research in cognition and deafness: Studies often reflect very disparate methods and stimulus materials, which leads to a significant difficulty in drawing generalizations from the literature. At this time a meta-analysis of the research literature in deafness and cognition would lead to highly ambiguous results (Kavale, 1984).

An equally disturbing methodological weakness within the literature on such important representational processes as short-term memory encoding is the apparently casual manner with which deaf subjects are sometimes selected for study. The degree or severity of hearing loss and the type of educational and communication background that subjects bring to an experiment can have critical influences upon cognitive processing (Conrad, 1979; Wolk & Allen, 1984). However, these factors are often not adequately considered or systematically studied. Thus, the interpretation of the results of such research is often clouded by the influences that subject characteristics have played in the cognitive processing of both the stimulus materials and the information conveyed in the task directions and procedures. Unlike sample characteristics in the general cognitive-research literature, degree of deafness and type of educational and communication training are not only strata along which a general population can be defined, but also may be critically intrinsic to the dependent variable itself (i.e., cognitive structuring and processing).

Recommendations

Two recommendations follow from the preceding analysis. First, researchers in deafness and cognition must address the distinction between representational and executive cognitive processing. Belmont, Karchmer, and Pilkonis (1976), Rittenhouse and Spiro (1979) and Liben (1984) have all found that strategy guidance or training makes a significant difference in the performance levels of deaf students. However, in these studies the strategy guidance or training given to deaf subjects is often treated as more of a methodological procedure than a conceptual issue. The focus within these studies is still on the representational process of the deaf subject rather than the deaf subject's ability to develop and use an appropriate strategy for processing information. This point is particularly critical in the case of the research of Rittenhouse and Spiro (1979) and Rittenhouse, Morreau, and Iran-Nejad (1981).

Researchers in this field have used Piagetian conservation tasks and attribute-specific training to help deaf students conserve. This process involves teaching students to focus less upon the perceptual cues of the transformation and more upon the quality to be conserved. Conservation skills should relate to the executive system's ability to develop and use a nonperceptual, conceptual, and logical (identity, reversibility, compensation) strategy for reasoning through to an answer. Recently, Light and Gilmour (1983) have negatively evaluated the modified versions of standard Piagetian tasks, such as conservation, that have been given to hearing subjects. These authors have argued that *correct* conservation responses may not be truly indicative of logical reasoning but may instead represent contextually constrained responses to strong suggestions that are contained within task instructions.

In an effort to help deaf subjects process information effectively, some experiments train deaf subjects in strategies that they either do not appear to possess or fail to apply spontaneously. Other experiments offer strong contextual cues that seriously modify the cognitive requirements of the task. Both kinds of experiments tend to cloud rather than clarify a basic and important theoretical question: What are the critical external and internal conditions that explain a deaf subject's success or failure in developing and applying effective strategies for reasoning, thinking, comprehending, and problem solving? This question is fundamental in regard to the executive system's processing and interpreting of task requirements, as well as to the matching of an appropriate strategy (if available) to the demands placed upon the cognitive system. Both Liben (1984) and Wolk and Schildroth (1984) have addressed this question in their research. The possible answers to this question also appear to be critical to a thorough understanding of the overall processing and structuring characteristics of the deaf subject's cognitive system. More research is needed before the question can be adequately answered.

The second recommendation is a call for a more concerted effort to be made by the community of cognitively oriented researchers studying deafness to replicate and extend research methodologies. Definitions of subjects vis-à-vis major handicapping conditions (degree of deafness, presence of additional cognitively related handicaps) and educational communication background must be clearly specified and systematically studied. This must be done not only for purposes of enhancing the external validity of the research findings but also for analyzing the direct effects such subject variables may have upon both representational and executive processing.

The present era is a very exciting time to be conducting research in deafness. Those researchers who are pursuing questions concerning cognitive development and cognitive processing in the deaf and those educators who will apply the research findings will all benefit from clearer conceptualizations of cognition and more systematic and coherent sampling plans and operational definitions. It is with these standards in mind that I look foward with great excitement to the next International Symposium on Cognition, Education, and Deafness.

References

Anderson, B. F. (1975). *Cognitive pyschology: The study of knowing, learning, and thinking.* New York: Academic Press.

Anderson, J. R. (1980). *Cognitive psychology and its implications.* San Francisco: W. H. Freeman.

Austin, G. F. (1975). Knowledge of selected concepts by an adolescent deaf population. *American Annals of the Deaf, 120,* 360–370.

Beck, K., Beck, C., & Gironella, O. (1977). Rehearsal and recall strategies of deaf and hearing individuals. *American Annals of the Deaf, 122,* 544–552.

Belmont, J. M., Karchmer, M. A., & Pilkonis, P. A. (1976). Instructed rehearsal strategies influence on deaf memory processing. *Journal of Speech and Hearing Research, 19*(1), 37–46.

Conrad, R. (1979). *The deaf schoolchild: Language and cognitive function.* London: Harper & Row.

Dolman, D. (1983). A study of the relationship between syntactic development and concrete operations in deaf children. *American Annals of the Deaf, 128,* 813–819.

Furth, H. G. (1964). Conservation of weight in deaf and hearing children. *Child Development, 35,* 143–150.

Gagné, R. M. (1977). *The conditions of learning* (3rd ed.). New York: Holt, Rinehart & Winston.

Ginsberg, H., & Opper, S. (1969). *Piaget's theory of intellectual development: An introduction.* Englewood Cliffs, NJ: Prentice-Hall.

Kavale, K. A. (1984). Potential advantages of the meta-analysis technique for research in special education. *Journal of Special Education, 18*(1), 61–72.

Liben, L. S. (1984). The development and use of memory strategies by deaf children and adults. In D. S. Martin (Ed.), *International Symposium on Cognition, Education, and Deafness: Working Papers* (Vol. 1, pp. 239–256). Washington, DC: Gallaudet College.

Liben, L. S., Nowell, R. C., & Posnansky, C. J. (1978). Semantic and formational clustering in deaf and hearing subjects' free recall of signs. *Memory and Cognition, 6,* 599–606.

Light, P., & Gilmour, A. (1983). Conservation or conversation? Contextual facilitation of inappropriate conservation judgments. *Journal of Experimental Child Psychology, 36,* 356–363.

McCabe, P., Pehrsson, R. (1980). An examination of causal relationships as perceived and written by normally-hearing and hearing-impaired subjects. *Volta Review, 82,* 221–228.

Murphy-Berman, V., Witters, L., & Harding, R. (1984). Hearing-impaired students' performance on a Piagetian horizontality task. In D. S. Martin (Ed.), *International Symposium on Cognition, Education, and Deafness: Working Papers* (Vol. 1, pp. 34–46). Washington, DC: Gallaudet College.

Neisser, U. (1976). *Cognition and reality: Principles and implications of cognitive psychology.* San Francisco: W. H. Freeman.

O'Connor, N., & Hermelin, B. (1976). Backward and forward recall by deaf and hearing children. *Quarterly Journal of Experimental Psychology, 28,* 83–92.

Ottem, E. (1980). An analysis of cognitive studies. *American Annals of the Deaf, 125,* 564–575.

Quigley, S., & Kretschmer, R. (1982). *The education of deaf children: Issues, theory, and practices.* Baltimore: University Park Press.

Rittenhouse, R. K., Morreau, L. E., & Iran-Nejad, A. (1981). Metaphor and conservation in deaf and hard-of-hearing children. *American Annals of the Deaf, 126,* 450–453.

Rittenhouse, R. K., & Spiro, R. J. (1979). Conservation performance in day and residential school deaf children. *Volta Review, 81,* 501–509.

Somers, M. (1977). A distinctive features approach to analysis of speech of the deaf. *American Annals of the Deaf, 122,* 470–474.

Wallace, G., & Corballis, M. C. (1973). Short-term memory and coding strategies in the deaf. *Journal of Experimental Psychology, 99,* 334–348.

Witters-Churchill, L. J., Kelly, R. R., & Witters, L. A. (1983). Hearing-impaired students' perception of liquid horizontality: An examination of the effects of gender, development, and training. *Volta Review, 85,* 211–225.

Wolk, S., & Allen, T. E. (1984). A five year follow-up study of reading comprehension achievement in a national sample of hearing-impaired students in
  special education programs. *Journal of Special Education, 18,* 161–176.
Wolk, S., & Schildroth, A. (1984). Consistency of an associational strategy used on
  reading comprehension tests by hearing-impaired students. *Journal of Research in
  Reading, 7,* 135–142.

A Synthesis from Beyond the Field of Deafness

Irving E. Sigel
Richard P. Brinker

The issues and questions raised by the papers in this volume indicate that a strong and viable research effort is being made to come to terms with the many perplexing and complex questions facing investigators who are studying cognition and cognitive development in deaf learners. This research will serve as a basis for developing educational programs that will meet the needs of these children in the coming decades. From our perspective, the goal of the International Symposium on Cognition, Education, and Deafness can be specifically stated as follows: How can deaf students be educated so that they can take their rightful place as autonomous self-directed individuals in both hearing and nonhearing worlds? A related question seems to be implicit in the foregoing: How can these children be educated so that they can bridge the gap between the world of the deaf and the world of the hearing?

As we analyzed all papers, we shaped our discussion to take account of the diversity of interests, research models, and opinions regarding what should and should not be done. As researchers from outside the field of deafness, our perspective is limited to this particular group of papers; we are not so presumptuous as to present ourselves as experts in the field of deaf cognition and education. We come from a background of developmental psychology and mental retardation research, respectively. However, we shall use as our data base the papers written for this volume, as well as the comments made by their authors in the various sessions of the symposium. We have organized our points into six topic areas:

1. Theories and models of cognition and education.

2. Types of studies reported.

3. Epistemological differences among the research designs.

4. Gaps in the research on cognition, education, and deafness.

5. Future research directions that flow out of the discussions.

6. Social-political issues that seem to be implicit and explicit.

Before attending to each of these topics, we would like to address a problem we found with the key concepts that are the focus of this book: cognition and deafness. In all of the discussions we found little effort to define explicitly either the continuum of deafness or cognition. The reason for raising these two issues at the outset is because this omission posed a problem for us in organizing this synthesis. We had to create our own framework, which is expressed in the foregoing categories. But it is noteworthy that we did not discover an explicit model for a psychology of deafness. The prevalent approach observed in the papers was a more general model of human development that applies to deaf children as well as to hearing children. We shall have more to say about this later in the context of particular topics. As for the definition of cognition, we shall address this point in particular, but in general it posed a problem for us since cognition is a central theme of the papers. Without an overall clarification, we are left with the feeling that the definitions of each concept vary considerably among investigators. If this variety is the case, then the various papers addressing cognitive issues may in fact not be addressing the same problems. This point is critical because until we have a common understanding of just what it is we are talking about, we may neither hear nor be heard by one another. With this introduction let us proceed directly to the specific topics.

Theories and Models of Cognition and Education

The papers in this volume reflect two theoretical orientations toward cognition (Piagetian and information-processing) and two theoretical orientations toward education (Ausubellian and Feuersteinian). None of these theoretical orientations can be offered as competing alternatives because they were not developed to explain the same phenomena. Piagetian theory offers both a description and an explanation of how certain types of knowledge develop from infancy to adulthood. Information-processing approaches, on the other hand, analyze knowledge acquisition into several component processes, such as attention, perception, representation, memory, and problem solving. While the information-processing approach is now clearly an ascendant psychological paradigm, it is limited in its capacity to systematically study knowledge acquisition in the home and school contexts where it usually occurs.

Ausubel's theory considers how the content of systematized knowledge in academic curricula should be presented in the process of education so that the structure of the knowledge facilitates the learning process. Feuerstein's theory, which shares many assumptions of Piagetian theory, is a model for transmitting generalized problem analysis and problem-solving skills to individuals who have been culturally deprived of the appropriate mediating experiences. It should be clear that these theoretical orientations neither compete with one another nor focus on the same aspects of cognition or education.

Is it important to have an articulated theory? Is it important to articulate a model of instruction for the deaf? Here we inject our own bias and argue that it is very important to have such articulations because in this way a rationale is developed for future research and for instruction. Moreover, a theory makes explicit the definitions of phenomena and concepts that are within its purview. We come with the basic belief that research without a definite theoretical base can be misleading. Findings obtained from such investigations do not inform us of their place in the scheme of things, nor do they inform us of the appropriate limitations on the generality of the results. Without a theoretical framework it is very difficult to determine the validity of results except in an ad hoc fashion, correlating these results with some other results.

While the importance of a theory for guiding research cannot be under-estimated, it is important to clarify whether such application is to improve upon the theory or whether such application is to solve some practical problem. For example, within Piaget's theory there is a distinction made between figurative knowledge and operational knowledge. Comparative research with deaf students may clarify the interplay between figurative and operative knowledge in Piaget's theory if the condition of deafness causes some atypical use of figurative knowledge in situations normally handled by operational knowledge. Such research should be conducted because the deaf population may offer a unique test of these aspects of the theory. Results of such basic research would illuminate the theory more than illumi-nating the knowledge of deaf persons, since a very narrow aspect of such knowledge has been investigated. Alternatively, if one were interested pri-marily in solving the educational problems of deaf students' symbolic repre-sentation of objects, for example, Piaget's theory would not be very helpful. There is very little discussion within his theory of alternative symbol and language systems which might persist beyond the preoperational period.

While these papers reflect various theoretical positions, it is not always clear why these positions are conjoined with deaf populations. For example, is there a reason unique to the condition of deafness that Ausubel's advance organizer model of teaching (see Biser, pp. 84–87) is particularly relevant? Or is the model simply useful to any teacher seeking to clarify instruction by making an explicit reference to the structure of knowledge in her or his domain?

None of the theories explicitly or implicitly referred to in these papers appear to have developed with deaf persons as subjects; nor do they account for the performance of deaf individuals. Thus, it becomes difficult to ascer-tain the extent to which such theories should either inform educational practice or constitute the starting point for alternative theories about deaf-ness and cognition, which would in turn inform alternative educational practice.

Lest we seem particularly harsh on this point, let us quickly add that the issue is not unique to those interested in the psychology of the deaf or the education of the deaf. Rather, it is a general problem in the use of theory as a basis for developing pragmatic approaches to education, particularly when the theory was not developed for that specific purpose. The same problem emerges in reviewing research on mentally retarded, learning-disabled, blind, or physically disabled populations. Certainly it is interesting to know how different populations behave in certain situations and on certain tasks that have been carefully researched with normal populations. But such differential research should explicitly state whether the purpose is to define the limits of generality for a phenomenon of theoretical interest or whether the purpose is to clarify the psychological nature of a handicapping condi-tion. It has been our experience that borrowing a paradigm from research with normal populations rarely illuminates the nature of a handicapping condition because such conditions are associated with social, psychological, and emotional differences that may be offered as competing explanations for performance in the research paradigm.

How are we to adapt a psychological theory or approach to the needs of deaf children, if in fact such adaptation is possible? We believe such adaptation requires an analysis of the educational impediments facing a deaf child in becoming an independent thinker and problem solver in the world of the deaf and in the world of the hearing. We saw very little discussion of such impediments or the relevance of theoretical aspects that specifically address the deaf person's problems.

In these papers we generally see only passing reference to a grand theory such as Piaget's. More frequently the research stems from mini-theories that tend to focus on components of cognition. If one accepts the idea that cognition is made up of a number of processes such as attention, memory, perception, language, and problem solving, this volume does indeed reflect just such interests. Each component has been studied, and the results are presented here. Since there is no overall theory of cognition, we are in effect addressing particulars, each of which is important. But unless we come to terms with how each of these particulars fits into the over-arching notion of cognition (specifically, how deafness affects the scaffolding of cognition), we will not be able to complete the jigsaw puzzle that we have in effect created. Even in addressing each of these components, there is a need to conceptualize them into a coherent whole. While some of the authors address this question, there is no final resolution of the inherent problem of such a diverse perspective. However, what we have observed in this regard is not unique. We reiterate that the state of applied developmental psychology in general is indeed reflected in our discussion of these particular papers.

Types of Studies Presented

Two types of studies were presented, *experimental* and *descriptive*. While both are necessary, each poses unique problems for the educator.

Experimental Research

Laboratory studies are conducted under highly controlled conditions that are necessary to identify experimental effects, that is, consequences of a particular treatment. In view of the controlled nature of experiments, one question is always raised by practitioners: How can these results be applied to the classroom? Essentially they cannot be directly applied. For example, studies on determining the effectiveness of cued text in teaching pronoun references (see Campbell, pp. 121–123) may not be easily incorporated into an ongoing language curriculum. Assuming that the results are in the expected direction, how can the teacher apply this specific knowledge to the classroom? It must be translated in terms of the curriculum objectives, which may or may not be compatible with the experimental findings. However, this point does not invalidate the experimental findings. The major task for the researcher and the practitioner is to establish lines of communication that lead to transforming the research findings into practice. The major function of the research is to establish substantial and valid facts. The practitioner has to find ways to incorporate these new results into actual practice. This incorporation necessitates the flexibility to modify practice accordingly.

Descriptive Research

By descriptive research we mean research that is systematic, carefully thought out, and free of manipulations. Mann's study on children's play (pp. 27–29) and Pien's study on early communication (pp. 30–33) are excellent examples of such work. Here the researchers carried out a systematic observation of different types of young children's play and communication styles.

One could say that the teacher is a researcher in the sense that he or she does careful observations and comes to know how the children will characteristically behave. The differences between the practitioner and the researcher in this regard are often in the effort expended by the researcher on developing systems of observation that are as unbiased as possible. The researcher selects categories for observation that are consistent with the theoretically important issues. The generality of such categories for describing a variety of children's behaviors often strikes teachers as a weakness in terms of capturing the individuality of a specific child. The bias (if we wish to call it that) is conceptual; it derives from a theory that defines what is important. The practitioner often concludes that investigators select rather trivial categories, frequently those most easily amenable to observation.

Lest it be thought that research can be relegated to the trivial, it should be pointed out that some of the most useful research conducted by developmental psychologists has been in the form of descriptive studies of children's social behavior, children's play behavior, and children's language. Much of Piaget's research can even be classified as observational, even though he gave children tasks to perform. Piaget asked children to explain or describe events that were not manipulated in the sense of an experiment, but where changes in the tasks were done in the presence of the child. The child was then asked to explain what happened. For example, in the classic conservation-of-mass studies, Piaget gave a child two equal-sized balls of clay; after the child attended to the balls equivalence, one of the clay balls was deformed. The child was then asked whether the two clay balls were still of equal amount. There is no treatment in this case; the children are not given any training or any new experiences.

The important feature of descriptive studies is that they enable both researchers and practitioners to consider systematically a variety of behaviors emitted by the child. Thus, performance data need not be reduced to simple categories of right and wrong, single measures of speed, or percentage of correct responses. Rather, the quality and type of response can be considered, and the vast variety of responses from different children can be organized into a coherent and meaningful picture of how children treat various types of situations. These experiments provided a tremendous

213

amount of information that became the basis of many additional descriptive and experimental studies. Often the greatest scientific progress occurs when a consistent and comprehensive description of phenomena is translated into an experimental paradigm that captures that phenomena and provides a more consistent, replicable measurement than would be possible in purely descriptive studies.

Again, the question at issue is, How can the practitioner use this information? It is evident that the practitioner can gain from such studies to the extent that they capture and resonate with the types of children's behaviors observed in response to the activities of the teacher. The difference between the practitioner and the researcher in this case is the conceptually based and rigorously defined categories for observation and the systematic methods of recording.

Epistemological Differences Implicit in Research Designs

A common thread among the papers is that both the experimental and the descriptive studies were essentially comparative descriptions of hearing and deaf children. This research design has three implications.

1. There is an implicit assumption that we need to compare deaf and hearing children and that hearing children form the norm.

2. There is an assumption that such research will inform us of the capabilities of deaf children.

3. Presumably, knowing about such differences will then facilitate the education of deaf children.

We shall address these implications collectively. That differences exist between deaf and hearing children in areas of language and other language-based cognitive skills is obvious. Although such research has its value, both theoretically and practically, the issue becomes one of priorities relative to education of the deaf. Deafness is not an all-or-none proposition.

Variation in onset and intensity of deafness is considerable. In addition to onset variation, there is also variability in etiology and accompanying neurological difficulties. Thus, studies comparing hearing children with deaf children provide information only in terms of the subset of deaf children in that particular study. We always have to ask the question, What type of population is used as the deaf group? Why not instead carry out more studies comparing children of various subgroups of deaf children, thus comparing populations that share specific characteristics (e.g., age of onset)? This idea of a within-population design may be most appropriate for deaf populations. In effect, there is reason to suggest that within-population research designs can provide important data on the nature of variability among deaf children and their level of functioning relative to the severity of their handicap.

214

The problem with the between-population approach, which compares a deaf population to a hearing population, is that we may be led to spurious conclusions about the deaf. Comparison of various papers presented in this volume leads to confusion that can only be clarified by including a variety of deaf groups, characterized at the very least by variety in (a) degree and onset of impairment, (b) types of communication and language systems used both for instruction and for social interaction, and (c) social milieu and its communicative/linguistic support (e.g., deaf parents who sign vs. hearing parents who do not sign). Without such comparisons we will never know how to practically apply research results.

Several studies reported here suggest that deaf individuals process information better when it is represented in visual/spatial signs. Rodda et al. (pp. 94–99) demonstrated that lipreading may reduce the information-processing capacity available for short-term memory storage, while total communication and manual signing provide higher information transmission rates. Morariu and Bruning (pp. 88–90) demonstrated that severely-to-profoundly prelingually deaf students remember stories better if they are presented in the syntax of American Sign Language rather than in written or signed standard English. Remarkably, their results apply also to a written form of American Sign Language even though it has a very different word order than English syntax and was perceived as a peculiar form of writing by deaf subjects. Nevertheless, subjects were better able to recall stories written in this peculiar way in comparison to stories written in standard English.

These studies, along with the studies of cherological versus phonological confusion in short-term memory (see Hamilton, pp. 91–93), suggest that the manual mode of encoding temporal symbolic information is the more natural mode for some deaf persons. The practical implication here is that a manual sign language be considered as the first language for some deaf persons and that the structure of English be introduced as a foreign or second language. This issue, of course, remains controversial.

Other studies resulted in quite different practical implications. Hanson (pp. 108–110), Lichtenstein (pp. 111–114), and Kusché (pp. 115–120), working from research on reading problems of deaf students, found that the best readers used some form of phonological code based on representation in terms of the normal speech articulators. The practical implication is that in order for deaf persons to learn to read, they must represent the orthography of printed words in terms of articulatory translations.

It is possible that we, as naive outsiders in regard to the field of deafness, are confused about the apparent differences between these two lines of research; are we comparing apples and oranges, or are these obtained differences really attributable to differences in types of deaf persons (e.g., orally trained vs. manually trained, good readers vs. poor readers)? During the symposium in which these papers were presented, few discussions of apparent conflict between results were noted. Perhaps the conflict was intentionally avoided because different results imply different types of educational practice, and these practices have previously been the source of heated philosophical debate. We will return to the issue of the social and political context of research with deaf persons at the end of this paper.

Gaps in the Presented Research

We believe that contradictory research results will be clarified when investigators employing different paradigms converge precisely on the issue creating the conflict, and then proceed systematically to explore the limitations of their results in terms of subpopulations of deaf individuals. Such an effort requires collaboration across schools of thought in order to obtain samples of deaf individuals stratified in comparable ways. Such convergence is indeed rare, and its rarity is not unique to research focused on deaf individuals. For example, in the area of reading research, one school of thought characterizes reading as primarily a problem of symbol recognition, symbol integration, and automatic association of strings of symbols with morphemes and words of the language (Liberman, 1983). A second group accuses the first group of teaching children to "bark at words" and argues that reading is a process of constructing meaning not only from an understanding of printed words, but also from a general understanding of how the world works (Goodman & Goodman, 1977). Probably there are learning-disabled readers in each of these categories, and each group benefits from one of the alternate approaches. In fact, research with learning-disabled readers is beginning to converge upon a paradigm in which subtypes of poor readers are systematically identified and subtype-by-treatment interactions are explored (Lyon, 1983).

Thus the conceptualization of deafness as a psychological-biological state of the individual (a state which has a wide range of variation across deaf individuals) is essential both for clarifying our current knowledge and for advancing this knowledge. Embedded in this conceptualization should be the cognitive variables that are relevant for the deaf. For example, how do children who are born deaf differ from children who become deaf at age 2, 4, or 6? It would seem reasonable to suppose that such differences would be of considerable importance. The reason for this assertion is that in the first group, deafness is a way of life without any alternative experience, while in the latter groups there may well be an acute sense of loss, thereby requiring a different type of adjustment to the new status. The severity of the sense of loss may well vary with the age of the individual. Studies of this type are not found among the papers included here.

Perhaps because the symposium focused on cognition, there was little discussion of the interactions between social development, affective development, and cognitive development. Psychologists are beginning to realize that there is a critical interaction between affective, social, and cognitive development (Flavell & Ross, 1981; Lewis & Michalson, 1983; Sigel, 1985). For a comprehensive psychological theory of deafness, it will be necessary to consider the affective and social development of the deaf along with their cognitive development. The absence of papers at this symposium on the interactions between cognitive, social, and affective development reveals a gap in the research that may be filled by future research. Let us turn to that question now.

Directions for Future Research

Our recommendations for future areas of research were formulated on the basis of reading the papers and listening to the discussions at the various symposium sessions. We have checked our observations with various knowledgeable participants and found that our observations were essentially consistent with theirs. We do not claim that our conclusion is scientifically arrived at after an exhaustive search of the literature; however, it is based upon our observations and readings, as well as upon our understanding of similar problems that have emerged from studies of other handicapped populations.

Although we have presented a number of ideas for future research in the preceding comments, let us consolidate those comments into this section. First, we find a gap and, therefore, a suggested topic for further conceptualization and empirical work in the development of a true psychology of deafness. This area should incorporate not only the cognitive aspects of variation among subjects, but also the social and affective components considered in the framework of the child's ecology. A cognitive theory of deafness is only one step into the problems of deafness in a hearing society. The affective features, such as anxiety, sense of inferiority, and problems in coping with the demands of both the deaf and the hearing worlds, are reasonable concerns for any youngster. These factors may well impinge on the child's intellectual development. There is a vast body of literature on hearing children that demonstrates the relationship between affect and learning, affect and test taking, and affect and interpersonal problem solving. These variables might well be incorporated into a large-scale conceptualization of the psychology of deafness. Within this broader context, relevant research problems can be identified for empirical study.

Basic to a clarification of cognition of the deaf is the definition of cognition itself. One way to conceptualize the problem of the cognition of deaf persons is to focus on the process of representation (i.e., the transformation of experience into some type of symbolic system). All experience is broad and extensive, and it is condensed into manageable units by generating representations. These experiences become internal representations that are subsequently transformed into external representations such as language, gesture, art, etc. When difficulty arises in such transformations, individuals often employ metaphors as a means of presenting an idea. Since one of the key areas with which deaf children must deal is communication, not only among themselves but with the nondeaf world, issues of representation and symbolic understanding gain prime importance. For example, just the processes of learning to read and communicate in writing require an understanding of symbolic systems.

Although we cannot go into great detail in discussing the issues inherent in the field (there are some studies dealing with orthography and reading), many questions requiring study immediately come to mind. For example, it is essential now to have studies of deaf children's development of the meaning of different types of symbols, whether they be icons (see Knobloch-Gala & Kaiser-Grodecka, pp. 76–78), manual signs, printed words, or lipread words. Future research should be designed to examine interactions between types of deaf persons and methods of representation.

Of course, to understand how these competencies develop requires careful study of a descriptive nature. In this way the researcher and the teacher can come together to deal with the problems of the deaf child. The teacher can identify areas in which he or she has difficulty in achieving the desired outcomes, and the researcher can begin to identify some problems for research on representations.

One of the key functions of research on cognition, as observed in this volume, is to inform practitioners about ways of teaching or, in broader terms, how to structure learning environments for deaf children. Educators cannot wait for researchers to produce definitive studies on how to educate and how to vary programs according to every child's needs; in other words, educators have to work with the state-of-the-art techniques to meet the immediate needs of the children. However, it is still important to establish a greater communicative bond between educators and researchers in order to answer some critical questions. In fact, it may be impossible to conduct the type of within-population designs that we are suggesting unless researchers are in close communication with teachers of the deaf who know which subtypes of deafness they have in their classes.

In addition, practitioners may assist researchers in piloting new types of representational systems which enable deaf children to communicate in a modality that is familiar to the hearing community. For example, Prinz and Nelson's work (pp. 124–127) with microcomputers opens an exciting area of research in which children communicate with the hearing world through writing. It may be that such new technology can be of considerable value in informing practitioners how children think and reason, in essence, how they generate representational thought.

While it would seem presumptuous to identify the specific research problems that (in our view) need addressing, we believe there are some areas that are notable by their omission. This lack relates to comparative studies evaluating the teaching of communication skills, especially different types of sign langauge. It seems that herein resides one of the most important types of research programs, that is, relating the teaching of sign language to the cognitive level of the child. For example, in using a Piagetian-type model of cognitive development where cognitive growth moves from sensorimotor to preoperational thought to operational thought, it seems reasonable to ask what the relationship is between the child's cognitive level and his or her ability to learn particular sign systems. Research of this type can contribute to our understanding of symbolic development, and it also has a practical use in informing practitioners concerned with the teaching of communication skills.

Other topics provide a dual service—one for theory building and the other for practice. The contribution of some of the research with the deaf contributes to our general knowledge of cognitive development (e.g., the role of conventional language and thought, which is an area fraught with controversy). How deaf children come to develop inferential thought and the differential domains of competence is another important question for our general understanding of development. Specifically, do prelingually deaf children perform differentially in areas involving language as compared to areas involving numeric symbols?

This topic leads to the assessment of cognitive competence among these children. The identification of profiles of competence (e.g., spatial-relations thinking as compared to numeric thought or perceptual problem-solving tasks), can tell us much about the various cognitive strengths as well as the obvious weaknesses. Again, as we come to know more about deaf children, this knowledge will contribute to the theoretical and the practical as we come to understand the complexities involved in the deaf child's cognitive growth.

Social-Political Issues

In closing we would like to comment on the social and political issues implicit in both the education and research programs for the deaf. As with so many organizations and conferences where researchers and practitioners come together, there was a gap in communication and acceptance evident at the symposium. From our observations, the practitioners often needed help to receive adequate answers to their questions on the significance of the research and how it fit into the broader perspective of their understanding of the tasks involved in providing education to deaf students. The problem seems to involve two issues: communication and identification of topics of common interest. Researchers are often oblivious to the implications of their research for practice, and educators are at times unwilling to listen to the research studies and to use their imaginations for applying research findings to their own educational efforts.

Communication requires people not only to listen to each other, but also to be willing and able to take the other's perspective and come to understand it. For example, we noted the tremendous emotional response that was aroused in some of the groups during discussions of sign language versus oral language. We also saw intense differences of opinion over issues such as which particular sign language to use for education. Yet, in all this discussion we could not summarize the empirical basis for the controversy. It seems as though individuals were unable to see each other's perspectives.

The summary of this volume will not be complete, we believe, until we address some of the policy issues that are raised both explicitly and implicitly. The issue concerning preference for different types of communication in education is the best exemplar. Not only were the limitations of data never mentioned relative to the advocacy of various systems for teaching, but points of view were presented with passion, thereby limiting the amount of cautious rational discussion. Our point is that many of these issues pose important questions for research.

A second policy question concerns not only the education of the children in the classroom, but also the role of parents. In our previous discussion we paid very little attention to parents and parent education other than to say that there are differences in children's development, depending on whether they are born into deaf or hearing families. Yet, there is considerable data demonstrating the significance of parents in children's educational development and school performance. In fact, Meadow's (1980) research demonstrates quite clearly the significance of parents in deaf children's cognitive development; her results are consistent with those of other investigators working with hearing children. Clearly there are policy issues involved in how to work with parents. Should hearing parents be required to learn to sign, and if so, which system should they use and how can they best learn it? What other types of help do parents need? These can become research questions, both of a descriptive type and of an experimental type, the former in terms of observing parents interacting with their children, the latter using various types of parent-education models as guides for such interventions.

In this regard there are models for both of these types of activities that could be very useful in conceptualizing family functions in regard to the child's development. The role of the family, both parents' and siblings' roles, is underplayed in these papers. There is a growing body of literature on these matters in studies of normal and handicapped child development (Dunn, 1983; Lamb, 1976; Sigel & Laosa, 1983).

Conclusions

In summary, we would emphasize that communication among the behavioral disciplines is necessary if we are to come to terms with some of the problems facing educators of the deaf. We see as one mission of this volume the identification of ways to enhance educational programs for the deaf child. To that end we have emphasized the role of research. What is noteworthy for us, who are in essence outsiders, is the degree of fractionation of a group that is apparently dedicated to a common goal. Our attention was drawn to the divisions within the group only because so many of the arguments presented for advocacy were not data based. A research conference has a primary interest in the use of data and in contributing such data to the solution of the problems that brought the people together.

We hope that these comments do have the positive effects which they are intended to have. We share a bias: No single discipline, nor one subdiscipline, can make much of a mark on a complicated educational and social problem. How to enhance the quality of life for the deaf person through education is the fundamental goal bringing us all together; in order to make the most progress in the shortest time, we will require the efforts of educators, scientists, parents, and of course, the children themselves. With a group such as those represented in this book working cooperatively, we should see such progress in the future.

References

Dunn, J. (1983). Sibling relationships in early childhood. *Child Development, 54,* 787–811.

Flavell, J., & Ross, L. (1981). *Social cognitive development: Frontiers and possible futures.* Cambridge, England: Cambridge University Press.

Goodman, K., & Goodman, Y. (1977). Learning about psycholinguistic processes by analyzing oral reading. *Harvard Educational Review, 47,* 317–333.

Lamb, M. (Ed.). (1976). *The role of the father in child development.* New York: John Wiley & Sons.

Lewis, M., & Michalson, L. (1983). *Children's emotions and moods: Developmental theory and measurement.* New York: Plenum.

Liberman, I. Y. (1983). A language-oriented view of reading and its disabilities. In H. Myklebust (Ed.), *Progress in learning disabilities* (Vol. 5, pp. 81–101). New York: Grune & Stratton.

Lyon, G. R. (1983). Learning disabled readers: Identification of subgroups. In H. Myklebust (Ed.), *Progress in learning disabilities* (Vol. 5, pp. 102–133). New York: Grune & Stratton.

Meadow, K. (1980). *Deafness and child development.* Berkeley: University of California Press.

Sigel, I. E. (1985). Cognition-affect: A psychological riddle. In D. Bearison & H. Zimiles (Eds.), *Thinking and emotions.* Hillsdale, NJ: Lawrence Erlbaum Associates.

Sigel, I. E., & Laosa, L. M. (Eds.). (1983). *Changing families.* New York: Plenum.

Reactions from the Practitioner's Point of View

Mary Hockersmith

We all appreciate the perspectives presented by Sigel and Brinker, their keen observations, and their challenge to those of us in the educational trenches.

The jigsaw puzzle of the components of cognition, developmental process, and educational practices is indeed an inherent problem in our field. Sigel and Brinker have suggested that researchers and practitioners need to establish an ongoing dialogue. However, before dialogue can be meaningful, some common information must be shared.

First, I charge college and university training programs with the task of laying the foundation for this common dialogue. When I was in college, courses in human development, cognition, and learning theory were usually not offered in the education department. One was required to cross-register into psychology or home economics for a child development course. No one mentioned the basics of research design to me until I was in graduate school. I submit that all teachers in training should be required to take coursework in human development, cognition/learning theory, and the vocabulary of basic research. Additionally, coursework must stress the application of these areas to classroom management, to curriculum design, and to systematic observation and descriptions of human behaviors.

What about those of us who have completed the rigors of preservice training? My next charge is to school boards and school administrators. They can assist practitioners in acquiring and incorporating the research information that is available by doing any or all of the following:

1. Support the teaching of thinking and problem solving. Please STOP supporting fact-and-memory education.

2. Support training in the application of cognitive and learning theory for our inservice teachers.

3. Support and demand an analysis of curriculum in order that higher-order thinking skills are stressed. Then provide the financial and organizational support for the curriculum revisions resulting from that analysis.

4. Support and encourage an environment where questions (Why? What do *you* think?) and intellectual challenges are welcomed from students.

5. Encourage and support research efforts.

6. Provide the time and incentive for practitioners to read the research studies.

Inherent in the study of human development is the study of interrelationships between the biological and psychosocial aspects of development. Sigel and Brinker have indicated an omission of these interactions in the papers in this volume. Those of us who are practitioners sometimes believe that both researchers and assessment personnel sometimes overlook these affective components. My third charge, then, is to the school psychologists and assessment personnel who provide much of our raw data. They must stop talking to teachers in numbers or test scores and tell us instead about student potential—about areas of expectation for success. They need to help us learn how to be better observers of behavior and to give us some ideas for classroom strategies. For example, when they tell us that a student has difficulty with the skill of visual transport, they should also tell us that this child will probably have difficulty looking from a paper on a desk to an overhead projection or chalkboard. Then, let us work out strategies together and discuss the results of our instructional modifications.

School administrators and school boards also have a role to play. School psychologists/counselors and assessment personnel must have a reasonable caseload before there will be time to do what we are requesting. A caseload of 80 to 100 students is too much to allow for active collaboration.

Finally, I wish to address the classroom teachers. We must stop talking so much. We need to become involved with our students to find out what they like and do not like. We need to know what their expectations are and what is relevant to them. We must observe how students accomplish a task and then document our observations. Only then may teachers begin planning how to build on student strengths so that students can taste success. Teachers should also plan lessons and materials that are relevant to the students, their lives, and their goals; and teachers must give students some responsibility for their learning. Teachers may plan their own assessment carefully by asking, "Am I testing what I am teaching, and am I teaching what I am testing? Why am I teaching this? Is my instructional sequence in accordance with developmental expectations?"

Regardless of the cognitive theory to which any of us may subscribe, there is now overwhelming evidence that successful development occurs through interaction with the environment. As practitioners, it is our responsibility to help to create that interactive environment. We must also actively seek an ongoing communication link with researchers and assessment personnel. Practitioners must ask questions, be specific about their observations and concerns, and tell the researcher what they need in the classroom.

This volume is certainly a beginning. Armed with some new information, new friends, and a new determination, we can contribute to the development of creative, inquiring minds among those we serve. We cannot afford to teach them what we know. We must prepare them to open doors that we did not even know were there and to dream dreams that we never dared to dream.

Reactions from the Researcher's Point of View

Donald F. Moores

The perspective I would like to give is not that of a basic researcher or a researcher who is interested in deafness from an experimental viewpoint. Rather, it is the perspective of an educator of the deaf who happens to be doing research.

I came into the field of education of the deaf as a trained behavioristic psychologist. As a behaviorist, my perspective was that speech and language (by which I meant English) and cognition (or intellectual functioning) were all the same; the implication was that one develops a child's speech, language, or intellectual functioning simply by manipulating contingencies of reinforcement.

I was disabused of this idea very quickly when I became a football coach in a high school for the deaf. I found that quality of speech, English skills, and cognitive functioning were not necessarily consistent for any particular child. In other words, I found all combinations and I realized how incredibly difficult it is to really synthesize in a field such as ours.

It is clear that the environment of a deaf individual is different from that of a hearing individual. The interaction of a deaf individual with other deaf people as opposed to hearing people also is different. It is clear that the social cognitive demands placed on deaf individuals differ in quantity and quality from the demands placed on hearing individuals. However, what comes across to me, and apparently to most of the people who have written papers for this volume, is the essentially normal functioning of deaf people in our society.

My own experience as a teacher at the elementary, high school, and college levels and from postgraduate research I have done shows continuously that deaf people function in a normal way. Research that I have been involved in with deaf children, deaf adult workers, and regular classroom teachers having deaf children in their classes consistently supports the idea that deaf children and adults are able to meet the conceptual demands of our society.

In many cases we find that deaf people are rated as being superior to hearing students or hearing workers in their environment, probably because deaf people are academically underemployed and underplaced. The problems that come up again and again deal with communication and not with basic conceptual abilities. Results of research on intelligence tests and on cognitive functioning, which I treat separately, indicate that deaf individuals are able to function at abstract levels as well as anybody else. Unfortunately, in our society and in every other industrial society, the deaf have been a relatively powerless group. Deaf people do not develop our cognitive tests; they do not develop our IQ tests; they do not set up our experiments. These tests have been made, administered, and interpreted by hearing people.

Even at the international symposium upon which this volume is based, where there was a liberal and open acceptance of deafness, only 1 of the 40 or so writers in the several theme areas was deaf.

In this volume, I write as a hearing person telling the reader about cognition and deafness. We should keep in mind that whether or not I have empathy for deafness, I have not lived through the environment that a deaf person experiences.

My first reaction to the content of the papers in this volume is similar to Sigel and Brinker's call for a clear definition of cognition. I found the content was much broader than I had anticipated, especially in the areas of reading and language. I felt that many of the papers could have been written for a conference on reading and/or language.

I was also curious as to whether or not the deficiency model would come across very strongly in this collection of papers. In our field, we tend to have cycles dealing with issues such as speech, language, American Sign Language, cognition, etc. For example, some linguists have spent the first 10 or 15 years of their careers trying to prove that sign languages are essentially the same as spoken languages; they then turn around and concentrate on the differences between sign language and spoken language.

The same thing happens when we talk about cognition. There are differences between deaf and hearing people, of course, but the question is whether these differences are really essential.

There were some surprising omissions among these papers. First, there was little reference to Ottem's (1980) review of literature that appeared in the *American Annals of the Deaf*, which was the most comprehensive short article on this topic.

Also, because Piaget's work received so much emphasis, Furth's work (especially the thinking laboratory that he established several years ago in Washington, D.C.; 1973) did not receive enough attention. And, as an offshoot of that, Sidney Wolff's *Games Without Words* (1973) was not mentioned at all. Probably the biggest discrepancy in relation to theory and its applications was the rare reference to the work of Vygotsky (1962, 1978).

Vygotsky developed the model that has been the basis for curriculum material used with deaf children. His work, of course, is the basis of Soviet deaf education and of much of Soviet special education. His ideas of the social bases of intellect, the concepts of a second-signaling system, and verbal control of behavior were not mentioned. One of the elements we might consider when we talk about simultaneous communication is Vygotsky's concept (actually the Soviet concept) of the *motor-impellent analyzer*, where the excitation of one system will also evoke another system. The argument, for example, is that the use of fingerspelling would be so integrated with speech that the beginning of one would cause the other to start. I am curious to find out if such a phenomenon is really happening with American children using simultaneous communication.

Although Barbara Bodner-Johnson's work (1982, 1984) dealing with family environments has not been widely circulated, it is surprising that it was not broadly cited. Her work is especially relevant when writers discuss elements that can be manipulated in the home (e.g., the importance of simultaneous communication in the home as the most influential predictor of reading achievement in deaf children). She has found that the emphasis in families with deaf children who are good readers is not on the handicapping nature of the children's hearing loss. Rather, the parents accept the hearing loss as a personal characteristic integral to the being of their children. In other words, the parents of those children concentrate on what their children can do and what the children are, not on what the children cannot do and what the children are not.

Some mention should have been made of the work of people (e.g., Pressley & Levin, 1983) in the area of functional cognition. When one tests children in an experimental paradigm, or when one observes children and finds that they do not spontaneously use strategies, this finding does not necessarily mean that they cannot use the strategies; it just means that perhaps the children may not know under what circumstances they are expected to use them.

When we look at deaf children, it is possible that much of what we find governing academic failure is more related to what the children do not do, not to what they cannot do.

Professionals might also look at Walberg's work (1984) in general education. Some of the most important factors in learning involve classroom climate and the use of reinforcement by teachers. The issue of reinforcement should be considered in light of what we do with so many of our deaf children—from the negative ways that we teach them speech, to the ways that we teach them English, to the ways that we interact with them by concentrating on their misarticulations. We tend to focus on negative elements, whereas we should know by now that positive reinforcement is a very powerful factor.

Walberg has reported findings similar to Bodner-Johnson's; that is, alterable family environments can be very important after one factors out certain effects. For example, parents helping children with homework accounts for much of the variance in school learning, regardless of family socioeconomic status.

The work of Rittenhouse, Morreau, and Iran-Nejad (1981) and Rittenhouse and Spiro (1979) also should receive more attention, especially their work on the cognitive functioning of deaf children. Many of their results would suggest that intellectual capacities of deaf children are much higher than have been recorded in the past. This point is true primarily because Rittenhouse himself has proficiency in ASL; thus, because of his fluency and ease of communication, he has found that explanation of causality in deaf children is equivalent to that of hearing children, whereas other researchers have frequently reported that deaf children cannot make these explanations.

It is also important to examine the classic review of cognition and deafness developed several years ago by Patrick Suppes (1972) of Stanford University. One of the points that he made was that the most developed forms of inference are not primarily auditory in nature, they are visual; very little development of mathematical concepts occurs in a purely auditory fashion. The fact that the child that we deal with functions for the most part in a visual modality does not mean that he or she might be retarded in the development of inferential skills.

Another area we should concentrate more on is classroom strategies in the teaching environment. There is much to be said for a compensatory interactive model in which deaf children can utilize their strengths to reach the same levels as other children.

We really must examine the different environments of deaf children as they go through integrated as well as self-contained classroom programs. We may find completely different demands—intellectual, social, and cognitive—being put on children in various placements. Ideally, we should have an idea of the social and cognitive demands facing deaf children.

Several steps are needed to improve the education we give to deaf students.

1. We must accentuate the positive when we deal with children, concentrate on their strengths and not their weaknesses, and reinforce them as much as appropriate.

2. We must involve the family, not solely as caretakers but also as teachers.

3. We must involve deaf people in the research.

4. We must move as quickly as possible out of the laboratory.

5. We must throw away the last vestiges of the deficiency model, which has enabled educators to blame the children and not ourselves.

6. We must always—always—be suspicious of low test scores.

In summary, the range of papers leads me to conclude that there is consensus that deaf people have the same potential as hearing people to function cognitively, although they are frequently exposed to environments that are far different from those in which hearing people find themselves. The principles that facilitate optimal development in hearing children also operate in the same way in deaf children. Children do not fail, but we may fail them. It is our responsibility not to become obsessed with perceived limitations but rather to build upon the strengths of our children to help them realize themselves. I am confident that one of the benefits of this volume will be a reaffirmation of that responsibility.

References

Bodner-Johnson, B. (1982). Describing the home as a learning environment for hearing-impaired children. *Volta Review, 84*, 329–337.

Bodner-Johnson, B. (1984). *The family environment and achievement of deaf students: A discriminant analysis.* Manuscript submitted for publication. (Available from author, Department of Education, Fowler Hall, Gallaudet College, 800 Florida Avenue, NE, Washington, DC 20002)

Furth, H. (1973). *Deafness and learning: A psychological approach.* Belmont, CA: Wadsworth.

Ottem, E. (1980). An analysis of cognitive studies with deaf subjects. *American Annals of the Deaf, 125*, 564–575.

Pressley, M., & Levin, J. (1983). *Cognitive strategy research.* New York: Springer-Verlag.

Rittenhouse, R. K., Morreau, L. E., & Iran-Nejad, A. (1981). Metaphor and conservation in deaf and hard-of-hearing children. *American Annals of the Deaf, 126*, 450–453.

Rittenhouse, R. K., & Spiro, R. J. (1979). Conservation performance in day and residential school deaf children. *Volta Review, 81*, 501–509.

Suppes, P. (1972). *A survey of cognition in handicapped children* (Tech. Rep. No. 197). Stanford, CA: Stanford University, Institute for Mathematical Studies in the Social Sciences.

Vygotsky, L. S. (1962). *Thought and language.* Cambridge: MIT Press.

Vygotsky, L. S. (1978). *Mind in society.* Cambridge: Harvard University Press.

Walberg, H. (1984). Improving the productivity of America's schools. *Educational Leadership, 41*, 19–30.

Wolff, S. (1973). *Games without words.* Springfield, IL: Charles C. Thomas.

Index

Page numbers for definitions are in italics.